Pennsylvania Politics
1746-1770

Pennsylvania Politics

1746-1770

The Movement for
Royal Government and
Its Consequences

By James H. Hutson

Princeton, New Jersey
Princeton University Press
1972

Publication of this book has been aided by the
Whitney Darrow Publication Reserve Fund of
Princeton University Press

This book has been composed in Linotype Caslon Old Face

Printed in the United States of America
by Princeton University Press, Princeton, New Jersey

To My Parents

Acknowledgments

I SHOULD like to record my great debt, personally and professionally, to Professor Edmund S. Morgan, Sterling Professor of History at Yale University. I belong to that small but growing company of scholars whose interest in American colonial history was kindled in Professor Morgan's undergraduate course, and I learned such of the craft as I now command in his graduate courses. For my colleagues of six years on the editorial staff of the Papers of Benjamin Franklin, Professor Leonard W. Labaree and Miss Helen C. Boatfield, I feel the most lively affection and admiration: two more learned, devoted scholars and decent human beings do not exist.

I wish to thank the staffs at the Historical Society of Pennsylvania, the American Philosophical Society, and the Yale University Library, where much of the work for this volume was done. I owe thanks also to Mrs. Alice Lucas of the Institute of Early American History and Culture, who typed this manuscript in her spare moments, and to Mr. Nicholas B. Wainwright, Director of the Historical Society of Pennsylvania and Editor of that venerable and excellent journal, *The Pennsylvania Magazine of History and Biography*, for permitting me to include material that appeared in two of my articles, cited in the footnotes, which were published in the *Magazine*.

The friendship and kindness of numerous individuals have been a comfort and an inspiration to me, and to them I want to express my deepest appreciation: Mrs. Hattie Miller, Mrs. Fannie Weber, Mr. and Mrs. David Hutson, Mr. and Mrs. William Lilley, III. To Mr. Tracy Weber,

Acknowledgments

Jr., whose long and loyal friendship I cherish, I should like to record a special debt of gratitude. The superb editorial assistance of Mr. Sanford G. Thatcher of the Princeton University Press spared me numerous mistakes and infelicities. Finally, I wish to thank my wife, whose unfailing good humor has been more valuable than any scholarly source.

JHH
Williamsburg, Va.
16 June 1971

Contents

Pennsylvania Politics
1746-1770

Introduction

THIS BOOK attempts to describe the contours of Pennsylvania politics between 1746 and 1770. While it professes to comprehend the principal drifts and movements of provincial politics during these years, it does not pretend to be comprehensive in the sense that every prominent provincial politician is introduced and every passing political episode is inventoried and explained. The book's focus is on the year 1764 and on the campaign for royal government which, from only the faintest adumbration at Thomas Penn's accession as proprietor eighteen years earlier, reached its crescendo in that year.

The attempt of the Quaker Party of Pennsylvania to overturn the province's proprietary government in 1764 and replace it with royal government commands attention for four reasons. One, the Quaker effort produced profound political turmoil in the province which engaged unprecedented numbers of people; as such massive perturbations in the body politic always do, it offers a rare opportunity to understand the society in which it occurred. Two, the campaign against the proprietary government provides a heretofore unexploited platform for observing the Paxton Boys, the disaffected frontiersmen who marched on Philadelphia in February 1764. From this new vantage point the conventional view that their march produced a coalition with their underprivileged urban brethren which ripened into the province's revolutionary vanguard a decade later appears untenable; what does appear is that the Paxton Boys had a major impact on provincial politics which has never before been perceived. Three, the attempt to overturn proprietary government produced the most significant realignment of political parties in the province's history. Twice the previously preeminent Quaker Party was fragmented and by 1770 it was in eclipse, fighting rearguard actions from rural bastions; those who deserted it gravitated to the new and aggressive Presbyterian Party—not to be confused, as historians usually do, with the Proprietary Party—which by 1770 had assembled all the elements which supported American independence in 1776. Four, the campaign against proprietary government prefigured with remarkable fidelity the campaign which Pennsylvanians and their fellow Americans conducted against the government of George III in the same and in the following decade. The terms of both conflicts were the same: could a theoretically superior authority in the metropolis, either proprietary or royal, impose its will upon British citizens in the colonies, who were accustomed, and determined to continue, to enjoy a large measure of autonomy? Each conflict developed in the same way: dogged resistance to the exertion of external authority, coupled with petitions, dispatches of agents, and more petitions, pleading for its abatement. And the results of both were the same: an effort, after all attempts at accommodation had failed, to overthrow the offending authority.

Politics in Pennsylvania appear, then, to have exhibited a remarkable consistency before, during, and after 1764. What this seems to suggest is that Pennsylvanians were prepared for revolution as early as 1764, that the crucial revolution "in the minds and hearts of the people" which John Adams believed "was effected before the war commenced" was effected in Pennsylvania, one of the most moderate of colonies, by the time of the Sugar Act. By extrapolating from Pennsylvania's revolt against proprietary government, one can apply the same conclusions to Americans in other colonies. Thus, the attempt to erect a royal government in Pennsylvania in 1764 was an event whose importance transcended the boundaries of the province. In that year Pennsylvania was a thermometer, measuring the revolutionary temperature across the colonies, and it should have received a scholarly reading long before now.

CHAPTER I

Troubles with Thomas Penn

THOMAS PENN, a forty-five-year-old ex-mercer who became the principal proprietor of Pennsylvania in 1746, was a reformer who aspired to restructure the government of his province. Specifically, he wanted to reduce the power and privileges which the Assembly had acquired under his predecessors and thereby end what he considered its intolerable preponderance in Pennsylvania's public affairs. Concurrently, he wanted to increase his own power so that it would at least match that of the House and produce a "balanced government" in which each branch possessed sufficient power to check the arbitrary designs of the other in the interest of the public good.[1] Thus, his plan for reform was beneficent in intent and not a blueprint for despotism, as the Assembly often charged. It was a strategy befitting William Hanna's description of him as a man having "a deep respect for representative government and the political institutions and rights accepted by most Englishmen of the eighteenth century."[2]

[1] The best account of Penn's political objectives—on this score it is a major contribution to the literature of Pennsylvania colonial history—is William Hanna's *Benjamin Franklin and Pennsylvania Politics* (Stanford, 1964), esp. 16-19, 36-42.

[2] *Ibid.*, 17. Penn was evidently sincere when he made statements of the following sort to his supporters: "you know my Love of freedom and that I wish not to abridge any part of the Constitution granted by my Father, but would preserve it to after Ages." To William Allen, 8 Dec.

Actually, Penn's political attitudes were considerably more ambivalent than Professor Hanna allows. Although he paid intellectual fealty to the concept of representative government, he had difficulty accepting it when he confronted it in a robust incarnation like the Pennsylvania Assembly. Toward its members he behaved like anything but an admirer of the institution they represented. He simply could not bring himself to trust them; rather, he exhibited a kind of visceral suspiciousness toward them and a capacity for misunderstanding their motives so profound that it bordered on paranoia. Consider, for example, the function the Assembly exercised in 1746 which offended him most, its exclusive control over the public tax dollar. As a close student of provincial affairs, Penn should have known that the Assembly had acquired its power in this area as much by default as by design—during the early decades of the eighteenth century someone had to pay for the administration of government, for gifts to Indians, and for other expenses and, the proprietary family being impoverished, the Assembly was obliged to step into the breach, raise the money, and do the job. But when Penn became proprietor in 1746, he professed to believe that the Assembly's control over the public monies had been acquired with hostile intent, that it had been malevolently "usurped" to deprive him of his lawful prerogatives. This unreasonable attitude informed his entire proprietorship. It led him into some enormous political blunders, the foremost being his refusal after Braddock's defeat to allow his

---

1764, Penn Papers, Historical Society of Pennsylvania; hereinafter cited as Hist. Soc. Pa.

lands in Pennsylvania to be taxed for fear that the wicked Assembly would saddle him with the whole cost of the war while letting its constituents go scot-free.[3] And it helped doom his plans for reform, for the Assembly always sensed his suspicion of it and repaid it in kind. Distrust, as it always does, bred distrust.

Penn was especially resentful of the Assembly's control over the public revenue because he believed that it was the key to its disproportionate power in the province; "there is nothing," he wrote Governor James Hamilton, "but the power of appropriating the Publick Money that can give those People any weight."[4] His conclusion rested on the following reasoning: the House received approximately £6,000 annually from the excise and from interest on its loans to the public of the provincial paper currency;[5] with

[3] According to Franklin, Penn expressed these apprehensions in a hearing before the Privy Council in the summer of 1760. *Preface* to Galloway's *Speech*, 11 Aug. 1764, in Leonard W. Labaree *et al.*, eds., *The Papers of Benjamin Franklin* (New Haven, 1959-   , 15 vols. to date), XI, 279; hereinafter cited as Labaree, ed., *Papers of BF*. He also expressed them in his 21st instruction to Governor Denny, laid before the Assembly on 31 Aug. 1756. *Pennsylvania Archives*, 8th ser., V, 4302; hereinafter cited as 8 *Pa. Arch.*

[4] Penn to Hamilton, 29 July 1751, Penn Papers, Hist. Soc. Pa. Typical of Penn's analysis of the baleful consequences of the Assembly's control over the public money was his letter to Hamilton of 31 July 1749, where he complained that the executive power in Pennsylvania was "too weak already" and that the "great cause of all is the Assembly having the disposition of the publick money." *Ibid.* See also Hanna, *Franklin and Pennsylvania Politics*, 40-43.

[5] This was the Assembly's own estimate with which Governor Hamilton agreed. Hamilton's successor, Robert Hunter Morris, placed the House's annual income at £7,000. See 8 *Pa. Arch.*, IV, 3446, and V, 3712, 3798, 3834, 3846; also Hamilton to Penn, 18 March 1752, Penn Papers, Hist. Soc. Pa. Half of the £6,000, the Assembly estimated, derived from interest on loans, the other half from the excise, although, theoretically, the interest should have yielded £4,000, since the entire supply of the

this money, which it controlled exclusively, it maintained an agent in England liberally supplied with funds to defend its "usurpations" and to combat his efforts to erase them,[6] bought the affection of the people by purchasing goods and services and by supporting projects they approved,[7] and deprived his governors of any bargaining power or leverage by being too affluent to need favors.[8] It followed, then, that the way to reduce the Assembly's power was to cut its financial tap. Accordingly, on 29 July

province's currency, £80,000 as of 1739, was loaned to the inhabitants at 5% yearly interest. The failure to collect the full amount of interest reflected the House's leniency with its debtors, a practice the proprietary partisans assailed as yet another method by which the Assembly used its control over the provincial currency to buy the affections of the people and ensure its preponderance in the province. 8 *Pa. Arch.*, v, 4035.

[6] The Assembly constantly feared that Penn would try to deprive it of the wherewithal to support an agent. See its reports of 14 and 23 Sept. 1756, 22 Feb. 1757, in Labaree, ed., *Papers of BF*, VI, 518, and VII, 139; 8 *Pa. Arch.*, v, 4322. That its apprehensions were not ill-founded is shown by a letter from Penn to Gov. John Penn, 30 Nov. 1765, conveying the following command: "You will be particularly careful not to allow one shilling of Money to be disposed of without your consent that Franklin [then Pennsylvania's agent in London] may have no more." Penn Papers, Hist. Soc. Pa.

[7] Penn and his faithful spokesman, the Rev. William Smith, both disapproved the Assembly's financial support of several worthwhile projects. Penn believed that the House had "misapplied" public money for "their hospital, steeple, bells, unnecessary library with several other things, [which] are reasons why they should not have the appropriations to themselves." Smith criticized the House for using their money "to distress all who oppose their Measures, and for building Hospitals, purchasing Lands, Libraries &c." Theodore Thayer, *Israel Pemberton King of the Quakers* (Phila., 1943), 38n; [William Smith], *A Brief State of the Province of Pennsylvania* (2nd edn., London, 1755), 20.

[8] James Hamilton expressed this part of the proprietary complaint quite well when he protested to the Assembly, 17 May 1754, that its control over the public money tended "to render him in a great Measure unnecessary to them during the Continuance of those Acts." 8 *Pa. Arch.*, v, 3711.

9

1751 Penn instructed Hamilton to pass no more excise bills or bills to emit paper money on loan unless he were given a veto power over the expenditure of the money they produced. This instruction (hereafter called the expenditure instruction) remained in force, binding one governor after another, until Penn died twenty-four years later.[9]

Penn's assessment of the source of the Assembly's strength furnished another example of his misunderstanding of Pennsylvania politics, for the notion that the House's power was based on its bankroll was belied by the very success of his policies. By adamantly adhering to his instructions, his deputies succeeded by 1762 in drying up the Assembly's funds. Deprived of both the excise and the interest money, the House was forced to rely on its reserves and other sources of revenue, which it quickly exhausted; by the end of 1763 all of its money was gone and it was, to put it crudely, flat broke.[10] Penn now had the

[9] The letter of 29 July 1751 was not a formal instruction, although Hamilton regarded it as having the authority of one. Penn embodied its command in a formal instruction on 30 May 1752, which he rescinded temporarily on 28 March 1753 but reactivated, for good, on 1 Nov. 1753. All the documents just cited are in the Penn Papers, Hist. Soc. Pa.

[10] In 1756 the Assembly emitted £30,000 in paper money and sunk it by extending the excise for ten years. The excise rate was set so low, however, that it would yield almost no yearly surplus and, if it did, it could not be spent but by act of Assembly, which would, of course, require the governor's consent. In 1746 the Assembly passed an act re-emitting on loan the province's stock of £80,000 in paper currency. The statute stipulated that, beginning in 1756, one-sixth of the £80,000 would be sunk during each of the next six years, so that by 1762 there would be no more paper money on loan and, naturally, no interest from it. See *The Statutes at Large of Pennsylvania from 1682 to 1801, Compiled under the Authority of the Act of May 19, 1887* . . . (Harrisburg, 1896-1911, 15 vols.), V, 7-15, 243-61; hereinafter cited as *Statutes at Large, Pa.* See also *Minutes of the Provincial Council of Pennsylvania* . . . (Phila., 1838-53, 16 vols.), IX, 382; hereinafter cited as *Pa. Col. Recs.*

House exactly where he wanted it, stripped of what he assumed to be the sinews of its strength. But, contrary to what he seems to have expected, instead of sinking into submissiveness it mounted against him the angriest and most ambitious campaign in Pennsylvania history, attempting throughout 1764 to terminate his government and install a royal government in its place. Clearly, the Assembly's muscle did not come from its money; rather its strength and dynamism stemmed from its embodiment and articulation of the attitudes and aspirations of its constituents, the people of Pennsylvania. But Penn, in whose perception the pound sign predominated, never grasped this point.

When Hamilton received the proprietor's expenditure instruction, he was thunderstruck. Could Penn really believe that the Assembly would acquiesce in his efforts to obtain a veto power over its spending money? That he was feeding on fantasy the governor informed him in no uncertain terms. The province would be "thrown into a Flame" by his demands, he wrote him on 18 March 1752; the Assembly would "bounce violently, and be very angry" and in retaliation might encourage a quit rent strike.[11] Proprietary Party chieftain William Allen and Attorney General Tench Francis corroborated his warnings, predicting that any attempt to implement the instruction would "raise such a Flame in the province as would not be quench'd in many Years."[12] Writing in an even more apocalyptic vein, Francis prophesied that "the moment this Instruction should be known it would occasion a down-

---

[11] Hamilton to Penn, 18 March 1752, Penn Papers, Hist. Soc. Pa.
[12] Hamilton to Penn, 9 Feb. 1753, *ibid.*

right Civil War in the Province, the people would hold out to the last as pro Aris & Focis. . . . The Governor and his Friends would be publickly branded as Deliverers up of the People's Rights. . . . In fine it could not be imagined to what Lengths an enraged people might go."[13]

Hamilton was prepared to brave the antipathy which he anticipated he would arouse by pressing the expenditure instruction if as few as three influential men in the province supported him. No one backed him, however. Instead, men like Allen and Francis urged him "most ardently" to conceal the instruction and use subterfuge to reject the Assembly's money bills.[14] With considerable reluctance he followed their advice, fearing, perhaps, that he would be deficient in the practice of deceit. Events proved that he was, for the subterfuge he invented in 1752 and 1753 to kill the House's bills to emit paper money on loan were so transparent that the members immediately recognized them for what they were and concluded, in line with long-standing suspicions about the influence of Penn's private instructions, that Hamilton was inhibited by them.[15]

[13] Quoted in Mabel P. Wolff, *The Colonial Agency of Pennsylvania 1712-1757* (Phila., 1933), 153. See also Richard Hockley to Thomas Penn, 4 Aug. 1754, in which he wrote that the citizens "understand he [Gov. Morris] inform'd the Lords of Trade and King in Council that unless the Publick Money rais'd in the Province was in the disposal of the Govr & Councell no good cou'd be expected to be done . . . which may be all right, but notwithstanding they cou'd cut his throat for it." Penn Papers, Hist. Soc. Pa.

[14] Hamilton to Penn, 9 Feb. 1753, Penn Papers, Hist. Soc. Pa.

[15] For Hamilton's amateurish use of subterfuge and for the suspicions it induced, see James H. Hutson, "Benjamin Franklin and Pennsylvania Politics, 1751-1755: A Reappraisal," *Pa. Mag. Hist. and Biog.,* XCIII (1969), 320-21, 323, 325, 327-30.

The fostering of a popular mentality which attributed unpopular executive actions to secret proprietary instructions came close to wrecking the proprietary cause in 1764, although no one could have foreseen this development during Hamilton's administration. For the creation of this attitude the governor himself, by his inept use of artifice, was, to some extent, responsible. But the real culprit was Thomas Penn. Had he been familiar with the temper of his province, he would not have ordered a deputy to implement an instruction which was so unpopular, so potentially inflammatory, that all of his advisers abhorred it and implored him to conceal it. Rather, he might have expected the subordinate to yield to the entreaties of his associates and to do business by deceit, thereby sowing the seeds of hypersuspiciousness among the people of the province. If he really wanted his instruction implemented, as he apparently did, Penn should have come to Pennsylvania to lead the fight for it personally, instead of ordering his governors to force the issue from the safety of his closet in England. To urge his deputies to do his dirty work from a distance of three thousand miles was to invite trouble. He might, it is true, have raised a furor by coming to Pennsylvania and pressing his monetary policy, but he would also have proved that proprietary government was a government of candor and not of concealment, and in the long run he would have profited more by making this impression than by staying in England and avoiding the storm.

On 3 Oct. 1754 James Hamilton was replaced by Robert Hunter Morris, who was bound by the same expenditure instruction, who was advised by the same men to conceal it for the same reasons, and who followed their advice, as Hamilton had.[16] There were major differences between the two administrations, however. Hamilton had been plagued mainly by the Assembly's desire to expand the volume of the province's currency by emitting more money on loan at interest. Morris's problem was caused by the fact that throughout his administration the province either was threatened with invasion by the French and Indians or was actually the victim of their incursions. Thus, he was confronted by the Assembly's efforts to raise money to defend itself, which it tried to do by emitting paper money and sinking it with an excise on spirituous liquors. An even more significant difference between the two administrations was the state of the Assembly's knowledge about the instructions Penn had given his governors. Whereas the Assembly only suspected that Hamilton's opposition to its money bills was dictated by secret instructions from Penn, no guessing was needed about Morris's instructions, because one of the House's agents in England, Robert Charles, had "come at" them (through means which he refused to divulge) and had sent intelligence about them to the members, who had received and digested it by the time Morris arrived in Philadelphia.[17] The Assembly, therefore, knew precisely what the new governor was up to when he began, in the December 1754 session, to reject excise bills on the grounds that they violated a royal instruction of 1740 or did not conform to the New England Currency Act of 1751. It was as though it were watching

[16] For an analysis of the Morris administration which amplifies many of the points which follow, see *ibid.*, 335-63.

[17] Morris to Penn, 26 Oct. 1754, Penn Papers, Hist. Soc. Pa.

through a keyhole as he manufactured these subterfuges. The effect on the House of observing Morris hide Penn's instruction and defeat its bills with artifice was to confirm the already powerful and mischievous suspicion it had developed during Hamilton's administration, that all proprietary governors were held in leading strings by secret instructions and that all unpopular or controversial executive actions could be attributed to them.

The Assembly was not prepared to suffer Penn's instruction in silence and declared in a message to Morris of 3 January 1755 its "great Dislike" for it and railed against all proprietary instructions as "void," "illegal," "absurd," and "impracticable."[18] The main reason for its indignation was that it considered the interest and the excise money Pennsylvania's private property; the people of the province alone paid it, and to allow an outsider like Penn, who had contributed nothing to it, to control its disposition seemed unjustifiable, unreasonable, and unnatural. Consequently, in several uncompromising messages to Morris the Assembly protested that, in ordering his deputies to seek a veto power over its expenditure of the province's interest and excise money, Penn was violating a precious "natural Right," the right of people "to dispose of their own Money, by themselves or their Representatives."[19] (That a right to spend the public money inhered in any legislative body would have astonished the Assembly's model in matters of parliamentary practice, the House of Commons. The policy in Great Britain, the constitutional-

---

[18] 8 *Pa. Arch.*, V, 3832, 3839.

[19] See, e.g., the Assembly's messages of 19 Aug. and 29 Sept. 1755, *ibid.*, 3991, 4027.

ity of which not even the most fervent commonwealthmen challenged, was that the executive branch of government collected and spent all public money, subject to account to the legislature which voted it.)[20] On 7 January 1755 the Assembly carried its protest against Penn's pretensions even further by petitioning the King-in-Council against his instructions, charging them with preventing Morris from passing a £20,000 excise bill, with sabotaging the British interest in North America, and with violating the royal charter of 1681.[21]

It was folly for the Assembly to make these accusations, for it could not prove any one of them. For the public record it could profess to know only as much about Penn's instructions as Morris revealed, because if it attacked them before an official British tribunal with information obtained by spying or other unscrupulous means (as Charles's obviously was), it would compromise its case morally and ensure its defeat. But Morris, acting with what seemed to the Assembly to be perverse obstinacy, refused to disclose his instructions, and therefore the House could officially know nothing about their nature. Thus, there was no way for it to prove the allegations of its petition. What it should have done was to wait for Morris to reveal his principal's orders and then remonstrate against them. But in January

---

[20] The Board of Trade spelled out the British practice unequivocally to the Assembly in a report of 24 June 1760 in which it warned the Assembly that by attempting to spend the public money it was "usurping . . . one of the most inviolable Prerogatives of the executive Power, not countenanced by any Example of the British Representative, who always consider the Application of the Publick Money subject to Account as one of the most undisputed Powers of the Crown." Labaree, ed., *Papers of BF,* IX, 143.

[21] See *Pa. Col. Recs.,* VI, 448-50.

1755 the members were furious about Penn's instructions, and their anger drove them to the precipitate and self-defeating act of sending to England a petition full of accusations they could not substantiate.

The Assembly's agents in England, Charles and the venerable Quaker merchant Richard Partridge, who were charged with presenting the petition, realized the weakness of their case, but instead of trying to make the best of it, they ignored the House's complaints and concentrated their fire upon the royal instruction of 1740, which Morris had used as a subterfuge to conceal Penn's instruction and defeat the £20,000 defense bill. These tactics failed miserably and on 30 May 1755 the Board of Trade frostily dismissed the Assembly's petition.[22] Disappointed with both the Board and its own agents, the House concluded from this fiasco that, if it were compelled in the future to seek relief from the continuation of Penn's expenditure instruction or from his efforts to subject it to another kind of external control, it would be necessary to employ other men to present its case and to appeal to other agencies or persons within the British government. Because of Braddock's defeat, it was obliged to apply this lesson much sooner than it expected.

On 24 July 1755 Morris informed an emergency session of the Assembly of the rout of Braddock's army. Recognizing that this catastrophe placed Pennsylvania in unprecedented jeopardy, the House responded on 25 July by resolving to grant an unprecedented sum for defense, £50,000, which it proposed to raise by means equally un-

---

[22] For the prosecution of the petition in England, see Wolff, *Colonial Agency*, 165-70.

precedented, a general land tax. Moving with dispatch matching the province's danger, it passed the £50,000 bill on 2 August and sent it to Morris the same day. On 5 August the governor returned it with a message signifying his refusal to pass it unless Thomas Penn's estate was exempted from the land tax, claiming the next day that he was compelled to make this demand by a clause in his commission which forbade him to consent to any act "whereby the Estate or the Property of the Proprietaries may be hurt or encumbered." This explanation the Assembly refused to believe, because on 29 July, in an attempt to raise a force of volunteers to march westward against the French, Morris had offered, as bounties, gifts of proprietary land, ranging from 200 acres for privates to 1,000 acres for colonels. Here was an offer which could cost Penn hundreds of thousands of acres—hardly an inconsiderable hurt to his estate—and yet the Assembly was apparently supposed to believe that Morris was authorized to make it, but was not authorized to consent to a land tax which by common estimate would cost the proprietor little more than £500. This conundrum seemed to be susceptible to only two solutions: either the offer of land bounties was made without authority, or the restriction allegedly imposed by the proprietary commission on hurting and encumbering the proprietary property was a subterfuge to mask proprietary instructions prohibiting the taxation of Penn's estate. The Assembly and the province, convinced by recent experience that secret proprietary instructions dictated all unpopular executive actions, were certain that the second answer was the correct one. But on this occasion they were wrong: Morris had, in fact, no instructions from

Penn prohibiting the taxation of his estate. But their absence did not mean that he approved such levies; it simply indicated that he had not expected the Assembly to try to impose them. When Morris's successor, Captain William Denny, arrived in the province in August 1756, he was freighted with instructions from Penn prohibiting the taxation of virtually his whole estate.[23]

Penn's refusal to submit to taxation shocked the province, for not even his most implacable detractors had ever imagined him capable of refusing to contribute to the cost of repelling a foreign invader.[24] Many Pennsylvanians actually believed that the royal charter of 1681 obliged him to assume the entire cost of provincial defense and even though numbers (as well as the authorities in England) disagreed, no one doubted that his position as Proprietor and Captain General of the province imposed inviolable obligations to assist in the defense of his dominions. Penn was also expected to contribute to provincial defense because he would benefit more from the defeat of the French than any other man in the province. The vast tracts of land he owned in central Pennsylvania were worthless as long as a foreign army lay entrenched along their western extremities. But let the French be driven away and their value would skyrocket. Finally, Penn was expected to pay the tax because no man in the British Empire, not the first peer of the realm, not the King himself, was exempt from levies on land. Still, no matter how compelling Pennsylvanians believed his obligation to contribute to the com-

[23] 8 *Pa. Arch.*, V, 4298-4306.

[24] For the bitter contention between Morris and the Assembly which followed Braddock's defeat, see Hutson, "Franklin and Pennsylvania Politics," 356-60.

mon defense was, no matter how grave the threat from the French and their Indian allies appeared, Morris insisted on the immunity of proprietary property from provincial taxation.

The indignation against Penn for dodging his taxes was incandescent. Witness, for example, the Assembly's diatribe against him on August 19: "Vassals must follow their Lords to War in Defence of their Lands," the House fumed, but "our Lord Proprietary, though a Subject like ourselves, would send us out to fight for him, while he keeps himself a thousand Leagues remote from the Danger! Vassals fight at their Lords Expence, but our Lord would have us defend his Estate at our own Expence! This is not merely Vassalage, it is worse than any Vassalage we have heard of; it is something we have no adequate Name for; it is even more slavish than Slavery itself."[25] The anger at Penn did not diminish as time passed, for it was periodically fanned by other episodes of tax dodging and in 1764 was one of the major factors impelling the Assembly to attempt to abolish proprietary government. A mock epitaph composed by Franklin for Penn in the summer of 1764 captured the popular indignation against him (and his brother), indignation which was never more intense than in the wake of Braddock's defeat:

Be this a Memorial
Of T[homas] and R[ichard] P[enn]
P[roprietors] of P[ennsylvania]
Who with Estates immense,
Almost beyond Computation,

[25] 8 *Pa. Arch.*, v, 3998.

When their own Province,
And the whole British Empire
Were engag'd in a bloody and most expensive War,
Begun for the Defence of those Estates,
Could yet meanly desire
To have those very Estates
Totally or Partially
Exempted from Taxation,
While their Fellow-Subjects all around them,
Groan'd
Under the universal Burthen.
To gain this Point,
They refus'd the necessary Laws
For the Defence of their People,
And suffer'd their Colony to welter in its Blood,
Rather than abate in the least
Of these their dishonest Pretensions

. . .

A striking Instance
Of human Depravity
And an irrefragable Proof,
That Wisdom and Goodness,
Do not descend with an Inheritance
But that ineffable Meanness
May be connected with unbounded Fortune.[26]

Morris's insistence on exempting Penn's estate from
taxes roused the Assembly's ire on another score, too. Arguing by analogy from Penn's charter of 1701, which
granted it "the Powers and Priveleges of an Assembly,

[26] Franklin's *Preface* to Galloway's *Speech*, in Labaree, ed., *Papers of
BF*, XI, 298-99.

according to the rights of the Freeborn Subjects of England," the Assembly claimed that, like the British House of Commons, it possessed the right to have its supply bills accepted or rejected by the executive without amendment. This right it lauded as "one of the most valuable" which British subjects possessed, asserted that it was "essential to an English Constitution," and declared that it could not "be given up, without destroying the Constitution." That Morris ridiculed this pretension as "new and lofty" and as "unknown to former Assemblies" made no impression on the members, and therefore, when he attempted to amend their £50,000 supply bill by exempting Penn's estate, they were convinced that he was trampling on their constitutional rights.[27] And, to exasperate the House further, he demanded a voice in the expenditure of any surplus the bill produced, thus putting himself once more in the position of trying to abridge its self-proclaimed "natural right" to the exclusive expenditure of the public money.

The House felt threatened by this double assault on its rights because it knew that it was not coincidental. A pamphlet which appeared in the province at the end of April 1755 made this unmistakably clear. This pamphlet, *A Brief State of the Province of Pennsylvania*, was an anti-Quaker screed which, though written by the Reverend William Smith, was supposed by the people of the province to have been written by Morris while he was in England in the early 1750s in conjunction with or at the direction of Thomas Penn. Therefore, its major proposition— "in Proportion as a Country grows rich and populous, more Checks are wanted to the Power of the People; and the

----

[27] 8 *Pa. Arch.*, v, 3979, 4124-25, 4159.

government, by nice Gradations, should verge more and more from the popular to the mixt Forms"[28]—was assumed to reflect Penn's political ambitions for the province, a reduction of popular power, which in fact it did. Consequently, the Assembly construed Morris's efforts to abridge its constitutional and natural rights as an attempt, dictated by the blueprint in the *Brief State*, to check its powers and concluded from the governor's actions that Penn was not only a tax dodger but an aspiring despot as well. This impression, of course, caused the proprietor's popularity to plummet even further.

Morris refused to let the popular reaction to his or his principal's policies sway him. From Braddock's defeat until the end of his administration a year later, he rejected every supply bill which did not exempt Penn's estate from taxes and did not give him a voice in the expenditure of its produce. His intransigence put the House in a painful predicament: should it pass supply bills on his terms and thereby sanction proprietary tax dodging and sacrifice its rights; or should it refuse them and thereby deprive the province of protection and sacrifice the lives of its constituents? It managed to dodge the problem during August and September because during these months the French and Indians did not exploit their victory over Braddock by invading the settled parts of the province. But beginning in the middle of October the Indians attacked and ravaged the entire length of the frontier and fixed the House on the horns of this dilemma over defense.

To deal with the Indian attacks Morris called the Assembly into special session on 3 November 1755. Five days

[28] [Smith], *Brief State*, 6-7.

later the members passed a bill raising £60,000 for defense by taxing all estates in the province. As expected, Morris rejected it because it did not exempt the proprietary property. Then followed an angry fortnight in which he and the House fired the bill back and forth like ships exchanging broadsides, each hoping that the pressure of events would force the other to modify his stand. How long this war of nerves would have lasted is not known. Obviously, at some point the steady budget of bad news from the west, the stream of stories of scalpings, pillage, and burning, would have aroused the Assembly's compassion for its constituents to a pitch where it would have paid Morris's price to obtain legislation to defend them. Mercifully, the people of the province did not have to await the Assembly's capitulation because on 24 November two events occurred which broke the impasse between it and the governor and prompted the passage of a supply bill.

On the afternoon of the 24th Morris informed the Assembly that he had just received a letter from Penn announcing his intention to make a "free Gift" of £5,000 to the war effort.[29] The House could not help but regard this donation as an equivalent for the proprietary taxes, and it therefore agreed to pass the supply bill, granting the exemption which Morris had long demanded. Helping to produce this decision was the descent on Philadelphia of a band of frontiersmen, precursors of the Paxton Boys nine years later.

As the Indian attacks escalated in the fall of 1755, the anger of the frontiersmen and their threats against the Assembly for failing to protect them escalated propor-

---

[29] 8 *Pa. Arch.*, V, 4150-51.

tionally. Westerners, who on 31 October were warning that they might go to Philadelphia and "Quarter ourselves on its Inhabitants and wait our Fate with them,"[30] were threatening toward the end of November to go to the capital and cut the Assemblymen's throats, to "march down and tear the whole Members of the legislative body Limb from Limb, if they did not grant immediate Protection."[31] These threats were taken seriously in Philadelphia and the capital trembled when a mob, led by John Hambright, a Lancaster Pike tavernkeeper,[32] and estimated at between 300 and 700 men,[33] appeared in town on the evening of 24 November and "demanded protection in such manner as threatened outrage if it was denied."[34] Hambright's men differed from the Paxton Boys in several ways: there were more of them (only about 250 Paxtoneers are esti-

[30] Quoted in Arthur O. Graeff, *The Relation Between The Pennsylvania Germans and The British Authorities (1750-1776)* (Norristown, Pa., 1939), 128.

[31] [William Smith], *A Brief View of the Conduct of Pennsylvania for the Year 1755* (London, 1756), 52, 70.

[32] For Hambright's leadership of the mob, see [Joseph Galloway], *A True and Impartial State of the Province of Pennsylvania* (Phila., 1759), 143. He was the proprietor of the White Horse Tavern on the Lancaster Pike about twenty-five miles west of Philadelphia. In August 1762 Gov. James Hamilton conferred with the Delaware Indians on his premises. See "Governor Thomas Pownall's Description of the Streets and Main Roads about Philadelphia, 1754," *Pa. Mag. Hist. and Biog.*, XVIII (1894), 213; *Pa. Col. Recs.*, VIII, 750.

[33] In a letter to Penn, 28 Nov. 1755, Morris estimated the mob at 700 men. Labaree, ed., *Papers of BF*, VI, 280. In a letter to the proprietor, 27 Nov. 1755, William Smith put it at 300 men, but in a newspaper account of the affair, published the same day in the *Philadelphische Zeitung*, he numbered it at 600. Penn Papers, Hist. Soc. Pa.; Graeff, *Pennsylvania Germans and British Authorities*, 136-37. In his *Brief View*, 81, Smith estimated the mob at 400 men.

[34] Daniel Dulany, "Military and Political Affairs in the Middle Colonies in 1755," *Pa. Mag. Hist. and Biog.*, III (1879), 24.

mated to have crossed the Schuylkill and camped at Germantown);[35] they were mostly German (the Paxtoneers were predominately Scotch-Irish); and they were not as heavily armed. Yet the Assembly believed that the motivation of the two groups was identical—indeed, it later explained the march of the Paxton Boys by applying to it its interpretation of the motivation of this earlier group of "rioters." Hambright's men, in the House's view, were not genuine sufferers, petitioning their representatives for assistance, but were rather proprietary storm troopers who had been summoned by the governor and his lieutenants to march on Philadelphia with the aim of intimidating the Assembly into adopting Penn's unjust policies.[36] That this view was absurd—Morris was so far from controlling the "rioters" that he had to be restrained from fleeing Philadelphia in terror at their approach[37]—the Assembly did not discern, and its apprehensions at the appearance of the mob, coupled with the announcement of Penn's "free Gift," prompted it to pass the £60,000 supply bill, proprietary exemption and all, on 27 November.

The members regretted this action almost immediately, for they soon discovered that the proprietor's "free Gift" was a fraud. Instead of being an outright donation, it was to be collected from the arrearages of the proprietary quit rents. Penn, in other words, had assigned the Assembly his bad debts, a significant portion of which remained outstand-

[35] Brooke Hindle, "The March of the Paxton Boys," *William and Mary Quarterly*, 3rd ser., III (Oct. 1946), 478; hereinafter cited as 3 *WMQ*.

[36] [Galloway], *True and Impartial State*, 143.

[37] Richard Hockley to Thomas Penn, 16 Dec. 1755, Penn Papers, Hist. Soc. Pa.

ing as late at 1759.[38] But what troubled the members even more about passing the supply bill was that the war and the forces it had loosed had compelled them to capitulate to what they believed was Penn's instruction to Morris, demanding the exemption of his estate from taxation. Although it was rumored that Franklin would be sent to England to protest against the proprietor,[39] the House took no action for the time being. Morris steadfastly refused to admit that his demand for the proprietary exemption was dictated by instructions, and the members, profiting from the debacle of their earlier petition, shied away from an appeal which could not be supported by incontestable facts. Suspicion, no matter how strong, would not suffice, they had learned.

On 20 August 1756 a new governor, Captain William Denny, reached Philadelphia. As candid as Morris was coy, Denny took command at one of the darkest moments of the war. On 17 August the Assembly had learned that a body of French and Indians had captured and burned Fort Granville on the Juniata River,[40] one of the province's strongest western fortresses, and on the very day of Denny's arrival Colonel John Armstrong had written from

---

[38] In the spring of 1757 there was £2,840 outstanding, which the House attempted to recover by passing a bill on 31 March 1757 emitting this sum in paper money "to be sunk by Payments to be made by the Proprietaries Receiver General." Governor Denny refused to sign the bill, however. 8 *Pa. Arch.*, VI, 4555-56. The sum outstanding on 5 April 1759 was £600. Labaree, ed., *Papers of BF*, VIII, 304. The Assembly frequently voiced its indignation at the inordinate delay in receiving the money, often professing doubts that Penn ever intended to pay in full. See, e.g., 8 *Pa. Arch.*, VI, 4523, 4559-60, 4601.

[39] Richard Peters to Thomas Penn, 20 Nov. 1755, Peters Papers, Hist. Soc. Pa.

[40] 8 *Pa. Arch.*, V, 4286.

Carlisle, warning that Fort Shirley, another western stronghold, could not withstand a threatened attack. The same day Lord Loudoun announced the fall of Oswego and with it the loss of British control over Lake Ontario.[41] To make matters worse, Denny informed the House on 24 August 1756 that the £60,000 raised the previous November was exhausted and that there was no money to pay the troops on the frontier (whose salaries were already in arrears). For all he knew, these men would have to be "immediately disbanded."[42] If this happened, nothing could prevent the French and Indians from marching straight to Philadelphia and sacking it. A panicky Assembly resolved to pass a supply bill and, in view of its recent difficulties with Morris, asked to see Denny's instructions. On 31 August the governor obliged by presenting full texts of those relating to money bills.[43]

The instructions contained few surprises. Penn continued the expenditure instruction, by ordering Denny to demand a voice in the disposition of any money the House raised by taxes or by interest on loans of paper money. Furthermore, he instructed Denny to insist, in the event the House passed a general land tax, on the exemption of all but an infinitesimal amount of his property—everything, the House charged, but a "Ferryhouse or two, a Kitchen, and a Dog Kennel."[44] This instruction confirmed the House's suspicion that Morris had been bound by one exactly like it, which, in turn, strengthened a more general suspicion, hardening since the early days of Hamilton's administra-

---

[41] *Pa. Col. Recs.*, VII, 231-33, 234-35.
[42] 8 *Pa. Arch.*, V, 4292.　　　　[43] *Ibid.*, 4298-4306.
[44] Labaree, ed., *Papers of BF*, VI, 526.

tion, that secret proprietary instructions dictated all executive actions in Pennsylvania, an opinion which, as we have already observed, cost Penn dearly in 1764.

Having seen Penn's instructions, the Assembly asked Denny on 1 September whether he intended to abide by them. The next day he responded affirmatively, announcing that he could not recede from them "without risking both my Honour and Fortune,"[45] alluding with this last word to the financial sanction Penn used to compel obedience to his instructions, the £5,000 performance bond he exacted from each of his deputies. To the Assembly this bond was one of the most repugnant aspects of his instructions because it imposed upon his governors an inflexibility which immunized them against all legislative instruments of persuasion, forensic as well as financial, and thus made a mockery of popular government in Pennsylvania. The House was happy, nevertheless, to have a public admission from one of Penn's own representatives of the paramount influence of the performance bond in provincial politics.

After receiving Denny's answer the members began considering the perilous state of the province and on 8 September voted to emit £60,000 for defense, which they proposed to sink by extending the excise on spirituous liquors for twenty years. Denny rejected this bill on 13 September because it did not comply with his instructions in two important respects: it did not give him a voice in the expenditure of any surplus the excise might produce and it extended it twice as long as Penn prescribed.[46] The Assem-

---

[45] 8 *Pa. Arch.*, v, 4308.

[46] Penn's demand that the excise run no longer than ten years was

bly was indignant at the governor's stand and denounced it in the same terms it had used during Morris's administration. His effort to gain control over the excise money was a violation of the people's right "to dispose of their own Money, by themselves or their Representatives . . . a natural Right, inherent in every Man, or Body of Men, antecedent to all Laws."[47] His insistence on amending a supply bill was a violation of their charter rights and their rights as Englishmen. Penn's instructions in general were "arbitrary," "unjust," "tyrannical," "cruel," "oppressive," and "unreasonable," the malevolent instruments "whereby our Constitution and the Liberties of our Country are wounded in the most essential Part, and even violated and destroyed." But the House's fusillade was futile, because the military situation was so desperate that money for defense had to be raised no matter what the cost or condition. Consequently, on 16 September it announced its intention of waiving its rights and passing an excise bill (with a reduced yield of £30,000) on Penn's terms. But it expressed its anger at being forced to capitulate to his instructions by threatening to appeal to "the Justice of his Majesty, and a British Parliament," a threat it repeated a week later.[48] The House realized, however, that the £30,000 bill was a stop-gap measure, that a much larger supply bill would be

---

not contained in the instructions Denny laid before the Assembly on 31 Aug. 1756. Rather, it was transmitted to the governor orally. He made a written note of it, however, and showed it to Speaker of the House Isaac Norris and Benjamin Franklin. Richard Peters to Thomas Penn, 22 Sept. 1756, Penn Papers, Hist. Soc. Pa.

[47] For this and the quotations immediately following, see 8 *Pa. Arch.*, V, 4333, 4324, 4326, 4327, 4345.

[48] *Ibid.*, 4327, 4345.

needed in the near future, that it would have to embody a land tax, and that a land tax would provide a better vehicle for opposing Penn in England. Hence, it postponed action until Denny asked for more money.

This the governor did on 24 November 1756, handing the House a paper on that date in which he calculated the cost of defending the province for the coming year at £127,284 13s. On 23 December the members resolved to raise £100,000 by the only method which would produce such a sum, a tax on *all* estates in the province. Not until 22 January 1757, however, did they perfect and pass a land tax bill. Three days later Denny rejected it, as the House must have expected he would, because it did not conform to his instructions.[49] The next day the members adopted a remonstrance, demanding "it of the Governor, as our Right, that he give his Assent to the Bill," and at noon on 28 January they marched through the streets of Philadelphia en masse to present it to him at the Council chamber.[50] But Denny stood his ground and rejected the bill once more, again justifying himself by citing his instructions. As soon as the members returned to their own chamber, they resolved unanimously to appoint a commissioner or commissioners "to go Home to England . . . to solicit a Removal of the Grievances we labor under by Reason of Proprietary Instructions."[51] The speed with which they acted and the lack of debate demonstrate that the measure had been previously concerted and that the members had postponed adopting it only until they received

[49] *Ibid.*, VI, 4433, 4460, 4476, 4495-96, 4497-98.
[50] Labaree, ed., *Papers of BF*, VII, 107.
[51] *Ibid.*, 109-11.

irrefragable proof from Denny that he opposed the supply bill because of Penn's instructions.

The article in the instructions on which the House intended to base its case against Penn was not, surprisingly, his stipulation that his estate be exempted from taxes, galling though that was. Rather, it was that part of the 21st article (laid before the Assembly on 31 August 1756) in which he ventured to formulate precise guidelines for the taxation of the inhabitants.[52] He ordered that no tax run longer than one year, that taxes be laid on the annual rent or income of an estate, not on its "whole Capital" value (that is, its total assessed valuation), that individual assets be assessed at no more than three percent of their valuation, that within these limits no tax be heavier than four shillings on the pound, that no unoccupied lands, surveyed or unsurveyed, be taxed, and that assessors be chosen according to rules which he dictated. These regulations were ridiculous because, as the Assembly publicly complained and Penn's partisans privately admitted, if they were strictly followed, they would produce no more than £30,000 per year,[53] less than a quarter of the amount which Denny claimed on 24 November 1756 was absolutely necessary for defending the province. This monumental flaw in Penn's instructions convinced the Assembly that its commissioners would prevail over him in England, for who could be more vulnerable than a man who insisted that the people of Pennsylvania pass supply bills on terms which

[52] 8 *Pa. Arch.*, V, 4300-6.

[53] 8 *Pa. Arch.*, VI, 4526; Franklin to Robert Charles, 1 Feb. 1757, in Labaree, ed., *Papers of BF*, VII, 117; Richard Peters to Thomas Penn, 31 Jan. and 14 Feb. 1757, Penn Papers, Hist. Soc. Pa.

would prevent them from defending themselves and which could cause the King to lose one of his most valuable provinces?

Having obtained what it regarded as sufficient incriminating evidence against the proprietary instructions, the Assembly got down to the business of defending the province, passing on 3 February 1757 a £100,000 land tax bill which exempted Penn's estate from taxes and made as many other accommodations with his instructions as its financial needs demanded. Denny, however, insisted on one hundred percent compliance with the instructions, which the House refused, and an impasse developed which was broken only by a further deterioration in the military situation and by the intervention of Lord Loudoun. On 21 March Denny received an express from Fort Augusta, advising him that 800 French and Indians were preparing to attack it and that the garrison "refused to do Duty for want of Pay."[54] The governor immediately communicated this intelligence to Loudoun, who was already in Philadelphia, and rather than lose a crucial fort for want of funds, the general urged him to waive his instructions and pass the £100,000 bill as it stood, which he did.[55]

In the meantime, Benjamin Franklin, the commissioner whom the Assembly had appointed on 29 January to represent it in England, was preparing to embark for the mother country. His instructions have not survived, but his conduct in London demonstrates that the House's strategy was to have him first try to resolve its differences with

[54] *Pa. Col. Recs.*, VII, 453.
[55] Labaree, ed., *Papers of BF*, VII, 152-53.

Penn by negotiating with him personally and, if that failed, to have him appeal to Parliament.[56] Fortunately, the absence of Franklin's instructions do not deprive us of a statement of the House's grievances against Penn, these being set forth in a report of one of its committees, 22 February 1757, and in a bill of particulars, the "Heads of Complaint," which Franklin presented the proprietor on 20 August 1757.[57] The members' fundamental objection to Penn, which underlay the years of fulmination and denunciation we have just described, was that he was trying, and because of the crisis created by the French and Indian War finally succeeding, to dictate provincial policy from England, to subject them to rigorous external control, even though they were accustomed to, and craved to continue, the enjoyment of a large measure of self-government.

As in the past, the Assembly's attacks focused, not on the specific phenomenon of external control, but on the instruments by which Penn was trying to impose it, on his in-

[56] Franklin's son William, who accompanied him to London, confirmed that his father was under orders to try to redress the House's grievances first by negotiating with Penn. The proprietors "trusted," he wrote Elizabeth Graeme on 9 Dec. 1757 "that as my Father was obliged to a friendly Negotiation with them" they could abuse Pennsylvania with impunity. *Ibid.*, 290. That Franklin's second course of action was to appeal to Parliament seems to be confirmed by his letter of 10 June 1758, to the Speaker of the Pennsylvania Assembly, written just after he had given up hope of reaching an accommodation with Penn personally. He wrote that he had been advised to try to remove the prejudices against Pennsylvania "before we push our Points in Parliament." Franklin to Thomas Leech *et al.*, 13 May and 10 June 1758, *ibid.*, VIII, 68, 87. See also Franklin to Norris, 19 Jan. 1759, *ibid.*, 234, in which he mentions proposals Penn has made to the Assembly; "I am advis'd," he wrote, "to make no Application to Parliament till I hear farther from the House."

[57] *Ibid.*, VII, 136-42, 251-52.

structions. The committee report of 22 February upbraided him for using them "to deprive the Assembly and People of their Rights and Privileges, and to assume an arbitrary and tyrannical Power over the Liberties and Properties of His Majesty's Liege Subjects" and assailed their unconstitutionality and illegality.[58] Proprietary instructions were unconstitutional, the House had consistently contended, because they contravened a major component of what it considered to be its "constitution," section four of the royal charter of 1681. In that section Charles II had granted William Penn "and his Heirs, and his or their Deputies or Lieutenants, free, full, and absolute Powers, for the good and happy Government [of Pennsylvania], to make and enact any Laws, *according to their best Discretions*, by and with the Advice, Assent, and Approbation of the Freemen of the said Country."[59] Reading this clause with the opportunistic literalism characteristic of Americans of their generation, the Assemblymen persuaded themselves that it made the discretion of Penn's deputies absolute and prevented the proprietor from exercising any control over them (and through them over the province). Instructions by which Penn tried to bind his governors were, therefore, "unconstitutional," although what the Assembly really meant was that external control was impermissible.

That proprietary instructions were illegal the House averred on the authority of its speaker of an earlier day,

[58] 8 *Pa. Arch.*, V, 3832; Labaree, ed., *Papers of BF*, VII, 138.
[59] This is a slightly abbreviated rendering of section four, as contained in the Assembly committee's report on grievances, 22 Feb. 1757, *ibid.*, 137. The full text of section four can be found, among other places, in an Assembly message of 8 Aug. 1755 in which it was cited to impugn the validity of Penn's instructions. 8 *Pa. Arch.*, V, 3943. Italics supplied by the author.

David Lloyd, who in 1725 affirmed that the law of England governing the relationship between a principal and his deputy had been stated by the Court of King's Bench in a 1702 case, *Parker* v. *Kett*, involving the power of a high-sheriff to forbid an under-sheriff to serve executions above £20. According to Lloyd, the court had decided that the under-sheriff had "full Power to do any act or thing which his Principal may do . . . that a Man cannot be a Deputy to do any single act or thing, nor can a Deputy have less Power than his Principal, and if his Principal makes him Covenant, That he will not do any particular thing which the Principal may do, the Covenant is void and repugnant."[60] That the relationship between the sheriff of an English county and his deputy defined the nature of the bond between the proprietor of a transatlantic colony and his lieutenant governor seemed to Lloyd and to later Pennsylvanians, not a preposterous proposition, but an eminently reasonable one (in 1759 Joseph Galloway cited *Parker* v. *Kett* as good law)[61] and, therefore, in the 1750s the Assemblymen professed to believe that neither Thomas Penn nor an English sheriff could control or restrain their deputies. Binding instructions were accordingly denounced as illegal, although again what the Assembly meant was that external control was impermissible.

The House was reluctant to make an explicit public declaration of its reason for opposing external control—its desire to govern the province itself. About the closest it usually came to expressing this ambition was by comparing

[60] David Lloyd, *A Vindication of the Legislative Power* (Phila., 1725).

[61] [Galloway], *True and Impartial State*, 26.

itself to the House of Commons and by accusing Penn of trying to strip it of any resemblance to the British legislature by giving his deputies inflexible instructions, which it must either accept or reject at the cost of losing indispensable legislation. By operating in this manner, Penn was acting like a dictator, the House charged, and was trying to reduce it from a viable parliamentary body to a superfluous ornament. Under such conditions "We might as well leave it to the Governor or the Proprietaries to make for us what Laws they please," the members complained, "and save ourselves and the Country the Expence and Trouble. All Debates and all Reasonings are vain, where Proprietary Instructions, just or unjust, right or wrong, must inviolably be observed. We have only to find out, if we can, what they are, and then submit and obey."[62] Penn, the Assemblymen protested on another occasion, would not only deny "us the Priveleges of an English Constitution, but would, as far as in his Power, introduce a French one, by reducing our Assemblies to the Insignificance of their Parliaments, incapable of making Laws, but by Direction, or of qualifying their own Gifts and Grants, and only allowed to register his Edicts."[63] Indeed, some men thought the proprietor was trying to impose an Egyptian constitution, for by giving Denny instructions which prevented the people from raising sufficient money to defend themselves, he appeared to be trying to force them to make brick without straw.

[62] See the Assembly's message to Gov. Morris, 11 Nov. 1755, 8 *Pa. Arch.*, V, 4113; similar sentiments were expressed in a House report of 11 Sept. 1753, *ibid.*, 3826.

[63] Assembly message to Morris, 22-24 Nov. 1755, *ibid.*, 4177.

The Assembly wanted to be neither Egyptian, nor French, nor superfluous. It wanted to be what it proudly proclaimed itself in a message of 26 January 1757, "an English Representative Body."[64] It wanted no more or no less than what Penn's charter of 1701 guaranteed it, the "Powers and Priveleges of an Assembly, according to the rights of the Freeborn Subjects of England," which it construed to mean equal status with the House of Commons.[65] And since by the 1750s the Commons was well on its way to becoming the supreme governing body in Britain, the Assembly, by its claims of parity with it, was intimating that it was the supreme governing body in Pennsylvania. A more straightforward, but still oblique, statement of its pretensions was its insistence, in its grievance report of 22 February 1757, on "an original Right of Legislation" by which it meant that it should have the initiative, the primacy in running provincial affairs.

Why was the Assembly so reticent about declaring its objectives? Why did it not candidly state that the reason it was sending an agent to England to protest Penn's policies was that it wanted to govern the province itself and was not prepared to tolerate any form of external control? One reason was the vigilance of its opponents. Proprietary governors like Robert Hunter Morris and proprietary pamphleteers like William Smith pounced on its declarations that no principal could legally bind his deputy and that the charter of 1681 made the proprietary deputy's

---

[64] *Ibid.*, VI, 4499.

[65] For examples of the Assembly's interpretation of this phrase, see its report of 22 Feb. 1757, in Labaree, ed., *Papers of BF*, VII, 138; Franklin to Isaac Norris, 14 Jan. 1758, *ibid.*, 361; 8 *Pa. Arch.*, V, 4026, 4176.

discretion inviolable and concluded from them that the House was averse to all forms of external control, not only Penn's but George III's as well, and that it was, in fact, hankering after independence.[66] These men were not backward about broadcasting these charges, and the House, though denouncing them as slanderous and "heinous,"[67] realized that its statements lent a certain credence to them. It also realized that by articulating precisely its aspirations and its objections to Penn's policies it would give real plausibility to the accusations of seeking independence and that this would destroy its chances of having Parliament or the British bureaucracy redress its grievances against Penn, for neither would be willing to assist a group under suspicions of disloyalty and treason. Thus, as a matter of policy, the House chose to forego complete candor.

Its conduct was also motivated by considerations far less calculating. In the 1750s (and in the next two decades, too) the Assemblymen and their constituents considered themselves loyal subjects of the British King. And yet the positions they had taken against Penn, if followed to their logical conclusions, seemed shamefully insubordinate. For example, the House's opposition to a principal's control over his deputy was so unqualified that it clearly comprehended the relationship between the King and his governors in America. The result was that men who believed they were loyal to the King found, by scrutinizing their thoughts, that they were opposed to his exercising effective control in America. This realization produced among the

---

[66] See, e.g., Morris's messages to the House of 7 Jan., 16 May, 12 Aug., and 24 Sept. 1755, *ibid.*, 3844, 3894, 3962, 4017, and Smith, *Brief State*, 10.

[67] See, e.g., [Galloway], *True and Impartial State*, 41.

Assemblymen confusion, embarrassment, and guilt. And, consequently, it inhibited a clear statement of their position. What the Assemblymen needed was some formula which would affirm both their allegiance to the King and their desire for autonomy. The concept of dominion status would have been perfect, but it had not yet been conceived, and the pronouncements of Franklin and other American statesmen, espousing a similar kind of constitutional arrangement, were still at least a decade away. Hence, the Assembly's aspiration for autonomy had not received the respectability which articulation confers, and its leaders were loath to spell it out. Yet it was the driving force in the quarrel with Penn, producing the petition to the Board of Trade in January 1755, Franklin's mission to England in the spring of 1757, and, ultimately, the attempt to eliminate proprietary government in 1764.

CHAPTER II

The Decision to Request
Royal Government

BENJAMIN FRANKLIN, the Assembly's commissioner to England, arrived at Falmouth on 17 July 1757 after a smooth, swift voyage of twenty-seven days. His passage was a poor portent of his mission, which was long, tedious, exasperating, and ultimately a failure. For this result Franklin was not responsible, because the Assembly had set him an impossible task, nothing less than persuading Penn to give up the substance of his power in the province. Franklin defined his objective in the Heads of Complaint, an informal paper which he drafted and handed to Penn at their first business meeting on 20 August 1757. "Proprietary Instructions enforced by penal Bonds" was the province's principal grievance, he declared, the redress of which was simple, he suggested; Penn need only observe the royal charter of 1681 and leave his deputies free and unfettered, at liberty to act "according to their best Discretion," as that document put it. What Franklin was asking amounted to a request that Penn relinquish control over the province, that he abdicate, in effect, as proprietor. That he would do anything of the sort was inconceivable and, therefore, in its main objective Franklin's mission was bound to fail.

Even had his task been less formidable, his mission would have been difficult because of the animosity between

Penn and him. Having "a natural Dislike to Persons who so far Love Money as to be unjust for its sake,"[1] Franklin was disgusted by Penn's tax dodging and flayed him for it in the messages he wrote for the Assembly from 1755 onward. Penn knew that he was the Assembly's penman, regarded him as a character assassin, and vowed as early as 10 January 1756 that he would "always despise him."[2] Consequently, the initial meetings between the two men resembled a confrontation between diplomats of hostile nations; each protested his respect for the other far too much to conceal his antipathy and distrust. Franklin, in fact, was not sufficiently distrustful and allowed Penn to trick him at the very outset of their conferences.

It was in composing the Heads of Complaint, at Penn's request, that he became his dupe. We have previously described that document as informal, but that adjective dignifies it too much; it was, as Penn later complained, "a loose Paper," "neither dated, signed, or addressed to any Person."[3] It appears, in fact, that Franklin suspected something and deliberately gave Penn a paper fit only for use as a rough agenda of conversation. But he should have committed nothing to writing, because the Heads of Complaint, irregular though it was, suited Penn's purposes perfectly; all that he needed was something of Franklin's composition which his solicitor, Ferdinando John Paris, could use to draw up an account of his controversy with the people of Pennsylvania, which could then be submitted to Attorney General Charles Pratt and Solicitor General

---

[1] Labaree, ed., *Papers of BF*, VII, 14.
[2] To Richard Peters, Penn Papers, Hist. Soc. Pa.
[3] Labaree, ed., *Papers of BF*, VII, 251, and VIII, 184.

Charles Yorke for their opinions (Penn as proprietor was technically a royal official and hence entitled to the law officers' opinions; Franklin, as a representative of a provincial assembly, was not). Paris accordingly drafted a state of the controversy which amounted to nothing more than eleven "loaded" questions, each phrased so that the law officers could answer them in only one way, the way which favored Penn most.[4] The proprietary strategy was brilliant: it guaranteed the support of the most authoritative legal opinion in the land for Penn's side of the quarrel with Franklin and it also guaranteed victory for him in the event that Franklin appealed the case to the King-in-Council, for either the Council or the Board of Trade would have to refer his complaints on points of law to Pratt and Yorke and they, having already given their opinion on these matters in Penn's favor, would not reverse themselves. Penn had Franklin coming and going, and Franklin knew it and resented it. It was unfair, he complained, for one party in a case to present its side while denying the opposition the same opportunity;[5] this was tantamount

---

[4] Paris's questions and Pratt's answers to them, 10 Oct. 1758, are at the Hist. Soc. Pa., as are Yorke's answers, 13 Jan. 1758. An example of how Paris phrased the objections in the Heads of Complaint to serve Penn's interests is furnished by his handling of the Assembly's protest against proprietary instructions. In asking the law officers' opinion on the legality of his principal's instructions, Paris did not mention the royal charter of 1681 which, the Assembly claimed, guaranteed Penn's deputies' absolute discretion. Rather, he posed the question this way: "Whether the Proprietarys of Pensilvania, may not lawfully, restrain their Lieutenant Governor's power and authority, by Instructions, and enforce his observance of the same, by Bond, (supposing such Instructions to be, in themselves, lawful, just, and prudent)." Of course, he received an affirmative answer from both Pratt and Yorke.

[5] Labaree, ed., *Papers of BF*, VIII, 235.

to condemning a man or a cause unheard. But Penn was not about to let Franklin see the case as Paris had stated it,[6] or to revise it in the interest of equal justice. In his first encounter with Franklin, Thomas Penn had done the one thing to him which he could never forget or forgive: he had outsmarted him.

Penn's stratagem convinced Franklin that he had no intention of negotiating in good faith. His subsequent conduct confirmed this conclusion, for he absolutely refused to discuss the specific points in dispute until he had received both Yorke's and Pratt's opinions. Since the latter did not respond until 10 October 1758, there was no movement in the negotiations for fifteen months. And yet throughout this period Penn regaled all interested parties with declarations of good will and of his "sincere Desire of settling everything with the Assembly amicably on reasonable terms."[7] Franklin was greatly angered by what he considered to be the hypocrisy of these statements. Nor was his humor improved by having constantly to wait on Penn to discover whether the law officers had finally deigned to give their opinion, errands on which he often felt like an indigent courtier, strumming his fingers in a patron's anteroom. His resentment against the proprietor burst its bounds in a conference early in January 1758, at which Penn claimed that, in issuing his famous charter of 1701, his father, the late, lamented William Penn, had exceeded his powers under the royal charter of 1681 and that the thousands of people who had migrated to Pennsylvania on the faith of the privileges granted by the 1701 charter had been deceived. According to Franklin, Penn delivered this

---

[6] *Ibid.*, VIII, 3. [7] *Ibid.*, VII, 374.

opinion "with a Kind of triumphing laughing Insolence, such as a low Jockey might do when a Purchaser complained that He had cheated him in a Horse." He was "astonished," he said, "to see him thus meanly give up his Father's Character and conceived that Moment a more cordial and thorough Contempt for him than I ever before felt for any Man living—A Contempt that I cannot express in Words, but I believe my Countenance expressed it strongly."[8] The impression of this interview was still vivid a month later, when Franklin expressed the hope that "the Proprietors will be gibbeted up as they deserve, to rot and stink in the Nostrils of Posterity."[9]

A major turning point in Franklin's mission came at hearings before Yorke and Pratt on 20 and 27 April 1758 on a petition from the Reverend William Smith, praying for relief from imprisonment for libel by the Pennsylvania Assembly. At these hearings Penn actively took the parson's part and abetted the abuse his counsel heaped on the Assembly. According to Franklin, his actions were "look'd upon by every body as an open Declaration of War," and they dashed his last lingering hopes for an accommodation with Penn.[10] Henceforth, he made no more appointments with him and did not see him or his agents on official business until Paris handed him the proprietary answer to the Heads of Complaint on 27 November 1758.[11]

That answer, which conceded little to the Assembly, was about what Franklin expected, based as it was on biased legal opinion. He had, moreover, been informed some months earlier by his own counsel, Richard Jackson, whom

[8] *Ibid.*, VII, 362. [9] *Ibid.*, VII, 374.
[10] *Ibid.*, VIII, 68, 150. [11] *Ibid.*, VIII, 179-83.

he had picked because of his prodigious learning and pro-American sympathies, that in the main point in dispute, the permissibility of Penn's attempts to exercise control in Pennsylvania through deputies bound by inflexible instructions, the proprietor would be supported by all shades of official British opinion.[12] Therefore, he was not surprised by Penn's declaration that he would not alter his practice of giving his deputies instructions enforced by penal bonds. What did surprise him, though, was the asperity of the answer. As he later learned, it was caused by an information leak in Pennsylvania. Somehow, the Proprietary Party had obtained a copy of his letter to Norris of 14 January 1758, in which he had called Penn "a low Jockey." The proprietor, who received and read the letter by 5 July 1758,[13] was enraged, swore to have nothing more to do with Franklin, and eagerly sought an opportunity to repay his rancor. In answering the Heads of Complaint he saw his chance.

Paris, who wrote the answer, tried hard to make it a suitable vehicle of vengeance. Penn's problems with the Assembly might have been resolved, he declared, had he been negotiating with "cool, temperate Persons"; indeed, even at this late hour he was willing to try to compose his differences with the House if it would "forthwith authorise and impower . . . some Persons of Candour to enter into

[12] Jackson warned that, "as the Practice of Instructing is originally a Practice of the Crown, I doubt [i.e., assume] the Council will not condemn it in a Proprietor." As for Penn's practice of dictating the terms of a supply bill in detail in his instructions, Jackson did not think that it would be censured "as our Administration goes farther in framing Laws for Ireland." See his "Private Sentiments and Advice on Pennsylvania Affairs," 24 April 1758, *ibid.*, VIII, 22-27.

[13] *Ibid.*, VII, 363-64n.

free Conferences, and adjust those Matters in the most agreeable Manner," a proposal which Penn personally reiterated the next day by writing the House and calling for the appointment of "Persons of Candour" to come over and confer with him.[14] Clearly, his purpose was to have Franklin recalled in disgrace. Franklin perceived this (how could he not have?), but he was baffled by other parts of the answer to the Heads of Complaint and wrote Penn on 28 November, requesting enlightenment. A few days later he received a curt note from Paris, refusing further information and telling him that the proprietor could not "conceive it will answer any good purpose, to continue a Corrispondence" with him.[15] Thus, Penn avenged himself upon Franklin. Franklin, for his part, was eager to return the favor, for he had not endured such a string of personal indignities since the abrasive apprenticeship of his Boston youth under his brother James.

The failure of negotiations with Penn played an important role in Pennsylvania's attempt to overturn proprietary government in 1764, because it significantly narrowed the options available to the province's leadership during that year. Franklin kept the members of the Assembly fully informed about Penn's tactics by letter and, when he returned home in 1762, expatiated on them at first hand. By 1764 his colleagues shared his conviction that Penn was as averse to reform as any Bourbon in France. The proprietors, wrote Joseph Galloway in the spring of that year, had "cut off all opportunity of complaint to them," so that the people lacked "the least Hopes" of their "present Condition becoming better while Proprietary Interest and Power

14 *Ibid.*, VIII, 184-86.   15 *Ibid.*, VIII, 193-94.

are united and prevail." "We have often attempted to obtain Relief from Oppression, from the Proprietaries," he wrote on another occasion, "but in vain. They have forbid us even to address them. They have refused to hear us."[16] Consequently, when in 1764 the Assembly was once again aggrieved by proprietary policy, it did not even consider appealing to Penn for redress. Despairing of help from him or from the British bureaucracy, and determined not to acquiesce in his designs, it sought relief in the radical remedy of royal government.

Snubbed by Penn, Franklin prepared to appeal against him to the House of Commons, the alternative course of action prescribed by his instructions. The Pennsylvania Assembly had selected this secondary strategy because of its faith, which virtually everyone in America shared, that the members of the Commons were independent public servants with great empathy for their fellow citizens in the colonies, were, in effect, 558 ombudsmen for America. Franklin, who was full of this notion when he left New York, was not in England long before he was disabused of it (the disillusionment of Americans in general did not come until after the Stamp Act). So far from being independent, the majority of Commons members were, he discovered, either placemen or other ministerial satellites, who were rubber stamps in their masters' hands. "An Administration will probably for the future always be able to support and carry in Parliament whatever they wish to,"

---

[16] [Joseph Galloway], *An Address to the Freeholders and Inhabitants of the Province of Pennsylvania* (Phila., 1764), 3; *The Speech of Joseph Galloway, Esq. . . . in Answer to the Speech of John Dickinson* (Phila., 1764), 4-5.

Jackson told him on 24 April 1758, and, as with all of his pronouncements, Franklin accepted this one as gospel, gravely informing Speaker of the Pennsylvania Assembly Isaac Norris on 19 March 1759 that, "if the Ministry make a Point of carrying *any thing* in Parliament, they can carry it."[17] As for the sympathy which the House of Commons was supposed to have for the colonists, Franklin discovered that this, too, was a delusion and that many members, and alarming numbers of ordinary Englishmen as well, were scornful of them.[18] Given these unpleasant realities, Jackson advised him to do two things to make headway with Parliament: acquire influence with the ministry and dispel the prejudice of the legislators against Americans in general and Pennsylvanians in particular.

Although he tried, Franklin made no impressions to his or Pennsylvania's advantage so long as the Pitt-Newcastle ministry continued in office (29 June 1757–5 October 1761). Pitt never deigned to grant him an interview[19] and neither, as far as we know, did Newcastle. He did see some important ministers, but only on business, and with them he established no meaningful rapport. He found the president of the Privy Council, Lord Granville, a high prerogative man, so prejudiced against American pretensions that

[17] Labaree, ed., *Papers of BF*, VIII, 26, 296. On 17 Feb. 1768 Franklin wrote Galloway that he knew "that nothing is to be done in Parliament that is not a Measure adopted by the Ministry and supported by their Strength, much less anything they are averse to and indifferent about." Clements Library, University of Michigan.

[18] For the prejudice against colonials which Franklin and his son discovered, see Labaree, ed., *Papers of BF*, VII, 290, and VIII, 89, 295.

[19] See Franklin's Account of Negotiations in London, 22 March 1775, Library of Congress.

in one interview he insisted that the King's instructions were "the law of the land" in the colonies.[20] Besides, he was married to the sister of Thomas Penn's wife and was thus suspected of a familial bias against the Assembly. Lord Chancellor Hardwicke, second in command at the Council, appeared to have even more authoritarian views, and Franklin feared that Lord Halifax, president of the Board of Trade, was more reactionary still. He was reputed to believe that military governments were best for the colonies,[21] a sentiment which confirmed the Assembly's wisdom in not submitting another appeal to his tender mercies, as it had its petition against Penn's instructions in 1755. Far from obtaining influence with these men, Franklin rarely received an encouraging word from them.

In trying to dispel Parliament's prejudice against Pennsylvania, he was no more successful. The instrument he selected for this task was, characteristically, the pen—not his, but Jackson's. At his request and with his and his son's assistance, the lawyer wrote a long, partisan account of the Assembly's struggles with the proprietary family, *An Historical Review of the Constitution and Government of Pensylvania* (the misspelling was apparently deliberate), in which not even William Penn escaped censure.[22] Franklin had the book dedicated to Arthur Onslow, Speaker of the

---

[20] Labaree, ed., *Papers of BF*, VIII, 293.

[21] *Ibid.*, VIII, 293; Franklin, in fact, found the entire Board of Trade a hotbed of anti-colonial prejudice. "America has rarely, for many Years past, had a Friend among them," he wrote Joseph Galloway on 13 Dec. 1766. "The Standing Secretary [John Pownall] seems to have a strong Bias against us, and to infect them one after another as they come to it." Clements Library, University of Michigan.

[22] For information about the publication and reception of this volume, see Labaree, ed., *Papers of BF*, VIII, 89n, 360-62, 402, 448, 453.

House of Commons, and paid for a printing of 2,000 copies. Published on 29 May 1759, it sold poorly in England and did not move well in Pennsylvania either. Franklin was discouraged by its reception, but realized that a one-shot effort to convert public and parliamentary opinion was unlikely to bear fruit. He knew that winning the minds of men was a long-range proposition and, therefore, he counselled his followers in Pennsylvania to have patience.

Confronted by such bleak prospects for the success of his mission, Franklin began to toy with another solution to the Assembly's difficulties with Penn, one which became more appealing the more he considered it—the assumption of the government of Pennsylvania by the King. This idea was by no means original with him. Pennsylvania had experienced royal government in the 1690s and few years passed thereafter in which groups or individuals, unhappy with the way the province was being run, did not propose it as a solution to their problems. In the 1720s Sir William Keith was scheming to overthrow the proprietary government and have himself installed as royal governor.[23] Under Governor George Thomas (1738-47) the Quaker Party was constantly buzzing with plans for royal government; "it became a common practice for the Quakers and their sympathizers," William Shepherd observed, "when any carefully concocted political schemes were balked, to threaten to petition the king to assume the government."[24]

[23] Or so it was widely believed. See Thomas Wendel, "The Keith-Lloyd Alliance: Factional and Coalition Politics in Colonial Pennsylvania," *Pa. Mag. Hist. and Biog.*, XCII (1968), 295, 302.

[24] William R. Shepherd, *History of Proprietary Government in Pennsylvania* (New York, 1896), 551-52. Mabel P. Wolff has written that "for the first few years of the Thomas administration, there was, more-

Early in 1755, when difficulties with Penn began to intensify, Isaac Norris came out for royal government[25] (he later reversed himself) and Franklin apparently spoke approvingly enough of it in the Assembly to convince his opponents, and historians who credit their assertions, that he was a convert to its cause, that he was going to England with the "avowed intention" of procuring it, and that he thought negotiations with Thomas Penn would be a waste of time.[26] Although there seems to be little doubt that in 1757 Franklin considered royal government as one possible solution to the province's problems,[27] it seems equally clear that he went to England resolved to settle the quarrel with Penn by negotiations, because he approached them with good will and good faith and made no moves toward royal

---

over, a certain amount of agitation looking toward a petition to the Crown to change the Pennsylvania government from a proprietary to a royal form." *The Colonial Agency of Pennsylvania 1712-1757* (Phila., 1933), 102.

[25] William Hanna, *Benjamin Franklin and Pennsylvania Politics* (Stanford, 1964), 79.

[26] For contemporary charges that Franklin was resolved to obtain royal government at this time, see William Peters to Thomas Penn, 4 Jan. 1756; Richard Peters to Penn, 29 April 1756; Robert Hunter Morris to Penn, 8 Oct. 1756; Richard Peters to Penn, 31 Jan. 1757; and Richard Hockley to Penn, 20 Feb. 1757; all in Penn Papers, Hist. Soc. Pa. William Hanna has given full credence to these charges; see *op.cit.*, 115, 116, 119, 120.

[27] Besides the weight of the accusations of his opponents, Franklin and his coadjutor, Joseph Galloway, both admitted in 1764 that they had spoken for royal government earlier, presumably at this time. Franklin conceded that the measure "had often been propos'd in former Assemblies," while Galloway claimed that it "had been often thought of and proposed by the same Members [himself and Franklin] in preceding Assemblies." Franklin's *Preface* to Galloway's *Speech*, in Labaree, ed., *Papers of BF*, XI, 288-89; Galloway, *The Speech of Joseph Galloway . . .* , 2.

government until the proprietor's conduct at the hearings on William Smith's petition, 20 April 1758, convinced him that an accommodation was impossible.[28]

Once Penn had made that impression, however, Franklin lost little time in exploring the prospects for royal government. At his request Robert Charles composed a series of questions for Richard Jackson on 24 April about the status of the province's rights and privileges if it came under the direct government of the crown. Franklin was vastly, and indeed excessively, encouraged by Jackson's answer, which claimed that the ministry did not of itself have the authority to abridge in any way the province's privileges, that it could diminish them only by procuring an act of Parliament.[29] In a private opinion, which he prepared for Franklin alone, Jackson warned, however, that the ministry could obtain from Parliament whatever statutes it wished and that "they will almost always wish to extend the Power of the Crown and themselves both mediately and immediately."[30] Franklin ignored this confidential caveat and focused his attention on the response to Charles, which he chose to consider as tantamount to a guarantee that Pennsylvania would lose nothing valuable in a change of government. He sent Jackson's opinion to the members of the Assembly and, supplemented by his sanguine interpretation, it played an important role in stimulating the campaign for royal government in 1764.

Franklin also solicited the opinions of British bureaucrats about the prospects for ousting Penn. He appears to

[28] See above, pp. 45, 47.
[29] Labaree, ed., *Papers of BF*, VIII, 6-21.
[30] *Ibid.*, 26.

have succeeded only in obtaining the views of some second-line Treasury officials, most notably those of his friend, Grey Cooper, to which he again reacted with excessive enthusiasm. These men conveyed to him what by 1758 had become a widespread feeling among British politicians and public servants, that the proprietary governments of Pennsylvania and Maryland (and the charter governments of Connecticut and Rhode Island as well) were anachronisms which should be resumed by the crown in the interests of more efficient colonial administration.[31] Yet Franklin inferred from their statements a much stronger determination to abolish these jurisdictions than actually existed. "It is certain that the Government here are inclin'd to resume all the Proprietary Powers," he wrote Norris on 16 September 1758, "and I make no doubt but upon the first Handle they will do so." By 19 January 1759 he had become even more confident. Royal government "might without much Difficulty be carried," he wrote the Speaker, "and our Priveleges preserved."[32]

Events proved him a poor prophet. Three factors account for his miscalculation: the unauthoritative information on which his lack of access to the ministry forced him to rely, his overly optimistic disposition (which he himself later acknowledged), and, above all, his indulgence in wishful thinking. To amplify this last point: to convert Pennsylvania to a royal government appealed to him because it offered an opportunity to visit Old Testament ven-

[31] For a characteristic expression of this sentiment, see Thomas C. Barrow, ed., "A Project for Imperial Reform: 'Hints Respecting the Settlement for our American Provinces,' 1763," 3 *WMQ*, XXIV (1967), 118.

[32] Labaree, ed., *Papers of BF*, VIII, 157, 236.

geance on Penn, to turn from office a man who was trying to have the Assembly do exactly the same to him; this desire led him to grasp at insufficient evidence and convince himself that what he wanted to happen could happen; and then he tried to convince the Assembly that it would happen. It was in this way that the campaign for royal government in 1764 was colored by Franklin's personal animus against Penn, for the Assembly would not have petitioned for royal rule had he not convinced it that such a request would be favorably received, and his judgment that it would be was shaped by his desire to settle scores with Penn.

Franklin, in fact, did not wait for the Assembly's authorization to try to arrange the proprietor's downfall. By the beginning of 1760 he was scheming to use one of Penn's own kinsmen to subvert him.[33] His plan was founded on a belief which had been current in Pennsylvania since at least 1755, namely, that the agreement concluded in 1731 between William Penn III (1703-47), grandson of William Penn through his first wife, Gulielma Springett, and John, Thomas, and Richard Penn, sons of Penn by his second wife, Hannah Callowhill, by which the three sons purchased the proprietorship and soil of Pennsylvania, was illegal and that the rights to former were still vested in the elder branch of the family.[34] In 1760 its representa-

[33] Thomas Penn's cousin, Springett Penn. That Franklin knew and was manipulating Springett in 1760 is shown by a letter to Springett from Thomas Penn, 1 June 1760, declining to grant him an interview because of "Your being under an influence which I think is not for your honour or service." Penn Papers, Hist. Soc. Pa.

[34] On 22 Aug. 1755 Richard Hockley wrote Thomas Penn that the Assembly was "viley insinuating amongst the People that the Governm^t in right belongs to the Heir of Springet Penn deceas'd [i.e., William

tive was William Penn III's twenty-one-year-old son, Springett, who was also its last male member. In this young man the blood lines ran thin, both literally and figuratively. He was a pitiable specimen, a consumptive mama's boy who died of tuberculosis in 1766. But it was precisely his weakness which recommended him to Franklin, who intended to exploit it in the following way: He hoped to obtain opinions from Jackson and other reputable lawyers that the transfer of the proprietorship in 1731 had been invalid. Then he hoped to induce Springett to sue Thomas Penn, presumably in Chancery, to recover it; if the suit succeeded, he was certain that the young man would have no stomach for governing the province and would sell his rights to the Crown. Franklin was even prepared to supply a sale's price. In 1712 William Penn had agreed to sell the proprietorship to Queen Anne for £12,000 and had received a down payment of £1,000.[35] Thus, £11,000 was still due on this long-forgotten contract, the details of which Franklin had discovered during his first year in England,[36] and he was convinced that the sickly Springett would be happy to part with the proprietorship for that price, even though its value had appreciated enormously in the intervening forty-eight years. The young man would "willingly surrender to the Crown for

---

Penn's eldest son by his first wife]. one of the Members told me so himself and had assurance to add that I might one day or other see it disputed." Penn Papers, Hist. Soc. Pa.

[35] Shepherd, *Proprietary Government in Pennsylvania*, 544.

[36] The contract is mentioned in the queries Robert Charles prepared for Franklin on 24 April 1758 for submission to Jackson. Labaree, ed., *Papers of BF*, VIII, 18.

such a Sum," he predicted, because "he seems not able to contend for his Right."[37]

Franklin's scheme got nowhere. Evidently, he did receive some encouraging legal advice before he left England in August 1762,[38] because in the Assembly in 1764 his lieutenant, Joseph Galloway, declared that he had "seen the Opinion of some very great Men, his Majesty's Servants, often near his Person, That the Powers of Government is an Interest that cannot be transfer'd or alien'd [and thus] the Right of Government cannot be in our present Proprietaries, but in the elder Branch of their Family."[39] Nevertheless, no lawsuit was brought against Thomas Penn and, with Springett's death in the fall of 1766, the whole plan went up in smoke.[40] It was just as well that it did, for beneath its patina of plausibility it was poorly conceived. A suit in Chancery, had Springett initiated one, would have dragged on interminably, as Franklin, who was familiar

[37] Franklin to Jackson, 31 March 1764, *ibid.*, XI, 151.

[38] As late as 9 Jan. 1762 Franklin had not received a formal opinion from any of his lawyers. By the spring of 1761, however, he had learned informally "that some Lawyers here are of opinion, that the Government was not legally convey'd from the eldest Branch to others of the Family." Franklin to Edward Penington, 9 May 1761 and 9 Jan. 1762, *ibid.*, IX, 317, and X, 6.

[39] Galloway, *The Speech of Joseph Galloway* . . . , 43.

[40] The strangest episode in Franklin's relationship with Springett occurred during his first mission, when he persuaded the young man to "put his baggage on Board [ship] for Pennsylvania." Thomas Penn to William Allen, 15 Feb. 1765, Penn Papers, Hist. Soc. Pa. Perhaps Springett was going to Pennsylvania merely to satisfy his curiosity about lands he owned there, the full extent of which he suspected Thomas Penn of concealing from him, or perhaps Franklin intended him to go to Pennsylvania to be proclaimed proprietor by the Assembly, thus forcing the hand of the authorities in England.

with the decades of litigation between the Penns and the Baltimores, must have known. If things went according to form, a decision on the case would probably not have come until the nineteenth century. And even if Springett were finally declared proprietor, what assurance was there that he would sell his powers for a price set in 1712? His mother or others around him would probably have prevented him from being shortchanged and would doubtless have demanded a decent price from the crown. But who could be sure that the crown, which was usually strapped for money, would buy the proprietorship? In truth, there was little of substance in Franklin's scheme, and it was unfortunate that the Assembly, presumably at his instigation, chose to make a major element of it, William Penn's contract of 1712, a key part of its campaign for royal government in 1764.

The futility of Franklin's flirtation with Springett Penn was typical of the state of floundering impotence in which he found himself after Thomas Penn snubbed him in December 1758. He was adrift with no apparent way to accomplish the objectives of his mission and with no reason to believe that his prospects would soon improve. Fortunately for him, the Assembly came to his rescue on 17 April 1759 by bribing Governor Denny to ignore Penn's instructions and pass a £100,000 supply bill which taxed his estate.[41] Now Franklin's job was to see that the bill was confirmed by the King-in-Council. Royal confirmation would not, of course, accomplish the primary purpose of his mission; it would prevent Penn from exempting his estate from taxes, but in all other respects it would leave

[41] Labaree, ed., *Papers of BF*, VIII, 326-27n, 419-20n.

his power to dictate policy to his deputies through inflexible instructions intact. On the other hand, confirmation would be a substantial achievement which Franklin could claim as a successful conclusion to his mission. Then he could return home with honor.

When Thomas Penn heard of Denny's capitulation to the Assembly, he served notice that he would not acquiesce in it and would try to prevent the confirmation of the supply bill. Accordingly, in the winter of 1760 he petitioned the King-in-Council to repeal it (as well as several other bills which the House had passed in 1758 and 1759). As soon as Franklin learned of his action, he retained counsel to convince the King's servants that the bills ought to be confirmed. Hearings were held before the Board of Trade in May and June 1760 and before the Privy Council's Committee on Plantation Affairs in August. Both bodies decided what Franklin called the "grand Principle" of the supply bill in the Assembly's favor; Thomas Penn could no longer prevent it from taxing his estate.[42] The Board of Trade, however, conceived so many objections to other parts of the bill that it recommended its repeal. The Privy Council Committee was also distressed by certain of its sections, which it castigated as "fundamentally wrong and unjust," but it was not as ruthless as the Board of Trade. Led by Lord Mansfield, it devised a compromise; the act was allowed to stand in return for which Franklin and his co-agent Robert Charles signed a pledge[43] guaranteeing that the Assembly would amend it in six particulars, designed

[42] *Ibid.*, IX, 125-73, 196-211, and XI, 285.
[43] Penn spoke of their "engagements on the Council Books." To Hamilton, 18 Oct. 1760, Penn Papers, Hist. Soc. Pa.

to protect Penn from discriminatory taxation. (The idea of amending an act sixteen months after its passage was by no means whimsical; although £100,000 in paper money was emitted immediately after the supply bill passed, taxes to sink this sum were not scheduled to be laid until 10 March 1764.)[44] The six amendments, which the Privy Council Committee dictated and embodied in an order of 2 September 1760 were the cynosure of Pennsylvania politics until well into 1764, and a dispute over one of them precipitated the attempt to overthrow the proprietary government. They are printed here in full:

1. That the Real Estate to be taxed, be defined with Precision, so as not to include the unsurveyed waste Land belonging to the Proprietaries.

2. That the Located uncultivated Lands belonging to the Proprietaries shall not be assessed higher than the lowest Rate at which any located uncultivated Lands belonging to the Inhabitants shall be assessed.

3. That all Lands not granted by the Proprietaries within Boroughs and Towns, be deemed located uncultivated Lands and rated accordingly and not as Lots.

4. That the Governors Consent and Approbation be made necessary to every issue and Application of the money to be raised by Virtue of such Act.

5. That Provincial Commissioners be named to hear and determine Appeals brought on the part of the Inhabitants as well as of the Proprietaries.

[44] From which date they were to run for three years, sinking one-third of the £100,000 each year. *Statutes at Large, Pa.*, v, 379-96.

6. That the Payments by the Tenants to the Proprietaries of their Rents, shall be according to the terms of their respective Grants, as if such Act had never been passed.[45]

The Privy Council also decreed that, if the Pennsylvania Assembly ignored its agents' pledge, a £100,000 supply bill, signed by Governor James Hamilton on 12 April 1760, which taxed the proprietary estates in the same manner as the supply bill of 1759, would be "immediately repealed without any reference to the Board of Trade, and Parliament applyed to, to do it."[46] Finally, the Council decreed—Penn, at any rate, believed that it had—that all future supply bills would have to conform to the six amendments.

Pennsylvanians were astonished when they heard of Penn's opposition to the supply bill; even Franklin, who thought that he had seen the worst the proprietor could offer, was amazed that he could muster the "Face" to demand its repeal.[47] It was one thing to dodge taxes by refusing to pass an offending bill; the sum shirked, when spread over the entire population of the province, would not impose an insupportable burden on any citizen. It was quite another matter, however, to try to dodge taxes by repealing the bill which levied them. Suppose Penn had succeeded in having the supply bill repealed. The £100,000 in paper money emitted under it would have become

[45] Labaree, ed., *Papers of BF*, IX, 205-7.

[46] This threat was not written into the order-in-council of 2 Sept. 1760, however. Thomas Penn to James Hamilton, 30 Aug. and 5 Sept. 1760, Penn Papers, Hist. Soc. Pa.

[47] Labaree, ed., *Papers of BF*, IX, 16; see also *ibid.*, VIII, 396.

worthless and the thousands of people who had accepted it in good faith (mainly farmers and small tradesmen who had supplied goods and services to the army) would have been ruined, all sacrificed to proprietary greed. No wonder that the Assembly was "enraged"—the word was Provincial Secretary Richard Peters's[48]—when in January 1761 it received an account of Penn's actions. And no wonder that as late as the autumn of 1764 the people of Pennsylvania were still fuming over what one election broadside described as the proprietor's "iniquitous Scheme of getting one Hundred Thousand Pounds of Paper Money, condemned by the King in Council, in your Hands, that you might be deprived of so much of your Property, and thereby be more easily reduced to P[roprietar]y Slavery."[49] "As the Proprietors knew," wrote Franklin in the summer of 1764, "that the Hundred Thousand Pounds of Paper Money, struck for the Defence of their enormous Estates, with others, was actually issued, spread thro' the Country, and in the Hands of Thousands of poor People, who had given their Labor for it; how base, how cruel, and inhuman it was, to endeavour, by a Repeal of the Act, to strike the Money dead in those Hands at one Blow, and reduce it all to Waste Paper, to the utter Confusion of all Trade and Dealings, and the Ruin of Multitudes, merely to avoid paying their own just Tax!"[50]

[48] Richard Peters to Thomas Penn, 13 Jan. 1761, Penn Papers, Hist. Soc. Pa.

[49] *To the Freeholders and other Electors for the City and County of Philadelphia, and Counties of Chester and Bucks* [*Sept.*] *1764.* Evans microcards, No. 9857.

[50] Franklin's *Preface* to Galloway's *Speech*, in Labaree, ed., *Papers of BF*, XI, 279.

The individual amendments which the Privy Council dictated caused no rejoicing in Pennsylvania either. The sixth amendment was particularly unwelcome, because it decided in Penn's favor a controversy which had been agitating the province since 1723, when the Assembly issued paper money for the first time. Contrary to the members' intentions, but consonant with the laws of economics, the paper depreciated. By 1729 one Pennsylvania pound was worth only 67 percent as much as a pound sterling, by 1739 only 58.8 percent as much.[51] The Assembly, nevertheless, made the paper money a legal tender, acceptable, as its successive statutes stated, at face value "for the payment and discharge of all manner of debts, rents . . . and sums of money whatsoever." But in practice an exception was made for one kind of debts: sterling debts due to British merchants. These Pennsylvanians paid in specie or in paper money at the rate of exchange between Philadelphia and London, a custom which was recognized and enforced by the provincial courts.[52] The proprietary family's contracts with its tenants called for the payment of their quit rents in sterling, but Pennsylvanians flouted them and paid the rents, when they paid them at all, in depreciating legal tender paper. Believing themselves defrauded and discriminated against, the Penns cried foul and demanded in April

[51] I.e., in 1729 the rate of exchange between Philadelphia and London was 150; by 1739 it had risen to 170. *Votes and Proceedings of the House of Representatives of the Province of Pennsylvania*, III (Philadelphia, Franklin and Hall, 1754), 333.

[52] Franklin to the Pennsylvania Assembly Committee of Correspondence, 12 April 1766, in Labaree, ed., *Papers of BF*, XIII, 238; Franklin, "Remarks and Facts Relative to the American Paper Money," 11 March 1767, *Pa. Chronicle*, 25 May–1 June 1767.

1729 through their deputy, Patrick Gordon, that the Assembly make its constituents honor their contracts.[53] When Gordon got nowhere with the House, the Penns tried to avail themselves of the arrangement enjoyed by the British merchants.

Beginning in 1732, they made all purchasers of their lands sign contracts binding them to pay their quit rents in sterling or in "its value in Currency, regard being had to the rate of Exchange between Philadelphia and London."[54] Thus, the Penns agreed to accept Pennsylvania paper, but not at its face value. If a tenant owed 10*s.* sterling in rent and if the exchange rate was 170, as it was in 1732 and for many years thereafter, the proprietaries insisted on 17*s.* in Pennsylvania money. But as long as the Assembly continued to issue paper money as legal tender, this scheme was not worth the paper the new contracts were written on, for so long could tenants continue paying their rent in Pennsylvania money, at its face value, leaving the proprietaries no remedy but to sue for breach of contract in the rabidly hostile local courts, which was no remedy at all. Relief, if it were to come, would have to come from the Assembly; somehow that body must be made to protect the proprietary rents. Accordingly, Gordon's successor, George Thomas, was instructed not to sign any bill "for making,

---

[53] Gordon presented this demand at a conference with a committee of the Assembly on 4 April 1729. See *Votes and Proceedings . . . of Pennsylvania*, 81.

[54] Board of Trade Report, 24 June 1760, in Labaree, ed., *Papers of BF*, IX, 150. According to Charles P. Keith, Thomas Penn, who came to the province in 1732, personally "introduced the practice of reserving quit rents payable according to the exchange." *Chronicles of Pennsylvania from the English Revolution to the Peace of Aix-la-Chapelle 1688-1748* (Phila., 1917, 2 vols.), II, 790.

emitting, encreasing, or continuing" paper money unless the Assembly agreed that the "Quit-rents and other Rents due, and to be due to the Proprietaries" should be paid at the "true and real Rate of Exchange between the Cities of Philadelphia and London, at the Time of such Payment." Thomas first produced this instruction in the winter of 1739, when the Assembly was debating a bill to emit £80,000 in paper money. The Assembly refused to comply, but it persuaded Thomas to sign the bill by voting the Penns an indemnity of £1,200 and an additional £130 annually until 1749 for the losses they would suffer because of depreciation.[55] After 1749 the proprietors were unable to renew the bargain with the Assembly. They gave Governor Denny the same instruction as they had given Thomas, but the House spurned it.[56] All the paper money it issued between 1755 and 1759 was issued as legal tender and without indemnification.

Against this background it is easy to see why Thomas Penn rejoiced at the Privy Council's sixth amendment. By directing the Assembly to draw all future supply bills so that his tenants would be obliged to pay their rents "according to the terms of their respective Grants," the Council was ordering that he henceforth be paid either in sterling or in Pennsylvania currency at the exchange rate between Philadelphia and London. In other words, it was giving him what he had sought in vain from the Assembly since

[55] Both the £80,000 bill and the bill providing an indemnity for the proprietors were signed by Gov. Thomas on 19 May 1739. See *Statutes at Large, Pa.*, IV, 322-26, 344-59; see also *Votes and Proceedings . . . of Pennsylvania*, 338-44.

[56] Denny laid his instruction on the emission of paper money before the House on 31 Aug. 1756. 8 *Pa. Arch.*, V, 4300.

1729: exemption from the province's legal tender paper currency.

Pennsylvanians were indignant at this decision. There were few things about which they agreed more heartily than that paper money was one of the principal reasons for the province's remarkable prosperity. Even if it tended to sink in value, most people reckoned depreciation a small price to pay for the services paper money performed and tolerated it out of a sense of civic duty. Thomas Penn was thought to have less cause to complain about depreciation than any other man in the province, because he profited more from paper money than anyone else: the paper-primed prosperity buoyed up the price of land, of which he was the chief seller, and attracted swarms of immigrants, who swelled the ranks of purchasers and bid up land prices even higher; a substantial proportion of his tenants, moreover, improved their farms and habitations with paper money borrowed from the Provincial Loan Office; finally, without the huge emissions of paper money between 1755 and 1760 the province could not have raised and paid the troops who drove the Indians from his vast and valuable tracts in central and western Pennsylvania. At the very least, therefore, Penn was expected to accept depreciation with the good grace of the ordinary Pennsylvanian. But he did not, choosing rather to insulate himself against it with an order-in-council. What he was doing was clear enough, familiar enough, and, as far as the people of the province were concerned, maddening enough; he was shirking the burdens of citizenship, just as he had done between 1755 and 1759 by refusing to pay taxes for defense. And those who perceived that depreciation was itself a tax considered him to be continuing his tax dodging in only a slightly different guise.

Pennsylvanians discerned other threads of consistency in his conduct, too. Many feared that, if the largest creditor in the province (which Penn indisputably was) suddenly refused to accept its money at face value, the credit of the currency would collapse, as it had in Maryland, where the local paper was not legal tender for Lord Baltimore's quit rents.[57] Runaway depreciation (not the gradual variety with which the province had learned to live) would, of course, ensue—Maryland's currency, though issued against funds as sound as Pennsylvania's, was worth forty percent less—and thousands would be ruined. Concurrently rents would rise, for if Penn succeeded in collecting them at the exchange rate between London and Philadelphia and if that rate held at 170 (its level between 1760 and 1764), an increase of 70 percent would result. It seemed altogether possible that great numbers of tenants would be unable or unwilling to absorb such an increase and would leave the province, turning the trickle of Pennsylvanians daily emigrating to the cheap lands of Virginia and the Carolinas into a mass exodus.[58] Thus, it was feared that the

[57] For an informative comparison between Pennsylvania's and Maryland's paper money, see Franklin, "A Paper on the legal Tender of Paper Money in America," 13 Feb. 1767, Yale University Library.

[58] A Pennsylvania grandee like William Allen thought the quarrel over the rise in quit rents was trivial, a dispute about "Goats wool," as he put it. To a rich man like Allen the rise in rents would have appeared insignificant. Penn charged ½d. per acre, which amounted to a little more than £1 per 500 acres. Thus, the projected increase in rents on an estate of this size would have been only about 14s. But to the hosts of small farmers, for whom money itself was as scarce as goats' wool, any increase in rent, even the 2s. 11d. increase on a farm of 100 acres, was crucial and could serve as a catalyst to migration. For Allen's

distress created by precipitous depreciation would be compounded by mass migration and Penn, to make a few extra pounds, would have wrecked the province's economy, just as he would have done had he succeeded in repealing the £100,000 supply bill of 1759.

The congeries of objections to the sixth amendment practically guaranteed that the Assembly would dishonor its agents' pledge and refuse to enact it and the other amendments which the Privy Council had dictated. This Denny's successor, James Hamilton, discovered as soon as he requested the House to redeem the pledge (28 January 1761). First, the members appointed a committee "to collect and consider the State of the Proprietary Taxation through the several Counties of this Province."[59] Packed with "several particular Friends of the Proprietaries" to insure its impartiality,[60] the committee reported on 12 March 1761 that no injustice had been done in the taxation of Penn's property. Since this was the primary purpose of the Privy Council amendments—to prevent injustice to Penn—and since at no time had the Assembly ever intended him harm, it concluded that the amendments were unnecessary and refused to enact them. But the reason it gave Hamilton (on 10 April 1761) for rejecting them was not their superfluity, but rather than unconstitutionality.

---

comment, see his letter to Benjamin Chew, 9 Dec. 1763, in David A. Kimball and Miriam Quinn, eds., "William Allen–Benjamin Chew Correspondence, 1763-1764," *Pa. Mag. Hist. and Biog.*, XC (1966), 218.

[59] The committee was appointed on 4 Feb. 1761. 8 *Pa. Arch.*, VI, 5186.

[60] The foremost proprietary friend was William Allen. Franklin, *Autobiography* (published for the American Philosophical Society by Yale University Press), 266.

To accept the amendments, it declared, would be to forfeit its right as an Assembly of free-born Englishmen to pass supply bills unamended.[61] This was, of course, the same argument it had used in previous years against the policies prescribed by Penn's instructions, and it showed that in articulating its grievances it was nothing if not consistent. Its consistency also appeared in the very fact of its opposition to the amendments embodied in the Privy Council's order, for an order-in-council was an instrument of external control, just as a proprietary instruction was, and in resisting the one as well as the other the Assembly demonstrated that it was opposed to every kind of external control, no matter what its source or sanction.

Throughout 1762 and 1763 Hamilton urged the House to enact the amendments. But instead of treating the members with his customary tact, he assumed an air of superiority. He seemed entirely too eager, for example, to remind them that the Privy Council had branded the supply bill of 1759 "fundamentally wrong and unjust." This gloating rankled. "The words fundamentally wrong and unjust are the great Fund of Triumph to the Proprietaries and their Partisans," Franklin wrote angrily in 1764. "These their subsequent Governors have unmercifully dinn'd in the Ears of the Assembly on all occasions" to show the members what "Villains" they had been.[62] Penn poisoned the

---

[61] Compliance with the amendments, the House remonstrated, "must be esteemed a high Breach of Trust by the People, whose Rights and Privileges we are bound in Duty to preserve; it would be waiving, at least, if not giving up, one of their most reasonable and essential Rights," i.e., that of passing supply bills without amendments. See 8 *Pa. Arch.*, VI, 5238.

[62] Franklin's *Preface* to Galloway's *Speech*, in Labaree, ed., *Papers of BF*, XI, 278.

atmosphere further by a serious tactical blunder. When it became clear after the Assembly's message of 10 April 1761 that the members were not going to comply with their agents' pledge, he tried to frighten them into honoring it. The Assemblymen were terrified by the Privy Council's threat to repeal the £100,000 supply bill of 1760 unless the supply bill of 1759 was amended as it had directed. Penn could have relieved them by announcing that he opposed such a draconian measure, but he chose instead to keep them guessing about his intentions and to increase their apprehensions by deliberately deferring the presentation of the supply bill of 1760, hoping thereby to work up their fears of repeal to such intensity that they would cave in and enact the amendments, as Hamilton on his orders was pressing them to do. After it became apparent by January 1763 that this strategy would fail, Hamilton decided to see what effect a plain, unvarnished threat would have, telling the House on 18 January 1763 that the supply bill of 1760 would be repealed if its agents' pledge were not honored.[63] The House withstood this attempt at intimidation, however, and remained as intransigent as ever. But the damage done by Penn and Hamilton's heavy-handed tactics was enormous, for by keeping the Assemblymen in a constant state of anxiety about the repeal of the supply bill of 1760, they kept them constantly reminded that the proprietor would risk wrecking the provincial economy to save a few pounds in taxes, and this kept them constantly angry at him.

Despite the high level of hostility toward Penn between 1760 and 1763 and despite his attempts to force the Assem-

---

[63] 8 *Pa. Arch.*, VI, 5378.

bly to accept external control in the form of the six Privy Council amendments, the House took no action against him. It sent no anti-proprietary petitions to England, deputized no additional commissioners to remonstrate with him, and made no moves toward royal government. The reason for its passivity was the improvement in provincial security. During the early years of the French and Indian War, especially after Braddock's defeat, Pennsylvania appeared to be in real danger of subjugation. With their homes and possibly even their lives at stake, the Assemblymen were compelled to accept almost any proprietary condition, even the exemption of Penn's estate from taxes, to obtain money for defense. But by 1760 the fortunes of war had changed dramatically in Britain's favor and the province was no longer in jeopardy. On 8 September 1760 French forces at Montreal surrendered to General Jeffery Amherst, prompting the Assembly to boast that "all Canada is now reduced. Her Subjects have submitted, and taken the Oaths of Allegiance and Fidelity to the English Government. Her regular Forces either are, or will soon be, transported to Old France."[64] With the French humbled, no more trouble was expected from the Indians, who in any case had been quiet since General Forbes took Fort Duquesne (25 November 1758). The war, as far as Pennsylvania was concerned, was over, a fact which was immediately reflected in the Assembly's attitude toward military appropriations.

In letters of 17 December 1760 and 12 December 1761 William Pitt and his successor, the Earl of Egremont, requested Pennsylvania to raise troops to help guard British

[64] *Ibid.*, 5162.

conquests in North America, so that regulars could be released for action in the West Indies.[65] The Assembly responded to the former on 17 April 1761 by voting 500 men (Pitt had asked for 1,800) whom it proposed to pay by emitting £30,000 in legal tender paper money, and to the latter on 19 March 1762 by voting 1,000 men (Egremont had also asked for 1,800), whose expenses were to be covered by an emission of £70,000 in legal tender. In both cases the House ignored the Privy Council's sixth amendment, and Hamilton predictably refused to pass the bills until it was included. But this tactic, which Morris and Denny had used to compel the Assembly to exempt Penn's estate from taxes, did not work now, because the province, being in no danger, needed no supply bills. Hence, the Assembly let them die. And just here is the reason for its restraint toward Penn between 1760 and 1763: the absence of a threat to provincial security enabled it to reject his dictation, which would have inflamed it. But if renewed warfare were to force it to accept his demands as a condition for defending its constituents, the province would almost surely be convulsed; for external control would be opposed, as it always had been, but because of the failure of petitions and of Franklin's mission, moderate measures would be set aside and recourse had to radical remedies. Thus, any threat to provincial security which compelled a new instance of capitulation to external control would almost surely be the catalyst of a movement for royal government.

In the summer of 1763 a new threat did, in fact, imperil

---

[65] Pitt's letter was read before the Assembly on 3 April 1761, Egremont's on 16 Feb. 1762. *Ibid.*, 5226-28, 5306-8.

the province—an Indian war called the Conspiracy of Pontiac.[66] Hostilities, which took almost everyone in the colonies by surprise, began with an attack on Fort Detroit on 9 May 1763. During the rest of the month the war spread like an inkblot in every direction. By the beginning of June, after all British forts in the midwest except Detroit had fallen, Fort Pitt was besieged. Failing to carry that fortress, the Indians struck in northwestern Pennsylvania, where they easily overpowered the weak garrisons at Fort Venango (16 June), Fort Le Boeuf (18 June), and Fort Presqu'Isle (20 June). Then they began to range eastward, attacking Fort Ligonier on 21 June and slaughtering whatever luckless settlers fell into their hands along a broad arch in central Pennsylvania. As always happened in such cases, terrified pioneers and their families poured into the settled parts of the province, hungry, wretched, and haggard, and beseeched the Assembly for protection so that they could return to their farms and live with dignity.

The House, convened in special session by Governor Hamilton on 4 July 1763, was furious at the sneak Indian attack and voted two days later to raise 700 soldiers to serve until its September meeting. The members avoided a controversy with the governor about paper money by not emitting any; the troops were to be paid from funds in the hands of the provincial treasury, and if these were insufficient, the deficit was to be made up at the September meeting.

When the House convened in September, the war was

---

[66] The term is Parkman's. The best modern account is Howard H. Peckham, *Pontiac and the Indian Uprising* (Princeton, 1947).

still raging, making it impossible to disband the troops. And yet it was difficult to see how they could be kept in the field, for the treasury had no more money and there appeared to be no way of raising any except by an emission of paper money. Futile though the prospect seemed, the House on 27 September passed a bill raising 800 men and emitting £25,000 in *legal tender* paper currency to support them.[67] Considering Hamilton's position on paper currency, cynics viewed this vote as a public relations stunt. But the Assembly was not going through the motions merely for appearances' sake. It was gambling that the military crisis and the necessity of obtaining money to keep the troops in the field would force Hamilton to waive the sixth amendment. Hamilton used the same logic in rejecting the bill on 29 September; he hoped that the military crisis would force the House to capitulate and incorporate the amendment. But even though the war was heating up and moving eastward like a forest fire—on 16 September word reached Philadelphia that the Indians had struck in Berks County—the Assembly refused to budge. So repugnant was the sixth amendment that it resisted adopting it even at the risk of seeing the provincial troops quit their posts for want of pay. And so between the intransigence of the governor and the House the bill was lost. On 30 September the members adjourned and went home.

The Assembly always met for a few days in October to organize itself after the provincial elections on the first of the month. Customarily, no other business was conducted during this session, but because the military situation had worsened since September, Hamilton asked for action.

[67] 8 *Pa. Arch.*, VI, 5438-39, 5442, 5447, 5456-58.

What had happened was that on 8 October Captain Bull, son of the flamboyant dipsomaniac Teedyuscung, the self-styled "King of the Delawares," had led a band of marauders into Northampton County, where they murdered twenty-three men, women, and children and frightened the rest of the people so badly that they fled their habitations in droves to seek the safety of more settled areas. These raids, the deepest eastward penetration the Indians had yet made, roused Hamilton to deliver the Assembly a spirited speech on 15 October,[68] reminding it that the provincial troops, for whom it had made no provisions at its last session, would surely melt away unless they were paid and that, if this happened, the Assemblymen would have defaulted on their duty to defend the people of Pennsylvania. If they were serious about protecting their fellow citizens, he urged them to refrain from passing the kind of supply bill—one making paper money legal tender—which they knew he could not sign.

The governor's fight talk succeeded, with the result that on 21 October 1763 the House passed a bill raising £24,000 to keep the provincial troops in the field until the first of December. Finding the money was not easy, however. The parliamentary grant was tapped for £12,000 (to reimburse Pennsylvania for her contributions to the campaigns of 1758, 1759, and 1760, Parliament had granted her a total of £78,000 sterling,[69] which the Assembly had used to pay

---

[68] *Ibid.*, VI, 5476-77.

[69] For a discussion of the Pennsylvania parliamentary grants, see James H. Hutson, "Benjamin Franklin and the Parliamentary Grant for 1758," 3 *WMQ*, XXIII (1966), esp. 578n, 586n, 587. See also Labaree, ed., *Papers of BF*, x, 114n. The Assembly received a few pounds in excess of £78,000.

most provincial expenses since 1761); £7,000 was squeezed out of the excise on spirituous liquor by extending it for three years;[70] the goods and merchandise in the hands of the commissioners for Indian affairs were sold to raise £4,000; and the Assembly was obliged to take the unprecedented step of appropriating £1,000 which had accrued from the duties on the importation of slaves. Raising the £24,000 was a victory, but a Pyrrhic one. The draft on the parliamentary grant completely exhausted that fund,[71] while extending the excise for three years removed its availability as a revenue measure. Nor would Indian merchandise and slave money be available again. What the Assembly had done in raising the £24,000 was to exhaust all of its means of raising revenue except by the emission of paper money.[72] Thus, if a worsening of the war or some

[70] Actually, the £7,000 was "borrowed" from the £15,000 raised to protect the city of Philadelphia by an act passed on 14 May 1762 (which, to confuse matters further, raised a total of £23,500 by the sale of bills of exchange drawn on the parliamentary grant). The £7,000 was to be replaced by extending for three years the excise act passed on 21 Sept. 1756, which ran for ten years. Thus, the act of 21 Oct. 1763 actually extended the excise until 1769. *Statutes at Large, Pa.*, V, 243-61, and VI, 226-29, 311-19.

[71] Indeed, on 21 Sept. 1763 Hamilton had informed the House that the other colonies claimed that Pennsylvania had been overpaid in the grant of 1760 and owed them £10,947 sterling. In Jan. 1764 the Assembly, acknowledging the justice of this claim, passed a bill to reimburse its neighbors. See 8 *Pa. Arch.*, VI, 5441; Labaree, ed., *Papers of BF*, XI, 19.

[72] It would have been impolitic for the House to try to raise money by taxing real and personal estates, because heavy taxes of this kind were already being collected and to have increased them would have invited a taxpayers' revolt. In 1763 Pennsylvanians were still paying taxes on their real and personal property to sink the £100,000 of paper money emitted by the supply bill of 1758. The £100,000 emitted by the supply bill of 1759 was, we will recall, to be sunk by taxes laid between 1764 and 1767 (above, p. 60), and the £100,000 emitted by

other emergency forced it to raise money in the near future and if the proprietary deputy continued to stand adamantly on the Privy Council's sixth amendment (as there was every reason to suppose he would), the Assembly would be compelled to capitulate to him—an ominous prospect indeed. There was keen irony in all of this: at the end of October 1763 Penn had the Assembly where he had been trying to put it ever since he became principal proprietor of Pennsylvania in 1746—out of money and obliged to raise it on his own terms. He fondly believed that placing the Assembly in such a situation would reduce it to docility. The first months of 1764 would show how completely he had misjudged its temper.

The Indians did not fancy winter fighting, and after Captain Bull's incursions in October the war tapered off. A handful of frontiersmen were killed in November, but thereafter the province enjoyed a respite from the redmen until the next spring.[73] From its own people, however, it received no repose. The military appropriations which the House had impoverished itself to vote in July and October failed to please their intended beneficiaries on the frontier. Many westerners were actually insulted by the Assembly's efforts. They indignantly pointed out that the few hundred troops it put in the field were so far from being capable

---

the supply bill of 1760 was to be sunk between 1767 and 1770. Had the Assembly wanted to emit paper money and sink it with a tax on real and personal property, as a matter of practical politics the tax could not have been levied until 1770. This is, in fact, what the House did in its £55,000 supply bill of 30 May 1764. See *Statutes at Large, Pa.*, V, 339, 380-81, and VI, 8, 345.

[73] C. Hale Sipe, *The Indian Wars of Pennsylvania* (Harrisburg, 1929), 462, 470.

of protecting the whole province that they were barely able to defend a borough.[74] Even so, the frontiersmen contended, the troops might still have accomplished something had no limits been placed on their mobility, but the Assembly had foolishly and, in the opinion of many westerners, criminally restrained them from serving beyond the purchased parts of the province. Thus, when General Amherst asked permission to use provincial troops to reinforce Colonel Henry Bouquet's expedition to relieve Fort Pitt (August 1763), an expedition on which the fate of the frontier was thought to depend, he was refused. The west was outraged at the refusal and never forgave the Assembly for it.[75]

[74] *The Apology of the Paxton Volunteers* [March 1764] contains a strong statement of the westerners' displeasure. "'Tis true," *The Apology* admits, "that the Assembly last year voted 800 men to guard the Frontiers. But had the Design been to have sent so many men to have looked on the Ravages that were committed amongst the back Settlers without giving them the least assistance, it could not have been more effectually executed. They were prohibited by Law from going over the Boundaries of the purchased Lands after the Enemy. . . . Every Person in the Province saw that this was only to insult our Distresses. For 100,000 men could not have guarded 200 Miles of a Frontier against the Invasions of the Savages in this manner." John R. Dunbar, ed., *The Paxton Papers* (The Hague, 1957), 189; hereinafter cited as *Paxton Papers*.

[75] Amherst's demand was conveyed to the provincial commissioners by a Col. Robinson on or about 1 July 1763. For the Assembly's justification of its actions in this affair, see 8 *Pa. Arch.*, VII, 5563-64, and [Joseph Galloway], *An Address to the Freeholders and Inhabitants of the Province of Pennsylvania* [Phila., 1764], Evans, 9561. For the frontier's indignation, see "The Declaration of the injured Frontier Inhabitants. . . ," read before the Assembly on 17 Feb. 1764. 8 *Pa. Arch.*, VII, 5549-52. See also *The Apology of the Paxton Volunteers*, 189. Hugh Williamson claimed that even before Amherst's demand Governor Hamilton had asked the Assembly to "put it in his power to order the troops to the assistance of Col. Boquet" but had been refused. "Plain Dealer, III," *Paxton Papers*, 379-80.

Even within the narrow compass which the Assembly prescribed for its troops, they performed abominably. Absenteeism was chronic,[76] while those who stayed at their posts were generally useless, because they were "not acquainted with the Country, or the Indian manner of fighting." The garrison at Fort Augusta seems to have set some kind of record for incompetency, if the allegations of the people living in the neighborhood can be believed. The garrison, they charged, "neither helped our distressed Inhabitants to save their Crops, nor did they attack our Enemies in their Towns, or patrol our Frontiers."[77] To protect themselves, the westerners, even those living under the guns of a fort, were obliged to hire private bands of rangers to scour their neighborhoods.[78] The expense for many of them was insupportable. And so, too, was their anger against an Assembly which could sit in the safeness of Philadelphia and congratulate itself on the contemptible measures it had adopted. Consequently, many on the frontier threatened to go to Philadelphia and punish the legislators, whom they blamed for so unconscionably shortchanging them. Reports about the mood of the frontier filtered into Philadelphia; a typical one, recorded by the Reverend Henry Muhlenberg on 22 November 1763, affirmed that the "country people are becoming embittered because the authorities are taking no adequate measures for defense." "Now we are beginning to hear," Muhlenberg noted, "that

[76] This may be inferred from a petition presented to the Assembly on 11 Jan. 1764. 8 *Pa. Arch.*, VII, 5510.

[77] "A Declaration and Remonstrance of the distressed and bleeding Frontier Inhabitants," 13 Feb. 1764. *Paxton Papers*, 110.

[78] See, e.g., petitions from Northampton and Cumberland Counties, read before the Assembly on 9 and 11 Jan. 1764. 8 *Pa. Arch.*, VII, 5508, 5509-10.

the people from the country are about to come to the city in droves and destroy everything in revenge."[79]

With rumors like these ringing in their ears, the Assemblymen met on 19 December 1763, convened by special writ from Thomas Penn's thirty-four-year-old nephew, John Penn, who had arrived in Philadelphia on 30 October 1763 to replace a haggard James Hamilton as governor. Young Penn's appearance in the capital was as unexpected as Pontiac's attack on the frontier and was viewed by many with equal foreboding, an attitude which Nature itself seemed to affirm by producing "a violent Earthquake attended with a very loud roaring noise" two hours after his arrival.[80] The new governor was no stranger to the province, having spent three years there (1752-55) at the beginning of the preceding decade. The visit had not been his idea, but his uncle Thomas's. In fact, his stay in Pennsylvania represented a continuation of the exile his uncle and his father had imposed upon him after he had concluded, while still a schoolboy, an impetuous marriage to a girl whom they considered beneath his dignity. The two older men compelled him to repudiate the match and, to escape legal reprisals, sent him off to Geneva under the care of a tutor.[81] He remained in Europe for some years and developed a special affection for Italy. In 1752 at his uncle's suggestion he came to Pennsylvania. Here the glit-

[79] Theodore G. Tappert and John W. Doberstein, tr., *The Journals of Henry Melchior Muhlenberg*, 1 (Phila., 1942), 709.

[80] James Pemberton, "A Brief Account of some Public Occurences in the Province of Pennsylvania in the Administration of Governor John Penn," Penn Papers, Indian Affairs MSS, IV (1733-1801), Hist. Soc. Pa.

[81] For the early stages of John Penn's career, see Howard Jenkins, "The Family of William Penn," *Pa. Mag. Hist. and Biog.*, XXII (1898), 76-78.

ter of the Grand Tour was gone, and life seemed grey and dull. Young Penn soon fell into a deep depression and moped around, muttering against the province.[82] To relieve the dreariness of his days, he made friends with an Italian musician, "an Insinuating Fellow of debauch'd Principles," according to a local proprietary official.[83] Rumor had it that he paid his paisano's rent and gave him many of his personal belongings; often he stayed at his house "till 2 or 3 o'clock in the Morning with debauched Company." Proper Philadelphians were scandalized by this friendship, but Thomas Penn was more annoyed by his nephew's prodigality, for the young man "did not mind money" and fell into debt. This was the unpardonable sin in Thomas's eyes and, accordingly, he summoned him home in 1755. The grandson of William Penn had made an altogether ghastly impression in Pennsylvania, and the people of the province were amazed when his uncle sent him over as governor in 1763. "Whom the Gods would destroy they first make mad," marveled one veteran politician.[84]

Being in better spirits this time, John Penn appeared to better advantage. Yet he still did not strike people as a man who could steer the province through an Indian war

[82] Richard Peters wrote Thomas Penn, 19 Dec. 1754, that John Penn "looked as if he was in distress and inwardly grieves much." William Allen also observed that he was "depressed in his spirits." See Hubertis Cummings, *Richard Peters* (Phila., 1944), 169; David A. Kimball and Miriam Quinn, eds., "William Allen–Benjamin Chew Correspondence, 1763-1764," *Pa. Mag. Hist. and Biog.*, XC (1966), 212. On his expressing hatred for Pennsylvania, see Jenkins, "The Family of William Penn," 80.

[83] Richard Hockley to Thomas Penn, 5 Oct. 1755, Penn Papers, Hist. Soc. Pa. The next two quotations are from the same letter.

[84] William Logan to John Smith [1763], Smith MSS, Hist. Soc. Pa.

and a threatened frontier insurrection. To begin with, he was not a heroic figure; he was small, soft, and delicate of feature (a hostile pamphleteer called him effeminate).[85] He was also unabashedly "artsy-craftsy." He loved music and played a tolerable violin in a chamber music group which often met at his house.[86] His affection for the theater was equally ardent,[87] and he was a connoisseur and collector of fine art.[88] These qualities, which would be admired today, did not endear him to the grave citizens of the Quaker commonwealth, who regarded them as decadent and demeaning. Penn was also handicapped by a total lack of administrative experience and a widespread belief that he was not the brightest man in the British Empire.[89] His biggest shortcoming, however, was his indolence, a trait which in 1768 prompted a number of despairing proprietary officials to try to have him replaced by his brother

[85] [Isaac Hunt], *A Letter from a Gentleman in Transilvania . . .* (Phila., 1764), Evans, 9701. An expressive portrait of John Penn is reproduced in Labaree, ed., *Papers of BF*, XI, facing the title page.

[86] Carl and Jessica Bridenbaugh, *Rebels and Gentlemen Philadelphia in the Age of Franklin* (New York, 1942), 156; Harold D. Eberlin and Cortlandt Hubbard, "Music in the Early Federal Era," *Pa. Mag. Hist. and Biog.*, LXIX (1945), 105n. For a caustic appraisal of Penn's musical attainments, see [Hunt], *Letter from . . . Transilvania*.

[87] Thomas Wharton to Franklin, 7 Feb. 1767, APS. According to Wharton, Penn constantly attended plays and frequently invited the players to dine with him.

[88] Bridenbaugh, *Rebels and Gentlemen*, 214.

[89] Both contemporaries and historians have remarked on Penn's mediocre mental endowments. Hunt in his *Letter from . . . Transilvania* called Penn a "Man of weak Intellect," but his bitter partisanship was showing. The more temperate Peter Collinson concluded after meeting the young man that he did not "seem to have Strikeing abilities." Labaree, ed., *Papers of BF*, X, 332. The historians Charles P. Keith judged that Penn was "not mentally deficient," just "a weak character." *Chronicles of Pennsylvania*, II, 887-88.

Richard, who was thought to have "more of the Spirit of government in Him."[90]

Penn had no compunctions about letting his inexperience accommodate his indolence. Recognizing that the first handicap justified a heavy reliance on local advisers, he solicited their assistance and then turned the running of the province over to them, thus gratifying his desire for ease. Willingly and even eagerly he became a figurehead. The wisdom of his de facto abdication depended on the abilities of his advisers. Wise men produced wise policies, foolish men foolish ones. During 1764 Penn had both kinds of advisers and both kinds of policies.

On 20 December 1763 the new governor delivered his maiden speech, recommending sympathetic consideration for General Jeffery Amherst's plan for a two-pronged offensive into the Indian homeland in the summer of 1764: a northern column, composed of regulars and provincials from New York and New Jersey, was to strike westward from Albany toward Lake Erie and on toward the beleaguered Fort Detroit, while a southern column, composed of regulars and troops from Pennsylvania and Virginia, was to carry the war into the Shawnee and Delaware country. Pennsylvania was asked to contribute 1,000 men.

[90] Thomas Wharton to Franklin, 29 March 1768, Franklin Papers, Hist. Soc. Pa. Penn's indolence showed up during his first stay in Pennsylvania; at that time he told Richard Peters that "he could not do business." Jenkins, "The Family of William Penn," 80. On 7 March 1764 James Pemberton wrote Dr. John Fothergill that the governor was "too inactive." Pemberton Papers, Hist. Soc. Pa. Further evidence of Penn's lethargy is that during the crowded and tumultuous period between 1 Jan. and 1 June 1764 he wrote his uncle only two letters, much to the latter's dismay. See John Penn to Thomas Penn, 17 March and 5 May 1764; Thomas Penn to John Penn, 24 March, 13 April, 11 May, and 1 June 1764; all in the Penn Papers, Hist. Soc. Pa.

On 21 December, before the Assembly had had an opportunity to digest Amherst's proposal, Penn transmitted a shocking piece of intelligence: On 14 December a band of frontiersmen, supposed to be mainly from Paxton township near present-day Harrisburg and hence known to history as the Paxton Boys, had ridden into Conestoga Manor in Lancaster County and murdered in cold blood six Indians living there under the protection of the government; the remaining Conestogas, fourteen in number, had escaped their brethren's fate only because they had been abroad at the time, peddling baskets and brooms.[91] This news confirmed in the starkest fashion the rumors about the ugly mood of the frontier and proved that the men of the west were fully capable of carrying out their threat of mounting a punitive expedition against Philadelphia. Having avenged themselves on the Indians, might they not deal with the Assembly next? The slightest provocation might bring a horde of frenzied frontiersmen down on the capital, and a refusal to vote the 1,000 men requested by Amherst would be nothing if not a provocation, for an offensive against the Indians was the passionate wish of every man in the west. Therefore, in what was clearly an attempt to placate the frontier (and to put some of its hotheads out of circulation by giving them a chance to campaign in Indian country), the Assembly resolved on 22 December to raise the 1,000 men required of it. The catch was that it had no money to pay them, and when it adjourned for a short Christmas recess on 24 December without raising any, critics charged that its vote of 22 Decem-

[91] The best account of the Paxton Boys is Brooke Hindle, "The March of the Paxton Boys," 3 *WMQ*, III (1946), 461-86.

ber was nothing but a public relations gimmick. More sympathetic observers, fully cognizant of the difficulties attending the raising of funds, were of the opinion that it would take a miracle of the magnitude of that celebrated on 25 December to enable it to implement its resolution of 22 December. No one foresaw that another massacre would do just as well.

During the afternoon of 27 December a second band of armed men from the Paxton area rode up to the Lancaster workhouse, where the remaining Conestoga Indians had been confined for their own protection by the local magistrates, battered down the door, rushed in, murdered the Indians, and left. As the raiders rode off, they boasted that their next stop would be Philadelphia, their next victims some 140 "Moravian Indians" quartered in the pesthouses on Province Island under the surveillance of the government because of their alleged complicity in the murder of white settlers in Northampton County.[92] The As-

---

[92] In a letter of 27 Dec. 1763, reporting the murder of the remaining Conestogas, Edward Shippen told Governor Penn that "some people say they heard them [the Paxton Boys] declare they would proceed to the Province Island, and destroy the Indians there." Writing to Penn the same day, Sheriff John Hay of Lancaster County reported that it was "rumoured that the people with a Superior Force intend an Attack on the Province Island, with a vow to destroy the Indians there." *Pa. Col. Recs.*, IX, 100, 103. For threats against the Moravian Indians even before the second attack on the Conestogas occurred, see Edward Shippen, Sr., to Joseph Shippen, 19 Dec. 1763, Shippen Papers, APS. The so-called Moravian Indians were a group of Christianized Indians living on a Moravian mission at Wechquetanc on Head's Creek in present-day Monroe County. They removed to Philadelphia on 11 Nov. 1763 after the provincial commissioners reported (21 Oct. 1763) that there was good reason to suspect that they had been "principally concerned" in the murders in Northampton County and that, consequently, they should be brought to some place "where their Behaviour may be more

sembly learned of the annihilation of the Conestogas from a proclamation issued by John Penn on 2 January 1764. The next day the governor passed along reports from informants in Lancaster County that the Paxton Boys were "making great addition to their numbers" and were "actually preparing to come down in a large Body and cut off the Indians seated by the Government on the Province Island"; it was difficult, he concluded, "to determine how far they may carry their designs, or where the mischief may end."[93] One thing was clear to everybody: a descent on Philadelphia might touch off a civil war, which is exactly what many thought the frontiersmen wanted, since it would give them a chance to carry out their threats of avenging the blood of their murdered kinsmen on the parties whom they held responsible, the Quakers and the Quaker-dominated Assembly. Franklin, for example, believed that the Paxton Boys meant to kill the Indians and "to punish the Quakers"[94] as well. Joseph Galloway reported that they had threatened to massacre "some of the best Men in the Government."[95] William Logan, for his part, felt that their objective was the whole eastern power structure; they seemed determined, he wrote, "to come

---

closely observed." 8 *Pa. Arch.*, VI, 5482-83; John W. Jordan, "Biographical Sketch of Rev. Bernhard Adam Grube," *Pa. Mag. Hist. and Biog.*, XXV (1901), 15.

[93] *Pa. Col. Recs.*, IX, 109.

[94] To Dr. John Fothergill, 14 March 1764, in Labaree, ed., *Papers of BF*, XI, 102. The author of "The Paxton Boys, A Farce" had the same opinion, making one of his characters, a Presbyterian who symbolized the Paxton Boys, wish in the words of the Emperor Nero: "Oh! had they [the Quakers] but one Neck . . . that I might lop them off at one chop." *Paxton Papers*, 162.

[95] *The Speech of Joseph Galloway*, 36, 38, 39.

down" and "stem all opposition."[96] Contemporary pamphleteers considered their objectives more sweeping and more terrible still; had Philadelphia been threatened by the hordes of Attila or Tamerlane, they could have scarcely been more hysterical. "The Paxton Boys are coming down," wrote one scribbler, "to kill us all, and burn the Town."[97] The Paxtoneers intended "to pour out their Vials of Wrath and D[evili]sh[ne]ss on the Inhabitants of this City," wailed another. To a third "the City appear'd to be in the utmost Danger of Massacre, Plunder and Desolation."[98] "Intimidated by the reported threats of the back inhabitants,"[99] the authorities hustled the Indians off Province Island on 5 January 1764 and shipped them to New York under a military escort; a little while later Israel Pemberton, Joseph Fox, and several other prominent Quakers slipped out of Philadelphia for New Jersey.[100]

With the frontiersmen on their tiptoes ready to march against the capital, the Assembly dared not provoke them by refusing to implement its resolution of 22 December. Consequently, on 6 January it resolved to raise £50,000 to support the 1,000 men previously voted, but it still begged the question of where the money was to come from. Only on 10 January did it face the reality of its financial posi-

[96] Quoted in Brooke Hindle, "The March of the Paxton Boys," 474.
[97] [Anonymous], "A Battle! A Battle! A Battle of Squirt . . . ," *Paxton Papers*, 176.
[98] [Anonymous], "The Paxton Boys, A Farce," *ibid.*, 161; [Isaac Hunt?], "A Looking-Glass for Presbyterians," *ibid.*, 254.
[99] "Fragments of a Journal Kept by Samuel Foulke, of Bucks County," *Pa. Mag. Hist. and Biog.*, v (1881), 67.
[100] Richard Waln to Nicholas Waln, 10 March 1764, Richard Waln Letterbook (1762-66), Hist. Soc. Pa.; John Harris to James Burd, 1 March 1764, Shippen Papers, VI (1763-68), Hist. Soc. Pa.

tion and admit that it had no way of raising funds except by emitting paper money. The next day it occurred to some members that Thomas Penn, with a view to getting his nephew off on the right foot with the Assembly, might have modified his currency instructions;[101] therefore, they asked the governor to lay them before the House. Young Penn complied on 12 January, but to the members' mortification they discovered that his uncle had laid him "under greater restraints than any of his predecessors had been, in regard to paper Currency." "Whatever our Distresses are," remarked an exasperated Franklin, "the Proprietor has no Bowels; he never relents."[102] The governor was instructed to adhere faithfully to the Privy Council's sixth amendment, which his uncle interpreted for him in this fashion: he was to prevent the provincial paper money from being made "a Tender, or any Satisfaction or Discharge for any Quitrents *or other Sterling Payments* due, or to become due to us."[103] The phrase "other Sterling Payments" gave the Assembly a start, for the sixth amendment contained no such words and made legal tender paper unacceptable for quit rents only. Puzzled for an instant about the phrase's meaning, the Assembly quickly perceived that it referred to the proprietary purchase money,

[101] The House's thinking on this matter was described by Franklin. "It was thought," he wrote, "that they [the proprietors] would probably chuse to have his Administration made easy and agreeable, and to that End might think it prudent to withdraw those harsh, disagreeable and unjust Instructions, with which most of his Predecessors had been hamper'd." *Preface* to Galloway's *Speech*, in Labaree, ed., *Papers of BF*, XI, 287.

[102] The first quotation is from Foulke's "Journal," *op. cit.*, 68; the second is from Franklin's Speech, 13-14 Jan. 1764, in Labaree, ed., *Papers of BF*, XI, 11.

[103] 8 *Pa. Arch.*, VII, 5514. Italics supplied by the author.

Penn's set price, £15 10s., for 100 acres of land. As soon as the Privy Council amendments were promulgated on 2 September 1760, he allegedly instructed his commissioners of property in Pennsylvania to make all their "future Contracts for the Sale of Lands in Sterling."[104] By sneaking the phrase "other Sterling Payments" into the sixth amendment and by insisting that the Assembly enact it, Penn was trying to hoodwink the House into giving his purchase money the same privileged status as his quit rents. The result would have been to boost the price of Pennsylvania land, whose excessive cost was already a topic of popular complaint, by as much as seventy percent; with rents due for a similar rise if the sixth amendment were enacted, it was difficult to see who could resist the temptation to migrate to Maryland or Virginia—possibly the old, well-established farmers, but certainly not the younger generation or the ambitious immigrants, on whose future the province depended.

The shock of seeing Penn's instructions had not worn off when the Assembly resumed its deliberations on 13 and 14 January on the ways and means of raising the £50,000. On one of these days Benjamin Franklin proposed that it satisfy the sixth amendment by issuing nonlegal tender paper money on which it would pay five percent interest to prevent depreciation, a practice which the New England colonies had been following since 1751.[105] Franklin's proposal perplexed the House—in June he told Richard Jackson that it seemed "very strange to an Assembly to pay

---

[104] Franklin, "Explanatory Remarks on the Assembly's Resolves," 29 March 1764, in Labaree, ed., *Papers of BF*, XI, 142.

[105] See *ibid.*, 7-18; Franklin, "A Paper on the legal Tender of Paper Money in America," 13 Feb. 1767, Yale University Library.

Interest on Paper Money, who had been us'd to receive Interest for Paper that cost them Nothing"[106]—and for two weeks it mulled the idea over.

It was able to take its time because the pressure from the frontiersmen had abated since the objects of their wrath, the Moravian Indians, had left the province. These "Christian" Indians turned out to be almost as unpopular in New York as they had been in Pennsylvania—"a number of Volunteers" were proposed to Lieutenant Governor Cadwallader Colden "to go out against them to punish them for their Cruelties and perfidy"[107]—and, therefore, Colden refused to let them enter the province. New Jersey did not want them either, so back they were marched to Philadelphia. Their reappearance there on 24 January affected the frontier as a red flag affects a bull;[108] by 28 January reports reached the city that 1,500, and if need be, 5,000, men were gathering to come down and kill the Indians and "any other who should oppose them."[109]

Hoping that favorable action on the Indian expedition bill would soothe the troubled spirits in the backcountry, the Assembly on 31 January put Franklin's proposal for an issue of nonlegal tender paper money to a vote. By a narrow margin it was defeated.[110] No alternative now re-

---

[106] To Jackson, 25 June 1764, in Labaree, ed., *Papers of BF*, XI, 238.

[107] *Pa. Col. Recs.*, IX, 120.

[108] An anonymous Quaker reported, 29 Feb. 1764, that "whilst they [the Indians] were upon their march through the Jerseys, faction and clamour seemed to subside, but no sooner was it known that they were returned, than the spirit of discord began to operate afresh. At first, only a little murmuring was heard, then they began to threaten. . . ." Samuel Hazard, ed., *Register of Pennsylvania*, XII (Phila., 1833-34), 10.

[109] *Pa. Col. Recs.*, IX, 126.

[110] To Jackson, 25 June 1764, in Labaree, ed., *Papers of BF*, XI, 238.

mained for the House but to bite the bullet and enact the sixth amendment. Consequently, on 1 February it voted to do what no Pennsylvania Assembly had ever done before, to emit paper money which was not a tender for the "Proprietaries Sterling Rents."[111] To save some of its pride, it rejected Penn's attempt to collect his purchase money in sterling, but this act of defiance was poor compensation for surrendering a principle which its predecessors had upheld for decades.

The members hated what they had been compelled to do to appease the west. John Dickinson railed at the exemption granted Penn as being "fundamentally unjust" and "contradictory to the maxims of equity; and the spirit of liberty."[112] Samuel Foulke, a Quaker member from Bucks County, was so exercised at seeing his colleagues put "their necks under the Tyrant's foot, while his Mutes rivett on the Yoke,"[113] that he proposed the immediate abolition of proprietary government and the establishment of royal government in its place. Such a course, he believed, was "the wish of every one who retains a Just sense of Freedom." William Logan confirmed that the Assemblymen "incline strong to a Change of Government"[114] but doubted that they would act precipitously. An attempt to obtain a change of government at this time would, in fact, have been ridiculous, for the House would have had to

---

[111] 8 *Pa. Arch.*, VII, 5535.

[112] David L. Jacobson, *John Dickinson and the Revolution in Pennsylvania 1764-1776* (Berkeley, 1965), 12.

[113] Foulke's "Journal," 69.

[114] To John Smith, [31? Jan.] 1764, Smith MSS, Hist. Soc. Pa. Dated by its statement that Franklin's *Narrative of the Late Massacres*, which appears to have been published on 30 Jan. 1764, was published yesterday. See Labaree, ed., *Papers of BF*, XI, 47.

take its case before the King-in-Council, where it would have found itself asking that body to take away Penn's government as a punishment for obeying one of its own orders. But if the Assembly were forced to swallow another dose of external control, one not sanctioned by the British bureaucracy, then an appeal for royal government would be a virtual certainty. As Logan put it, the members "intend on the first Occasion that may offer as Grounds for such a Proceeding to apply for it at home."

To the Assembly's dismay, its £50,000 vote on 1 February made very little impression on the Paxton Boys, who had worked themselves up to such a pitch of anti-Indian hysteria that they were impervious to any efforts to appease them. On 4 February word reached Philadelphia that they were assembling to come down the next morning and "put to death all the Indians."[115] This information was passed on to John Penn, who responded characteristically by turning the defense of the capital over to Benjamin Franklin. (Though hardly a Horatius, Penn on this occasion did not deserve a hostile writer's comparison to Sardana Palus, a sybaritic king of the Assyrians, who immolated himself with his favorite concubine as the Medes were besieging his palace.)[116] At a public meeting at the State House on the afternoon of 4 February Penn urged the 3,000 people who had braved a "driving, cold rain" to join together to defend the city.[117] Then he called upon Franklin, who had the patent for forming voluntary associations in Philadelphia, to organize the citizens and offered him their com-

---

[115] *Pa. Col. Recs.*, IX, 132.
[116] [Hunt], *Letter from . . . Transilvania.*
[117] Foulke's "Journal," 69; *Journals of Muhlenberg*, II, 18.

mand. Although he refused any kind of title or name, the Doctor became their generalissimo in fact, signing the articles for a military association first and seeing that the citizen soldiers, many of whom had served under him in the Philadelphia City Regiment in 1756, were organized into six companies of foot, one of artillery, and one troop of horse.[118] These minutemen did not quiet the apprehensions of their fellow townsmen—a Quaker observed that those "who depended upon them for defence and protection, would have found their confidence shockingly misplaced"[119]—but the very fact that they were assembled and in being deterred the Paxton Boys from executing their design.

The fifth of February, the day on which the Paxtoneers were supposed to reach Philadelphia, passed without incident. That night, however, the ringing of the fire bells sent the inhabitants pouring into the streets, prepared to repel an assault. At midnight Penn ran to Franklin's house "with his Counsellors at his Heels, for Advice, and made it his Headquarters for some time."[120] Although it was presently learned that no more than 250 Paxton Boys had crossed the Schuylkill and encamped at Germantown, Franklin was up all night holding the governor's hand, and he was up the entire next night, too, which passed in conferences at Penn's house.[121] During this period he was, as he told

[118] Franklin to Dr. John Fothergill, 14 March 1764; to Lord Kames, 2 June 1765; both in Labaree, ed., *Papers of BF*, XI, 103, and XII, 161. *Pa. Gazette*, 9 Feb. 1764.
[119] Anonymous Quaker, in Hazard, ed., *Register of Pennsylvania*, 11.
[120] To Fothergill, 14 March 1764, in Labaree, ed., *Papers of BF*, XI, 103.
[121] Franklin to Richard Jackson, 11 Feb. 1764, *ibid.*, 77.

a friend later, "a kind of Dictator."[122] At the meeting on the night of 6 February a decision was made to send a delegation of prominent citizens to Germantown to confer with the "rioters," as they were now being called. Franklin and Joseph Galloway of the Assembly, Attorney General Benjamin Chew and William Logan of the Council, Mayor Thomas Willing, Daniel Roberdeau (a leading Philadelphia Anglican), and Dr. Carl Wrangel, a Philadelphia Lutheran minister, were selected for the mission. At five o'clock on the morning of 7 February they rode out from the capital, and after several hours of spirited negotiations with the Paxton Boys, whose ardor had been considerably dampened by the fighting face put on by the Philadelphians, a "peace treaty" was concluded, the frontiersmen agreeing to disperse in return for a promise that the Assembly would consider their grievances expeditiously. Despite some tense moments caused by a visit of 30 Paxton Boys to Philadelphia on 8 February, violence was averted and the frontiersmen peacefully melted away.

Two of their number, James Gibson and Matthew Smith, stayed behind in Philadelphia to deal with the Assembly. On 13 February 1764 they handed the governor a formal statement of the frontier's grievances—the so-called Paxton Boys' *Remonstrance*[123]—which he laid before the House on 15 February. Foremost among the grievances recited was the unequal representation of the west in the Assembly (the five frontier counties returned but ten members, whereas the three old counties of Philadelphia, Chester, and Bucks, where the Quakers were concentrated, re-

[122] To Fothergill, 14 March 1764, *ibid.*, 104.
[123] 8 *Pa. Arch.*, VII, 5543-47.

turned twenty-four). The Assembly's Indian policy was scored on several counts: the Moravian Indians on Province Island were accused of being "His Majesty's perfidious Enemies," and their expulsion from the province was demanded; the same treatment was requested for all other Indians living in or near the inhabited parts of the province on the grounds that red-white integration of any sort was "extreamly dangerous"; the frontiersmen insisted that Quaker Indian traders be put under tighter official restraints and demanded that trade with the redmen be stopped until all whites were redeemed from captivity; finally, they complained that the government had "damped the Spirits of many brave Men" by refusing to offer bounties for Indian scalps.

Before the Assembly answered the *Remonstrance*, it asked for and received Penn's permission to see another paper which had issued from the Paxton Boys, the so-called *Declaration of the distressed and bleeding Frontier Inhabitants*, which had been sent to the governor from Germantown on 6 February.[124] The reading of the *Declaration* on 17 February scandalized the House and produced more religious bitterness in Pennsylvania than anything since Gilbert Tennent's famous philippic against his fellow Presbyterians two decades earlier, his sermon *On the Dangers of an Unconverted Ministry*. The *Declaration* was a broadside against Quaker government in Pennsylvania, a tirade

---

[124] Information given Isaac Wayne, 2nd month [February], 1764, Pemberton Papers, Hist. Soc. Pa. *Paxton Papers*, 133. According to James Pemberton, the *Declaration* was transmitted to the governor by an assemblyman from one of the interior counties. Pemberton to Dr. John Fothergill, 7 March 1764, Pemberton Papers, Hist. Soc. Pa. The *Declaration* is printed in 8 *Pa. Arch.*, VII, 5549-52.

about the province's "unhappy Situation, under the Villainy, Infatuation and Influence of a certain Faction that have got the political Reigns in their Hand and tamely tyrannize over the other good Subjects of the Province!" Specifically, it charged the Quakers with enslaving the province to Indians, with despising and refusing to protect the people on the frontier, and with permitting refugees from Indian attacks to "starve neglected" while maintaining their fiendish foes in luxury and idleness (surely a novel description of the Province Island pesthouse). The Friends, loath to let such charges go unanswered, commissioned their Committee for Suffering to prepare an official response, which was published on 25 February.[125] Even before its appearance, however, self-appointed champions took the field to defend the honor of their persuasion and to retaliate against the Paxtoneers by attacking their religion.

It was no secret that the vast majority of the Paxton Boys were Scotch-Irish Presbyterians, nor had it mattered too much until the *Declaration* was brought to the public's attention. Certain Quakers, to be sure, had reviled the "rioters" before their march on Philadelphia as being of the "same Spirit with the blood-ran, blood-thirsty Presbyterians, who cut off King Charles his Head,"[126] while others had sneered at the insurgents after they reached Germantown as being a "presbiterian" faction, "that Society thro' out the province being tainted with the same bloody principles with respect to the Indians & of disaffection to

---

[125] Under the title of *The Address of the People call'd Quakers, In the Province of Pennsylvania, To John Penn, Esquire,* . . . , *Paxton Papers,* 133-38.

[126] *Pa. Col. Recs.,* IX, 126.

the Government.''[127] But the majority of Friends were not prepared to ascribe the Paxton aberration to the principles of its participants. To them the Paxtoneers were first and foremost "a lawless banditi" or a "Shabby Gang." Once they attacked Quakerism in the *Declaration*, however, this attitude changed and swarms of polemicists assailed Presbyterianism with a ferocity ill becoming their peaceful profession; they wrote, in fact, with the frenzy of dervishes. Their near-hysteria was caused by a fear of Presbyterianism which had been building in Quaker hearts since members of the Kirk began arriving in large numbers early in the eighteenth century. By 1729 James Logan was afraid that the Presbyterians would "make themselves the Proprietors of the Province"[128] and Quaker alarm mounted every year thereafter, especially as the Friends saw the sect flooding the province with ministers from its newly founded seminary in New Jersey and proselytizing with a zeal unmatched by other Pennsylvanians. The Presbyterians, it appeared, wanted to take over the province, and the march of their Paxton co-religionists seemed to confirm that suspicion. Accordingly, apprehensive Quaker writers gave them no quarter.

Insofar as the Paxton "riot" was an attempt to overthrow the existing government—and no opportunity was missed to represent it as such—it was pictured as the latest installment in a perpetual Presbyterian holy war against the mild and beneficent government of the Kings of Great Britain. Oliver Cromwell was portrayed as the archetypal

---

[127] Foulke's "Journal," 70.

[128] Guy S. Klett, *Presbyterians in Colonial Pennsylvania* (Phila., 1935), 235.

Presbyterian, whose example the Paxton Boys were accused of consciously imitating.[129] Other writers picked up the tale at the end of the civil war and compiled a catalogue of all the Presbyterian uprisings in Scotland and Northern Ireland from that period until the accession of George III, including campaigns as notable as Bonnie Prince Charlie's invasion of England in 1745 and commotions as obscure as the battle of Bothel Bridge in 1679.[130] The moral drawn from these events was that Presbyterians were and always had been "Quarrelsome, Riotous, Rebellious, dissatisfied with the publick Establishment" and enemies to "Kingly Government."[131] We shall find, thundered one writer, "that in the Annals both of ancient and modern History, Presbyterianism and Rebellion, were twin-Sisters . . . and their Affection for each other, has ever been so strong, that a separation of them never could be effected."[132]

The second point on which the pamphleteers hammered was the Paxton Boys' alleged intention to "extirpate" the Quakers "Root and Branch, and not leave one Soul alive."[133] "Bloody persecuting Principles" these were called, and sanguinary intolerance was declared to be as salient a historical characteristic of Presbyterianism as rebelliousness. Presbyterians, wrote one critic, could not abide

---

[129] [Anonymous], "The Paxton Boys, A Farce," *Paxton Papers*, 158, 159.

[130] See, e.g., [Isaac Hunt?], "A Looking-Glass for Presbyterians," *ibid.*, 245-55.

[131] [Anonymous], "An Answer to the Conduct of the Paxton Men," *ibid.*, 325; [Hunt?], "A Looking-Glass," *ibid.*, 249.

[132] *Ibid.*, 246.

[133] [Anonymous], "The Paxton Boys, A Farce," *ibid.*, 159; the next quotation is from *ibid.*, 164.

any "other profession or Opinion but their own, and never cease till they establish themselves in such a Manner, so as to exclude all other Sects."[134] Witness Scotland and New England, the writer continued, "Countries where their Religion has been propagated with the Sword." From whence, he derisively asked, "but from Mahomet" could they have learned such tactics? Constant were the references to the fate of the Quakers in early Massachusetts, those godly people who were used, as one Friend put it, "in the most cruel Manner, that the Serpentine Nature of Man could invent."[135] The whippings, cropping of ears, boring of tongues, and executions they suffered "for their faithful obedience to Christ" were recounted, and all the blame was put on the "Envious, Malicious, Hard-hearted Presbyterians" of the Bay Colony.

In abusing Presbyterianism when only a small group of that sect's communicants deserved censure, the Quakers employed the very tactics for which they excoriated the Paxton Boys: holding a whole people responsible and fair game for retaliation for the offenses of a few of their brethren. Their attacks offended every Presbyterian in Pennsylvania and rallied the entire denomination against them, with the result that they now found their active adversaries increased from a few thousand western pioneers to a society embracing the whole province and including perhaps a quarter of its inhabitants. Presbyterian penmen, never a

---

[134] This and the two following quotations are from [Hunt?], "A Looking-Glass," *ibid.*, 250, 246.

[135] This and the two following quotations are from [Anonymous], "The Quakers Assisting to preserve the Lives of the Indians, in the Barracks, vindicated," *ibid.*, 392.

diffident lot, began returning the Quakers' blows immediately. They concentrated on proving them hypocrites and on implicating them in the murders committed by the Indians on the frontier. They had a field day with the fact that on the afternoon of 4 February some two hundred Quakers, contrary to their society's ancient peaceable profession, took up arms and joined the association to defend the city.[136] And they were ecstatic over an episode two days later, when the Friends' main meetinghouse on Market Street was put at the disposal of a detachment of soldiers. These events made a mockery of the Friends' "fundamental Principles of Non-Resistance,"[137] exclaimed one writer, principles which had never before bent for the defense of King and country, which had stood proof against the menaces of Frenchmen and Spaniards, but which were now "chearfully sacrificed . . . as a Compliment to perfidious Savages." "No Excommunications now for the taking up Arms," raged the author of the *Quaker Unmasked*. "Behold the MeetingHouse converted into a Place of Arms! No Preaching nor Praying heard there, but the beating of Drums, and the confused clashing of Arms, by Men who knew not how to use them." Are these, the unmasker continued, "the People who are taught by immediate Inspiration that it is a heinous Crime to fight? What amazing Hypocrisy appears in their Profession! They must either confess that they have hitherto resisted the Holy Spirit, or impiously assert that the Spirit has changed his Mind,

---

[136] James Pemberton to Dr. John Fothergill, 7 March 1764, Pemberton Papers, Hist. Soc. Pa.

[137] [David James Dove], "The Quaker Unmask'd," *Paxton Papers*, 209.

and now directs them to War and Blood, contradictory to his former Inspirations. But this is to blaspheme God, and belie the Holy Ghost, yet such is their Conduct!"[138]

This line of attack was based on hard facts, which the Quaker apologists could not explain away. Of a very different character was the attempt to make the Quakers accomplices in the murders on the frontier. The indictments of the various pamphleteers were built on the following kinds of "evidence": a "French Indian," not otherwise identified, was supposed to have told two other Indians, who then told somebody else who had since died, that "the Quakers in Philadelphia gave him a Rod for the Indians on the Ohio, to chastise" the whites in western Pennsylvania;[139] the Quakers by virtue of their appearances at Indian conferences were accused of setting themselves up in competition with the governor and convincing the redmen that Pennsylvanians were a "pusillanimous Pack of old Women, divided among ourselves, without spirit or resolution," which impression was alleged to have encouraged the Indians to "commit what Outrages they pleased upon us"; the Quakers were supposed to have "persuaded the Indians that the Proprietor and the Traders had cheated them and therefore they ought to scourge the white people who live on the frontiers." And so it went, malicious inference and imagination converting everything to the conclusion that the "Quakers have stirred up the Indians to anger and even to murthering his Majesty's

[138] *Ibid.*, 212.
[139] *Ibid.*, 293n. The remaining quotations in this paragraph are, in the order of their appearance, from *ibid.*, 273, 375-76, 377, 212.

subjects in this province." Some writers went even further and made the Friends "secretly rejoice" when they heard of "whole Settlements murdered and destroyed."

The viciousness of the Presbyterian counterattack boosted the pamphlet warfare into an even more vituperative phase. Quakers ridiculed Presbyterian dogma, made ethnic jibes at the Scotch-Irish, and accused the leaders of the Kirk in Pennsylvania of studying "nothing more than the Distruction of God's People, by ushering into their [flock's] Minds, Vice, Immorality, Hatred, Envy, Evil speaking, bitterness of Heart and a perpetual dislike to all other religious Societies."[140] The Presbyterians replied in kind. Passions were so inflamed that Franklin told friends in England that he had never seen more "violent Parties and cruel Animosities."[141] In fact, he genuinely feared that the two groups would come to blows and that "civil Bloodshed" would ensue. This, fortunately, did not occur, but the Quaker-Presbyterian donnybrook produced two important results, nevertheless. One was the solidification of the Presbyterians. In 1741 the Great Awakening had rent them into New Side and Old Side, and the schism had not been officially healed until 1758. But formal reconciliation did not restore denominational cohesion; what did were the Quaker attacks in 1764, for they gave the Presbyterians a sense of common identity and forged a new feeling of community among them. To be sure, ill will remained—in places such as Lancaster County the New and Old Siders

---

[140] *Ibid.*, 395.
[141] Franklin to Jackson, 25 June 1764, in Labaree, ed., *Papers of BF*, XI, 239.

could not agree on a joint political ticket in September 1764[142]—but the Quaker abuse in the winter of 1764 closed the Presbyterian ranks far more effectively than the official agreement of 1758. The second result of the affray was related to the first: an epidemic of hyper-denominationalism, in which anything the Quakers proposed was automatically opposed by the Presbyterians and vice versa, a climate of opinion which, as we shall presently see, had a profound effect on the province's politics.

The *Declaration of the distressed and bleeding Frontier Inhabitants*, whose reading before the Assembly on 17 February touched off the Quaker-Presbyterian hostilities, infuriated the members of the House (twenty-two of whom were Friends) and closed their ears to the Paxton Boys' grievances.[143] They could not, in fact, wait to wash their hands of their emissaries, Messrs. Smith and Gibson. Accordingly, on 18 February they proposed to Penn that the two men be invited to joint public hearings (the governor's council was to participate, too) where a series of loaded questions would be put to them which "would naturally, by their Answers, show that the several Matters contained in those Papers [the Paxton Boys' *Remonstrance* and *Declaration*], respecting the Conduct both of the executive and legislative Powers of Government, were unjust, and without Foundation, and by that Means make it unnecessary

---

[142] See James Burd to Samuel Purviance, Jr., 17 Sept. 1759, Shippen Papers, Hist. Soc. Pa. See also Leonard J. Trinterud, *The Forming of an American Tradition: A Re-examination of Colonial Presbyterianism* (Phila., 1949), 153.

[143] William B. Reed, *Life and Correspondence of Joseph Reed* (Phila., 1847), I, 34.

to enter into any Argument with the Remonstrants on the Subject of their Complaints."[144] Penn, overriding the opinion of what were described as the "moderate" men on his council,[145] rejected the Assembly's proposition. Actually, it was Attorney General Benjamin Chew who rejected it, for in characteristic fashion young Penn had turned the control of domestic politics completely over to him. He admitted as much to his uncle, confessing that "I chiefly depend upon him" and calling him, in a classic of understatement, his "Assistant in drawing Messages."[146] Recognizing Chew's position in provincial government, Assemblymen dubbed him the "prime minister."[147] Few doubted, as James Pemberton put it on 7 March 1764, that he had "the sole direction of him [Penn] and the Affairs of the Government."[148] On Chew's advice Penn answered Smith and Gibson separately and "in Secret."[149] What he told them the Assembly never discovered, but whatever it was made the two emissaries "extreamly well satisfy'd with the

[144] House committee report, 21 Feb. 1764, 8 *Pa. Arch.*, VII, 5554.

[145] Franklin to Richard Jackson, 14 March 1764, in Labaree, ed., *Papers of BF*, XI, 107. Franklin evidently meant the Quaker councilmen, Shoemaker and Logan. James Pemberton noted that the House's proposal was "evaded thro' the influence of the Governor's chief advisers," Benjamin Chew, in particular. To Fothergill, 7 March 1764, Pemberton Papers, Hist. Soc. Pa.

[146] See John Penn to Thomas Penn, [5? May] and [15? June] 1764, Penn Papers, Official Correspondence, IX (1758-64), Hist. Soc. Pa.

[147] Foulke's "Journal," 73.

[148] To Fothergill, 7 March 1764, Pemberton Papers, Hist. Soc. Pa. See also [Anonymous], *The Substance of a Council held at Lancaster, August the 28th 1764*, Evans, 9848, where it is stated that Chew was supposed to have "govern'd our G[overnor]s thro ten Years."

[149] This and the following quotation are from Franklin to Jackson, 14 March 1764, in Labaree, ed., *Papers of BF*, XI, 107.

Governor." Left to its own devices, the Assembly uncere-
moniously sent Smith and Gibson packing. On 21 February it dispatched its clerk to the two men (the members
apparently considered such an errand beneath their dignity) to tell them that other matters before the House took
precedence over their business and, therefore, there was
"no further Occasion of their Attendance."[150] Not until 24
May did the Assembly get around to considering the Paxton Boys' complaints, and when a committee appointed to
look into the problem reported on 20 September, it confined itself to one grievance only, the underrepresentation
of the western counties in the Assembly, the redress of
which it refused to recommend.[151] Not until the spring of
1776, when revolution was imminent, was the Pennsylvania Assembly reapportioned.

The failure of the frontiersmen to obtain redress of any
of their grievances—a bounty for scalps being the sole ig-
nominious exception[152]—has caused historians to assume
what is apparently self-evident, that the march of the Paxton Boys yielded no immediate results (unless raising
Quaker blood pressures is counted as one) and that it had
significance only because in arousing the sympathy of the

[150] 8 *Pa. Arch.*, VII, 5556.

[151] Actually, the committee addressed itself to two grievances, the
underrepresentation of the west and the failure of the Pennsylvania
Supreme Court to hold sessions in western counties, thus obliging suit-
ors, jurors, parties, and witnesses to go all the way to Philadelphia for
trials. The latter grievance was not mentioned, however, in either the
Paxton Boys' *Remonstrance* or *Declaration*. It was cited in a petition
from "upwards of Twelve Hundred Inhabitants" of Cumberland
County, read before the House on 23 March 1764. See 8 *Pa. Arch.*, VII,
5580, 5608, 5636-37.

[152] Proclaimed by Penn, 7 July 1764. *Pa. Col. Recs.*, IX, 190-92.

Philadelphia lower classes it prefigured the frontier-urban coalition which established the new order in Pennsylvania in 1776.[153] It should become clear momentarily, however, that the Paxton Boys (broadly defined to include the irate frontiersmen both before *and after* the march on Philadelphia) did, in fact, produce important results in 1764.

Matthew Smith and James Gibson were incensed at being brushed off by the Assembly and stalked out of town making ostentatious "marks of Disgust."[154] Back on the frontier they related their tribulations to their comrades, who perceived at once that they had been duped by the city people, who had lulled them into dispersing with promises which were forgotten as soon as they disbanded. In the words of one wag: "they all agreed that they were jockey'd, Each cursed himself for being a blockhead."[155] Self-reproach was soon superseded by a desire for revenge, however, and angry men immediately began projecting another march against the capital, determined to make the Assembly pay for doublecrossing them and resolved to beat reforms out of the members, if necessary. Word of their intentions quickly reached Philadelphia; only a "few days" after Smith and Gibson left town, a Quaker Assemblyman noted in his journal that the Paxton people "had insolence enough to threaten the Legislature with returning, with redoubled force to procure for themselves satisfaction and redress of their pretended grievances."[156] On 29 February another Quaker observed that the "Paxton Chiefs are gone home without being heard, and we are daily threatened

---

[153] Charles H. Lincoln, *The Revolutionary Movement in Pennsylvania, 1760-1776* (Phila., 1901), 112-13.

[154] Foulke's "Journal," 72.   [155] *Paxton Papers*, 221.

[156] Foulke's "Journal," 72.

with a return of a more formidable force."[157] The persistence of the Paxton threat can be followed in Franklin's writings: the western mob is "soon expected down again" (14 March);[158] "tumults" are "threatened and daily expected" (31 March);[159] "we are daily threatened with more of these Tumults" (12 April);[160] "Reports [are] frequently spreading that the Frontier People are assembling to come down again" (1 May);[161] "the daily threats of these lawless People" continue (24 May).[162] In other words, from February until the end of May Philadelphia was assailed, day in and day out, with threats from the frontiersmen to return and chastise the Assembly. And many feared that, if they came again, they would not be satisfied unless they accomplished the putative aims of their first march: the murder of the Moravian Indians (who remained in Philadelphia until 20 March 1765) and the "massacre" of the Quakers.[163]

One might have thought that, having repelled the Paxton Boys once, the Quakers would have despised their renewed threats. Actually, however, they viewed them with trepidation. For one thing, the three companies of regulars, Royal Americans under Captain John Schlosser, who had made such an important contribution to defending the

---

[157] Anonymous Quaker letter, 29 Feb. 1764, in Hazard, ed., *Register of Pennsylvania*, XII, 13.

[158] To Richard Jackson, 14 March 1764, in Labaree, ed., *Papers of BF*, XI, 107.

[159] To Richard Jackson, 31 March 1764, *ibid.*, 150.

[160] "Cool Thoughts . . . ," *ibid.*, 160.

[161] To Jackson, 1 May 1764, *ibid.*, 185.

[162] *The Speech of Joseph Galloway*, 39.

[163] Franklin to Peter Collinson, 30 April 1764, in Labaree, ed., *Papers of BF*, XI, 181.

city in February, could not be counted on in another crisis, because General Gage was expected to recall them at any moment (Franklin, in fact, believed that the Paxtoneers would time their second march to coincide with the soldiers' departure).[164] Secondly, there were strong doubts that another voluntary association could be formed. The abuse the Presbyterians poured on the Quakers for joining the first one[165] and the reproofs the fighting Friends had received from their own brethren virtually precluded their participation during another emergency, and without them the viability of a volunteer association was questionable. It was possible, then, to envision a new horde of Paxton Boys marching into Philadelphia unopposed. The prospect of being at the mercy of these "Christian white savages" created profound anxiety in the capital. "The Mobs strike a general Terror," wrote Franklin on 14 March 1764, "and many talk of Removing into other Provinces, as thinking both their Persons and Properties insecure."[166] Indeed, some Quakers even considered moving to England,[167] testifying to the fact that from February through May Philadelphia (or at least the Quaker part of it) was gripped by greater fear than the city had ever known before (the

---

[164] *Preface* to Galloway's *Speech, ibid.,* 304.

[165] "Cool Thoughts . . . ," *ibid.,* 161; *Paxton Papers,* 301.

[166] To Jackson, 14 March 1764, in Labaree, ed., *Papers of BF,* XI, 107; to Collinson, 30 April 1764, *ibid.,* 181.

[167] "Unless we should have some Change in Government or men or measures I think our Weakness is so Great no man can be safe in Person or Property and shall therefore determine to move soon, if I live, into Yours [New Jersey] if my wife will not consent to go to England." William Logan to John Smith, [15? Feb.] 1764, Smith MSS, Hist. Soc. Pa.

panic caused by Braddock's defeat being the only possible exception).

To account for the western unrest, the Quakers and their political associates came up with a conspiracy theory. After the Paxton Boys returned home, they persuaded themselves that they had marched on Philadelphia, not because of indignation at the Indians quartered there or because of a desire for legislative reapportionment, but because they had been put up to it or had been hired, like extras in a movie, by certain persons in the capital (their fee was quoted at half a crown per day).[168] This theory was credible for three reasons: the Paxtoneers' precursors, the men John Hambright led into Philadelphia in 1755, were thought to have been organized and orchestrated by people in the capital;[169] while at Germantown, certain of the Paxton Boys were alleged to have confessed that they had been "invited and Encouraged by many Considerable persons" in Philadelphia, who had assured them that at their approach at least 400 city dwellers would rally to their standard;[170] and, lastly, the frontiersmen's rough, unkempt appearance persuaded the Quakers, who were prepared to believe the worst about them anyway, that they were a col-

---

[168] See [Anonymous], "The Author of the Quaker Unmask'd, Strip'd Stark Naked . . . ," *Paxton Papers*, 261. For another accusation that the Paxton Boys were in someone's pay, see [Anonymous], "The Quaker Vindicated . . . ," *ibid.*, 235.

[169] Joseph Galloway and the anonymous author of the *Address to the Rev. Dr. Alison, the Rev. Mr. Ewing* . . . drew parallels between the Hambright "riot" and the Paxton "riot." See *The Speech of Joseph Galloway*, 38, and the *Address to Alison*, Evans, 9892.

[170] James Pemberton to Dr. John Fothergill, 7 March 1764, Pemberton Papers, Hist. Soc. Pa.

lection of brutes, incapable of comprehending the gerry-
mandering at which they professed to be aggrieved, and
that, therefore, they must be the "tools" or the "dupes"
of others. As to who had manipulated them, there were
two schools of thought. Some suspected a conclave of Philadelphia Presbyterians who were aspiring to establish their
religion in the province,[171] either by intimidating the government with their armed co-religionists or by spiriting
them up to overthrow the old order completely and establish a theocracy in which "their Goddess Presbytery"
would reign triumphant. Others thought that the conspira-
tors were the leaders of the Proprietary Party whom they
contemptuously called "State Incendiaries" and "State
Physicians."[172] Specifically, "Prime Minister" Benjamin
Chew was considered by many to be the "chief counsiller
in the late Rebellion,"[173] the aim of which was assumed to
be the advancement of the proprietary political program
through the use of force.

Strengthening the suspicion that there was an alliance
between the Paxton Boys and the Proprietary Party was

[171] The writer of "The Author of the Quaker Unmask'd, Strip'd
Stark Naked," 261, subscribed to this theory.

[172] A proponent of this theory was Isaac Hunt. In his "Looking-Glass
for Presbyterians," No. II, *Paxton Papers*, 301, he attacked "some of
our State Physicians, who have been at work behind the scenes to encourage one part of the inhabitants to rise up in arms, and attempt to
draw blood of the rest." The people of the province, he continued,
"heartily and sincerely pity the poor despicable wretches [the Paxton
Boys] that were made Dupes of upon this occasion to serve the turn of
those shallow pated Statesmen." For the use of the term "State Incendiaries," see Foulke's "Journal," 72.

[173] James Pemberton to Dr. John Fothergill, 7 March 1764, Pemberton Papers, Hist. Soc. Pa.

John Penn's consistent forbearance toward the "rioters."
On 20 January 1764, for example, he had refused to endorse an Assembly demand that the sheriff, coroner, and
magistrates of Lancaster County be summoned to Philadelphia and interrogated about the identity of the ring-
leaders among the Paxton Boys, thus inviting insinuations
that he did not really want the murderers of the Indians
apprehended.[174] He had also refused to reduce the rioters
after they reached Germantown, a step urged by a number
of Quakers who were certain that an assault on their en-
campment would capture or annihilate the lot of them.
Penn, however, "greatly exasperated" these "meek, peaceful inspir'd Quakers" (a Presbyterian description) by opt-
ing to negotiate with the Paxtoneers,[175] a decision for which
he was vilified by Quaker writers as having "meanly
stoop'd to caress the rebels."[176] Also held against the governor was a speech made by a member of the Council to a
throng of Philadelphians on 7 February, just after the decision of the Paxton Boys to disperse had been announced.

[174] The Quakers and Franklin thought, at any rate, that the governor
had ignored the proposal. Actually, Penn referred it to the Council,
which considered it on 23 Jan. and 2 Feb. and on the latter day advised
him to reject it and instead charge the justices of the peace in Lancaster
County with examining the sheriff and coroner. Accordingly, on 4 Feb.
the governor wrote the Lancaster justices and ordered them to begin an
investigation. Of Penn's action the Quaker Party seems to have been
completely ignorant, although it would probably have censured it as
inadequate had it been apprised of it. 8 *Pa. Arch.*, VII, 5526-27; *Pa.
Col. Recs.*, IX, 124; 1 *Pa. Arch.*, IV, 160.

[175] Hindle, "The March of the Paxton Boys," 480; anonymous
Quaker letter, 29 Feb. 1764, in Hazard, ed., *Register of Pennsylvania*,
XII, 12; [David James Dove], "The Quaker Unmask'd . . . ," *Paxton
Papers*, 210.

[176] [Hunt], *Letter from . . . Transilvania.*

The orator called the Paxtoneers a "very worthy set of men,"[177] a description which shocked and revolted the Friends in the audience, who regarded them as bloodthirsty butchers. Most incriminating of all in Quaker eyes was the governor's rejection of the Assembly's scheme of publicly humiliating Smith and Gibson by feeding them a set of loaded questions and his arrangement instead of a secret interview with the two men which (rumor had it) radiated friendship and goodwill. Added up by the Quaker Party, Penn's actions toward the Paxton Boys amounted to this: he had dragged his feet in apprehending the murderers among them and had been reluctant to destroy them when they were in his power; rather, he had attempted to whitewash them, to pass them off as decent citizens, and had treated in secret with their emissaries to the apparent satisfaction of all concerned. Little wonder, then, that the governor was accused of striking a nefarious bargain with the rioters. Isaac Hunt decided that Penn "had promis'd them an act of Indemnity, and engag'd to take them into high favor, if they would turn their resentment upon the Delegates of the Province,"[178] a conclusion which Franklin strongly endorsed. "Impunity for their past Crimes," he charged, was "to be the Reward of their future political Services."[179] Elaborating to Dr. John Fothergill on 14 March 1764, he claimed that "strong Suspicions now prevail that those Mobs . . . are privately tampered with to be made Instruments of Government, to awe the Assembly

---

[177] Hindle, "The March of the Paxton Boys," 480.

[178] [Hunt], *Letter from . . . Transilvania.*

[179] *Preface* to Galloway's *Speech*, in Labaree, ed., *Papers of BF*, XI, 305.

into Proprietary Measures."[180] The leaders and Quaker
Party rank and file believed, in other words, that the Proprietary Party was conspiring to use the Paxton Boys as
storm troopers to intimidate the Assembly and, if necessary, to force it to adopt its legislative program. The re-
lentless threats from the west John Penn and his lieutenants were assumed to be orchestrating to keep the Assembly
fearful and, if possible, submissive.

The crystallization of this suspicion about the middle of
March generated a tremendous wave of moral revulsion
against proprietary government in Quaker circles, where
the tide was already running strongly against John Penn
for his stand on the £50,000 supply bill. This bill, it may
be recalled, was passed on 1 February to appease the frontier and prevent a march on Philadelphia. One measure of
its failure was that it was delayed in reaching the governor's desk because the appearance of the Paxton Boys at
Germantown disrupted the Assembly and prevented the
transaction of legislative business for the better part of a
week. Actually, the House had not passed the supply bill
on 1 February, even though the members talked as if they
had. What had passed on that date was simply a resolve,
exempting the proprietor from the obligation of accepting
the paper money issued by the bill as legal tender. But
since this conceded the only objection which James Hamilton or John Penn had ever raised against the bill, the
House believed that the vote on 1 February had as good
as passed it. By 10 February a committee had put it in
statutory language, and the further formality of voting on
it and sending it to the governor for his assent was taken

[180] *Ibid.*, 102-3.

care of by 24 February. To the House's utter astonishment, Penn returned it on 8 March with a totally new objection, never so much as hinted at before: the bill, he contended, contravened the Privy Council's second amendment of 2 September 1760 (above, p. 60) and could not be signed until it was made to conform thereunto.[181] The Assembly was flabbergasted, for it had taken the second amendment into account in framing the bill and had, as far as it was aware, complied with it. In fact, it had inserted the amendment practically verbatim into the bill. "The located uncultivated Lands belonging to the Proprietaries shall not," the bill stipulated, "be assessed higher than the lowest Rate at which any located uncultivated Lands belonging to the Inhabitants, *under the same Circumstances of Situation, Kind and Quality*, shall be assessed."[182] With the exception of the words in italics, the phraseology was identical to the amendment as promulgated by the Privy Council. The words in italics were precisely what Penn objected to, however; he wanted them deleted and the exact words of the amendment inserted. But let us give the devil his due; it was Attorney General Chew, the province's de facto chief executive, who insisted that the exact words be inserted.[183]

---

[181] For Penn's message of 7 March 1764, which he submitted to the House on 8 March, see 8 *Pa. Arch.*, VII, 5567-69. His second major objection to the bill was that it did not conform to the Privy Council's third amendment of 2 Sept. 1760, which stipulated that "all Lands not granted by the Proprietaries within Boroughs and Towns, be deemed located uncultivated Lands and rated accordingly and not as Lots." See above, p. 60.

[182] Labaree, ed., *Papers of BF*, XI, 111-12. Italics supplied by the author.

[183] For Chew's primary responsibility for the interpretation of the second amendment, see William Logan to John Smith, 17 and 25 March

A pettifogger's delight, they were a fair man's despair, for their literal meaning was that the best of the proprietor's located, uncultivated lands should be assessed no higher than the worst of the people's. Suppose Penn were living today and owned a vacant lot at the corner of Broad and Market Streets in Philadelphia; Chew was insisting that it be assessed no higher than a plot of the same size on a worked-out strip coal mine outside of Scranton. Or, as Joseph Galloway put it in April 1764, he was demanding that the proprietor's "Lotts in this City [Philadelphia] that do not contain half an Acre, and are worth from £1500 to £2000 shall be rated no higher than half an Acre of a poor Man's land at Juniata, not worth £5."[184]

1764, Smith MSS, Hist. Soc. Pa.; William Peters to Thomas Penn, 4 June 1764, Penn Papers, Hist. Soc. Pa.

[184] [Galloway], *An Address to the Freeholders,* Evans, 9561. Actually, Chew's interpretation of the second amendment did not promise to save Penn as much tax money as these two examples imply. For the purpose of assessment Pennsylvania divided its located, uncultivated lands into three categories. The poorest land it assessed at £5 per 100 acres, the next grade at £10, and the best land at £15 per 100 acres. Thus, although Penn would save some money by having his best lands assessed no higher than the people's worst, there would be a definite limit, a £5 floor, placed under his savings. Where he stood to make a killing was in having his vacant city lots assessed as located, uncultivated land, as the third Privy Council amendment ordered, although it is not clear exactly how much this ruling would save him. On 14 March 1764 Franklin cited an example of a city lot paying taxes of only 7½d. while in Penn's possession, but paying £7 as soon as it was sold to a local citizen. Thus, on this lot, Penn paid taxes at a rate of 224 times less than his purchaser. See Labaree, ed., *Papers of BF,* XI, 106. It is interesting to note that in the spring of 1764 a pro-Penn pamphleteer estimated that he would save only £110 in taxes by virtue of Chew's interpretation of the second amendment, while John Dickinson stated that no one, whether friend or foe, reckoned his savings at higher than £400 or £500. [Hugh Williamson], "The Plain Dealer," No. I, *Paxton Papers,* 346; John Dickinson, *A Speech Delivered in the*

The Assembly could not believe that the Privy Council, in promulgating the second amendment, had intended so egregious an injustice, and Franklin, who had represented it at the Council hearings in 1760, assured it that it had not.[185] Although the members were aware of Chew's influence over the governor, they did not attribute the amendment's interpretation to him. John Penn they considered unlikely to have independently conceived anything so audaciously wicked. Hence, there seemed to be only one person who could have been responsible—their old adversary, Thomas Penn. That he had recently doctored the Privy Council's sixth amendment in an effort to beat the province out of some extra pounds made him a prime suspect, but what principally caused the Assemblymen to point their collective finger at him was their experience with proprietary policy during the preceding decade. Having become accustomed during that period to attribute all unpopular executive actions to secret proprietary instructions and having seen their suspicion confirmed by the conduct of successive proprietary deputies—confirmed until it became a conviction, an article of faith about the workings

---

House of Assembly of the Province of Pennsylvania, May 24th, 1764 (Phila., 1764), 2, 3, 18.

[185] In his *Preface* to Galloway's *Speech*, in Labaree, ed., *Papers of BF*, XI, 280, Franklin assured the people of the province that "As to their present Claim, founded on that Article [the Privy Council's second amendment], 'that the best and most valuable of their Lands, should be tax'd no higher than the worst and least valuable of the People's,' it was not then thought of; they [the proprietors] made no such Demand, nor did any one dream, that so iniquitous a Claim would ever be made by Men who had the least Pretence to the Characters of Honorable or Honest." See also William Logan to John Smith, 25 March 1764, Smith MSS, Hist. Soc. Pa.

of proprietary policy—the members concluded that the outrageous interpretation of the second amendment had been enjoined upon John Penn, under pain of forfeiting the customary £5,000 performance bond, by secret instructions from his uncle.[186]

This time Thomas Penn was not guilty. He had no hand in Chew's interpretation of the amendment and knew nothing about it until a letter from his nephew, apprising him of it, arrived in England at the end of May. Immediately he conferred with his legal adviser, Henry Wilmot, who informed him that Chew's interpretation was unjust and should be repudiated. Since Wilmot's advice conformed to his own feelings on the matter, Penn eagerly accepted it and on 1 June wrote his nephew, ordering him to agree to the Assembly's interpretation of the second amendment and to allow his located, uncultivated lands to be assessed "at the lowest rate of the inhabitants under the same circumstances of situation, kind, and quality."[187] But by 1 June it was already too late to rectify his attorney general's mistake; irreparable damage had been done by it. The message of 8 March, coupled with the detection of John Penn's apparent alliance with the Paxton Boys, seemed to signal the complete moral bankruptcy of the proprietary

---

[186] See, e.g., the Assembly's 22nd resolve of 24 March 1764: "it is the Opinion of this House, that the Governor's rejecting the said [supply] Bill does not arise from its not being comfortable to that Report, but because it is not formed agreeable to Proprietary Instructions." Labaree, ed., *Papers of BF*, XI, 132. See also Franklin to Jackson, 14 March 1764, *ibid.*, 105, and the Assembly's message to John Penn, 22 March 1764, *ibid.*, 113.

[187] See Henry Wilmot to John Penn, 30 May 1764; Thomas and Richard Penn to John Penn, 1 June 1764; Thomas Penn to Benjamin Chew, 8 June 1764; all in Penn Papers, Hist. Soc. Pa.

cause. During the preceding decade Thomas Penn and his partisans had always tried to justify his tax dodging by arguing that the Quakers in the Assembly were out to "get" him for renouncing their faith and joining the Church of England[188] and that, if allowed to tax him, they would ruin him; let him be assured of fair taxation, they claimed, and he would gladly pay his proper share. Most Pennsylvanians were skeptical about the sincerity of Penn's fears and viewed them as a rationalization for avarice. The £50,000 supply bill of 24 February put his protestations to the test by taxing his property exactly as everyone else's, with as much impartiality as the wit of man could devise. And what was the result? Instead of paying up, John Penn used tactics befitting the province's slipperiest shyster to shirk his fair share. His actions gave the lie to all past proprietary professions and recalled, at the same time that it accentuated, a full decade of proprietary tax dodging.

More distressing still was the Assembly's conviction that the message of 8 March represented a culmination of Thomas Penn's efforts of over a decade to subject it to external control through the instrumentality of inflexible instructions. That Penn would succeed in imposing his will on this occasion no one doubted. Who, after all, would be willing to provoke the Paxton Boys by refusing to vote military supplies, especially in the critical month of March? On the frontier March meant two things: spring planting and the resurgence of Indian warfare. Farmers and redmen would be taking the field at the same time, with potentially disastrous results for the former; the tillers of

---

[188] See, e.g., Franklin's *Preface* to Galloway's *Speech*, in Labaree, ed., *Papers of BF*, XI, 279.

the soil would not be safe "from assassins or bush-rangers for a single day or hour," a Berks County man remarked, and would have "to remain together in groups with their families," while "their fields were lying idle."[189] The west, in other words, faced either starvation or the scalping knife unless the Assembly passed the supply bill to finance an expedition to clear the Indians from its doorstep. In this situation it would brook no excuses for legislative inaction. The supply bill must be passed, whatever the costs to the Assembly's sensitivities. Otherwise, said a frontiersman, swelling the flood of warnings which were cascading in from the west, "as soon as the attacks by the barbarians were resumed the frontier settlers from the four counties would flock to Philadelphia by the thousands and speak to the government." That their vocabulary would be one of violence was clear to all.

From the moment, then, that John Penn demanded that the Assembly assess the best proprietary lands no higher than the people's worst, the members perceived that pressure from the west would force them to accommodate him. The prospect of capitulating to so repugnant a demand galvanized sentiment for royal government, while the absence of the factors which had inhibited it in February guaranteed that the movement for it, so long in gestation, would at last materialize in March. One factor which had impeded a royal government movement after the capitulation to Penn on 1 February had been the House's need of the governor's cooperation in defending Philadelphia against the onslaught of the Paxton Boys and its reluctance

---

[189] *The Journals of Muhlenberg*, II, 55. The next quotation in this paragraph is from the same source.

to alienate him at that perilous moment by spearheading a movement to replace him. By March, however, suspicions about Penn's pact with the frontiersmen had changed the House's outlook. The members reasoned that by aligning himself with the Paxtoneers the governor had taken the most hostile step possible toward them and that, therefore, nothing further could be lost by alienating him. The second impediment to a royal government movement at the beginning of February had been the nature of the House's principal grievance against Penn at that time: his insistence that it accept the Privy Council's sixth amendment, exempting his quit rents from payment in legal tender. The Assemblymen realized that they would be laughed out of court if they appealed to England against Penn's adherence to the sixth amendment, for the only way the Privy Council could support them was by condemning itself. Penn's assessment demand appeared to be a different matter altogether, however, for they believed that it was based on a shameless perversion of a Privy Council amendment and that the Council would, consequently, welcome the opportunity to vindicate its honor by stripping Penn of his government.

By 8 March, then, the decks were cleared for a campaign for royal government, and the House initiated it on 10 March by appointing a committee, consisting of Franklin, Galloway, and six other members, to compose "Resolves upon the present Circumstances of this Province, and the Aggrievances of the Inhabitants thereof." Midst the welter of forces which contributed to the crystallization of the royal government movement the Paxton Boys predominated, for by forcing the House to capitulate to Penn's latest set of repugnant demands, they served as the catalyst for the movement, which, as we shall presently see, produced a decisive transformation in Pennsylvania's political life. Therefore, to say that the Paxton Boys had little immediate impact on politics in Pennsylvania is wrong; their impact was profound.

CHAPTER III

The Campaign for Royal Government

ALTHOUGH THE members of the Pennsylvania Assembly knew the moment they read John Penn's message of 8 March that they would be compelled to capitulate to his assessment demand, they decided to stiffen their backs momentarily in the hope that a streak of obstinacy would assist the royal government campaign. Consequently, they returned the £55,000 supply bill to Penn on 14 March (why £5,000 was added in the interim is not clear) without agreeing to his terms. By rebuffing him, they hoped to force him to be candid with them, for although everybody in the province knew the interpretation he placed on the Privy Council's second amendment, he was reluctant to make an explicit public declaration of his understanding of it, confining himself, as he did in rejecting the £55,000 bill on 19 March, to terse statements that the bill did not conform to the amendment. In response to Assembly messages of 19 and 20 March requesting that he explain himself, Penn refused, informing the House that "the English language does not afford Words more forcible, clear and explicit"[1] than those in which the amendment was written and demanding that they be inserted into the supply bill verbatim. This the House declined to do and kept the pressure on the governor by reminding him in a message

---

[1] This and the following quotation are from 8 *Pa. Arch.*, VII, 5576, 5579.

of 22 March "how absurd it would be for the two Branches of the Legislature to agree to pass an Act in Terms which both . . . understand very differently." Recognizing that the House could not be stalled forever, Benjamin Chew, who had been writing Penn's messages all along, chose to spell out, in a message of 23 March, the proprietary interpretation of the second amendment: "if Five, Ten, or Fifteen Pounds, is the lowest at which *any* such Lands of the Inhabitants are assessed, none of the located uncultivated Lands of the Proprietaries shall be assessed higher."[2] Here were the words the Assembly had been waiting for, words which could put the campaign for royal government into high gear, for by demanding that the best of the proprietary lands be assessed at the same rate as the worst of the people's, Penn gave the House the perfect partisan battle cry, the ideal self-incriminating political slogan. Hence, the Assembly lost no time in proceeding against him, unanimously adopting on 24 March twenty-six resolves which its committee of 10 March had prepared.[3]

The resolves naturally stressed the Assembly's principal grievance: Thomas Penn's effort to subject the province to external control. The first one went so far as to declare that, unless he came to Pennsylvania to govern personally, he had no authority in the province, that if he and his successors continued to govern through deputies, they could be "considered in no other Light than as private Owners

[2] *Ibid.*, 5585; for Chew's authorship of this message, see William Peters to Thomas Penn, 4 June 1764, Penn Papers, Hist. Soc. Pa.

[3] For these resolves, see Labaree, ed., *Papers of BF*, XI, 123-32. On 24 March the House adjourned until 14 May. After a fortnight more of sparring with Penn, it voted, on 29 May, to accept his interpretation of the second amendment and pass the £55,000 supply bill. *Ibid.*, 203-13.

of Property, without the least Share or constitutional Power of Legislation whatever." The next several resolves scored Penn's instructions and the "penal Bonds" with which he enforced them. Then, other grievances against the proprietary government were enumerated: Penn's deputies were accused of corrupting public morals by issuing exorbitant numbers of tavern licenses (for each of which they received a fee); the proprietor was attacked for appointing judges during pleasure, rather than during good behavior; his land policy was denounced; his nephew's refusal to pass a militia bill, unless given the appointment of officers, was criticized; and Penn was berated for "endeavouring to demolish and annihilate the Priveleges granted" by his father. The final two resolves spelled out the House's response to this catalogue of complaints: the government of Pennsylvania should be "lodged in the Hands of the Crown" and the members, for their part, would adjourn to consult their constituents to determine whether "an humble address" should be sent to the King, praying him "to take the People of the Province under His immediate Protection."

Actually, the intention of the members was not to solicit public opinion (as their last resolve implied), but to shape it. Since they met behind closed doors and forbade day-by-day publication of their proceedings, the people of the province knew precious little about their latest clash with John Penn. Therefore, the Assemblymen wanted to sell them their version of it, while their minds were still open. Consequently, when the House adjourned on the afternoon of 24 March, key members had planned and were prepared to execute what was perhaps the most intensive public relations campaign in the province's history, one which, as far as the state of the mass media permitted, intended to saturate Pennsylvania with royal government propaganda. Plainly visible in the plan was the hand of the province's foremost practitioner of the art of public persuasion and, by the testimony of friend and foe alike, the leader of the royal government campaign, Benjamin Franklin.[4]

The plan went into effect on 29 March with a "blitz" from the printing presses of Franklin & Hall. That day's issue of the *Pennsylvania Gazette* printed the messages which had passed between the Assembly and John Penn from 19 March onward and the resolves of 24 March. The same day 3,000 copies of these messages and resolves, printed separately as a broadside, were published and distributed to the people. Still on the same day 3,000 copies of "Explanatory Remarks," which Franklin wrote as a commentary on the resolves, were published and distributed.[5]

[4] In a protest, 26 Oct. 1764, against Franklin's appointment as agent to England, ten assemblymen accused him of being "the Chief Author of the Measures pursued by the late Assembly," i.e., of the campaign for royal government. In reply he wrote: "I shall not dispute my Share in those Measures." See Labaree, ed., *Papers of BF*, XI, 409, 431. For other affirmations of Franklin's leadership, see John Penn to Thomas Penn, 5 May 1764, Penn Papers, Hist. Soc. Pa.; George Bryan to ————, 13 April 1764, quoted in Burton A. Konkle, *George Bryan and the Constitution of Pennsylvania, 1731-1781* (Phila., 1922), 49; and *Pa. Journal*, supplement, 27 Sept. 1764.

[5] There is no conclusive evidence that the broadside was distributed to the public on 29 March. That it was is inferred from the billing date in the *Work Book* of Franklin & Hall. The firm billed the province for the printing of the piece on 12 April 1764. On the same day it billed the province for Franklin's "Explanatory Remarks," which were certainly published on 29 March. Therefore, it seems reasonable to suppose that the broadside, without which the "Explanatory Remarks" would have made little sense, was also published on 29 March. Labaree, ed., *Papers of BF*, XI, 133-34n, 134-44.

On 31 March Franklin & Hall printed 100 copies of a petition for royal government (which Franklin wrote),[6] and these were circulated at a mass meeting of the citizens of Philadelphia, held at the State House on either that day or on one of the first days of April.[7] Exactly how many people attended the meeting is not known, but no one could have pleaded ignorance for missing it, because the Assembly leaders sent "particular Messengers" to every house in town to announce it. Joseph Galloway, touted by his admirers as the "Demosthenes of Pennsylvania," was the principal speaker at the gathering. He harangued the crowd at length, poured "the most rank abuse" on the proprietors, and urged his auditors to bestir themselves and demand a royal government. "The way from Proprietary Slavery to Royal Liberty was easy," he declared. Later in April Franklin again took to the press, publishing a long anti-proprietary polemic, *Cool Thoughts on . . . Our Public Affairs*, which supplemented a shorter, more intemperate piece by Galloway, *An Address to the Freeholders and Inhabitants of . . . Pennsylvania*. Both pamphlets were "distributed gratis by the thousands" and were "thrown into the Houses of the several Inhabitants" of Philadelphia.[8] On 18 April Franklin & Hall recorded the printing of another 200 petitions for royal government.[9] In the counties these were circulated by the local Assemblymen, but in Philadelphia three of Franklin's cronies, Thomas Whar-

---

[6] *Ibid.*, 145.

[7] This meeting and the efforts of Assembly partisans to procure signatures to royal government petitions, discussed later in this paragraph, are described in a letter from John to Thomas Penn, 5 May 1764, Penn Papers, Hist. Soc. Pa.

[8] Labaree, ed., *Papers of BF*, XI, 154-57.

[9] *Ibid.*, 145.

ton, Philip Syng, and Philip Knowles, solicited signatures, going into "all the houses in Town without distinction, to give everybody . . . an opportunity of showing their Love for their Country in endeavouring to shake off Proprietary Injustice and Slavery." Liquor, dispensed by the Assembly party at an "open house" at one of the city's taverns, was used to prime prospective signers and, according to the opponents of royal government, deceit was also employed; many people, they alleged, "put their Names to blank Sheets of Paper, did not know that the Constitution of their Country was affected by what they did, and were told that it was only an Address of Duty to their Majesty to which their names were to be affixed."[10]

The result of these unprecedented efforts became apparent when the Assembly reconvened on 14 May. Petitions from all parts of the province were handed in, containing some 3,500 names.[11] A majority of the signatories were Quakers;[12] 1,650 signers were residents of Philadelphia

[10] *Pa. Journal*, supplement, 27 Sept. 1764.

[11] The figure of 3,500 was given in several publications of opponents of the royal government. Most significantly, Franklin, when commenting upon it directly, did not challenge its accuracy. See John Dickinson, *A Speech, Delivered in the House of Assembly of the Province of Pennsylvania, May 24, 1764* . . . (Phila., 1764), iv; *Pa. Journal*, supplement, 27 Sept. 1764; Remonstrance of the Inhabitants of Philadelphia, 26 Oct. 1764, 8 *Pa. Arch.*, VII, 5688-89. For Franklin's apparent acceptance of the figures, see his *Preface* to Galloway's *Speech*, in Labaree, ed., *Papers of BF*, XI, 290.

[12] It is virtually impossible to determine precisely how many of the signers were Quakers. The Quakers, in fact, circulated their own version of the royal government petition, which differed slightly from the one written by Franklin. Eight signed copies of it are in the Public Record Office, London. In that repository are also twenty-three signed copies of Franklin's petition. Many who signed this document are readily identifiable as Quakers, but since there is no complete roster of the

and its environs.[13] Despite the notorious imprecision of colonial population statistics, something can be made of these figures. The population of Philadelphia and its suburbs in 1764 was probably no more than, and perhaps somewhat less than, 20,000, while the population of Pennsylvania seems to have been in the neighborhood of 250,000.[14] Thus, an area with only eight percent of the province's population furnished almost fifty percent of the petitions' signatures. Consider the matter another way. Supposing that for each adult white male in Pennsylvania at this time there were three other people (probably a conservative estimate in an era of large families), there would have been about 5,000 potential petition signers in the Philadelphia area, and approximately 57,500 in the rest of the province; therefore, thirty-three percent of eligible Philadelphians would have signed the petition, whereas only three percent of the remainder of the inhabitants would have. Of course, these calculations are unscientific and hence suspect,

---

Quakers in Pennsylvania, it is impossible to determine precisely how many were Friends. To complicate the problem further, the petitions in the Public Record Office represent only a portion of the total number which were signed. Given these difficulties, one is forced to rely on contemporary testimony, such as James Pemberton's statement of 13 June 1764, that the Quakers "pretty generally" signed the petition, or George Bryan's statement of 26 April 1764, that "great numbers" of Friends signed, to establish the identity of the signatories. *Ibid.*, 145-46; James Pemberton to Samuel Fothergill, 13 June 1764, Pemberton Papers, Hist. Soc. Pa.; Konkle, *George Bryan*, 50, 51.

[13] Richard to Nicholas Waln, 3 June 1764, Waln Letterbooks, 1762-66, Hist. Soc. Pa.

[14] The population of Philadelphia is arrived at by extrapolating from Sam Bass Warner's careful estimate of 23,739 in 1775; see his *The Private City Philadelphia in Three Periods of Its Growth* (Phila., 1968), 11-12. For the population of Pennsylvania, see Labaree, ed., *Papers of BF*, XI, 290.

but compared with the somewhat more trustworthy conclusion that Philadelphia, with eight percent of the population, furnished fifty percent of the signatures, they demonstrate what appears to be a valid fact, that in the signing of the royal government petitions there was an urban-rural split, the province's major urban area providing a disproportionate amount of support for royal government and its rural areas providing overwhelming opposition. Contemporary testimony also documents this split. George Bryan observed that "in the country the petitions for a change of government are less liked, especially as you approach the frontier," and Israel Pemberton informed an English correspondent that, in contrast to the city Quakers, "very few Friends in the country had sign'd or Approved of these Petitions." Even among the Germans the division was apparent, the rural Germans opposing royal government, those living in Philadelphia (led by David Deshler and John Wister) favoring it.[15]

That such a split occurred should not surprise us, for the tension between rural conservatism and urban experimentiveness (one hesitates to use the term "liberalism" in the context of the royal government campaign) is an enduring phenomenon in American history. But were there not specific factors to explain it? One possibility is that most of the supporters of royal government, the Quakers, lived in

---

[15] Bryan to ———, 13 April 1764, in Konkle, *George Bryan*, 48; Israel Pemberton to David Barclay, 6 Nov. 1764, Pemberton Papers, Hist. Soc. Pa.; Thomas Penn to Richard Peters, 18 Nov. 1764, Penn Papers, Hist. Soc. Pa. Also relevant is the observation of William Bingham that in the counties outside Philadelphia the petitions "do not meet with that encouragement" their sponsors expected. Bingham to John Gibson, 1 May 1764, Shippen Papers, VI (1763-68), Hist. Soc. Pa.

Philadelphia, but the information we have about the distribution of Friends throughout the population, imperfect though it is, suggests that not an appreciably greater proportion of them lived in Philadelphia than in the remainder of the province. We are on firmer ground when we say that the composition of the Quaker Party contributed to the split.

Thus far little has been said about Pennsylvania's political parties. The struggle between the Assembly and the proprietor has been treated almost as though it occurred in a political vacuum betwen abstractions called "legislature" and "executive." This, of course, is misleading, because the Pennsylvania Assembly was controlled by the Quaker Party and its objectives, local self-government and provincial self-determination, were those of the party. The bulk of its members were, of course, Quakers, but by supporting popular rights in opposition to the proprietary prerogative, which it had done since the planting of the province, the party attracted the support of a wide variety of men—Presbyterians like George Bryan and Charles Thomson, Anglicans like Daniel Roberdeau and Thomas Leech, and nonsectarians like Benjamin Franklin—whom it wisely welcomed and used. In return for being included in the fold, it was tacitly understood, they would be expected to protect the position of Quakerism in the province. But this was hardly an onerous obligation, since it merely meant defending the religious freedom which had always existed.

Being considered the champion of "democracy" and having opened its ranks to successful self-made men like Franklin, the ex-printer, and John Hughes, the ex-baker, won the Quaker Party a substantial following among the lower socio-economic sectors of the population, which gave it a far broader base than most colonial political parties. In addition to the Quaker farmers and millers who dominated politics in Bucks, Chester, and Philadelphia counties and the Quaker merchants and professional men of Philadelphia, the party, prior to 1764, enjoyed the support of a majority of the lower-middle- and middle-class artisans of Philadelphia. Conspicuous among this element was the White Oaks, an organization of ship carpenters.[16] These men adored Franklin, who had risen from the leather apron ranks to fame and fortune, and served, as the occasion arose, as both his body guard and honor guard. Franklin was, in fact, the hero of the mass of the mechanics— "the great Patriot," they called him—and, at times, it appears that their first loyalty was to him personally and to the Quaker Party only derivatively. Responding to his call, the mechanics of Philadelphia—White Oaks, butchers, and porters—swelled the ranks of the volunteers who turned out to fight the Paxton Boys in February, and they dutifully supported Franklin by signing petitions for his favorite project, royal government. "A few Ship Carpenters and some of the lowest sort of people" signed the petition, sneered John Penn in May 1764.[17] Thus, the strong urban working wing of the Quaker Party accounted for an appreciable amount of the support which the royal government petition received in Philadelphia.

Another factor which contributed to the city's support of the petition was the fear of the return of the Paxton Boys,

[16] For the White Oaks and their activities in 1764 and the years following, see James H. Hutson, "An Investigation of the Inarticulate: Philadelphia's White Oaks," 3 *WMQ*, xxviii (Jan. 1971).

[17] To Thomas Penn, 5 May 1764, Penn Papers, Hist. Soc. Pa.

which plagued its population from February to the end of May. The advocates of royal government exploited this uneasiness by declaiming on the "present Insecurity of Life and Property" and on the "imminent Danger" to the people[18] and by reminding them that the proprietary government had no militia or police force at its command. A royal government, they promised, would not permit disturbances of the public peace, for the King's governor would be backed by the King's troops. Franklin, an enemy charged, even suggested that the King might quarter a regiment of regulars in Philadelphia to protect it.[19] It is clear that the fears of Philadelphians and the promises that royal government would allay them helped win the city's support for the petition to the King. Colonial politicians, no less than present practitioners, recognized the effectiveness of the law and order issue.

A final reason Philadelphians supported the petition for royal government was that they had been swayed by the public relations campaign on its behalf. They were available for public meetings, accessible to propaganda, and susceptible to proselytism. These conditions did not prevail in the rest of the province, where there were few cities and the population was dispersed on farms. Communications were so poor that some citizens did not know that royal government was being proposed, and those who did re-

[18] *The Speech of Joseph Galloway*, 35, 36.

[19] In *Cool Thoughts* Franklin stated that a royal government and a regular army would be welcome for "the steady Protection it will afford us against Foreign Enemies, and the Security of internal Peace among ourselves." Labaree, ed., *Papers of BF*, XI, 169. The charge that he suggested the quartering of regulars in the capital is in *Pa. Journal*, supplement, 27 Sept. 1764.

ceived only a fraction of the literature (and libations) which inundated Philadelphians. Therefore, the urban-rural split can also be explained as a cleavage caused by a communications gap.

Did the 3,500 petition signatures represent success to the proponents of royal government? Had they been spontaneous, they would have meant a considerable triumph; having been intensely solicited, they represented, in the opinion of friend and foe alike, a resounding failure. Opponents hooted at their paucity. "It is enough to say," wrote one, "that, after incredible pains, in a Province containing near Three Hundred Thousand Souls, not more than 3500 could be prevailed upon to petition for a change of government." "Such a small Number of Subscribers," wrote another, "in so populous a Province, and these procured in such a manner, instead of encouraging, ought immediately to have put a total Stop to this mad Attempt of the Assembly to change our Government."[20] The supporters of the petition were very defensive about these jibes and resorted to such stunts as drastically understating the population of the province—Franklin put it at 110,000—[21] to make their figures look better. But stratagems could not disguise their failure.

One principal reason the royal government campaign failed was that it did not answer the right questions. Its voluminous propaganda was strong on sloganeering and vituperation, but weak on reasoned explanation. Its main

[20] *Preface* to *A Speech, Delivered in the House of Assembly of the Province of Pennsylvania . . . by John Dickinson . . .* (Phila., 1764), iv; *Pa. Journal,* supplement, 27 Sept. 1764.
[21] Labaree, ed., *Papers of BF,* XI, 290.

purpose was to denigrate Thomas Penn by stressing his meanspiritedness and his "oppressions,"[22] by reviling him as an aspiring despot whose ambition was to reduce Pennsylvanians to the "servile Condition of the . . . worst slaves of the most absolute Monarch." The strategy behind this effort was to portray Penn as such a base and abandoned individual that any change in the government of Pennsylvania would be a change for the better. Not that the supporters of royal government pictured George III as just any ordinary alternative. The young king they affected to idolize as being "as just, benevolent, and amiable a Prince, as Heaven ever granted in his Mercy to bless a People." With him at the helm, they expected that "the direct and immediate Rays of Majesty [would] benignly and mildly shine on all around." Royal liberty would supplant proprietary slavery, as Galloway promised in his State House speech, and goodness and mercy would pour forth as the people of Pennsylvania's portion. Far more people within the range of this rhetoric signed royal government petitions than those beyond its reach. But even in Philadelphia, where it was most effective, approximately two out of three citizens were not converted to royal government and did not sign petitions requesting it. These people would not settle for slogans and panegyrics. They wanted specific answers to specific questions.

Although most of them were disenchanted with proprietary government and distressed with Thomas Penn's efforts to run the province from his Spring Garden study,

---

[22] *The Speech of Joseph Galloway,* 7, 8, 11, 40; the remainder of the quotations in this paragraph are in the order of their appearance, from *ibid.*, 19, 7-8, and from Labaree, ed., *Papers of BF,* XI, 301.

they wondered how royal government could redress the grievance of excessive external control, especially when it was being sold to them as an instrument to suppress the province's internal disorders. Their doubts were not allayed by reports that the government of George III intended to lay imposts, levy stamp duties, and deprive Pennsylvania of its paper currency. And the situation in the Delaware Bay, where British men-of-war, now at the service of customs officials, searched every ship afloat, was hardly reassuring. Nor was it clear how royal government would safeguard the province's singular political privileges—the right of its Assembly to sit upon its own adjournment, for example. And many feared for the freedom of religion (which the proprietary charter guaranteed) in the face of rumors that the King intended to install a bishop in the American colonies and establish the Church of England, tithes, spiritual courts, and all.[23] These problems the literature and oratory of the royal government campaign did not confront; tactically, they could not.

The architect of the royal government campaign, Benjamin Franklin, pinned his hopes for procuring a new regime and retaining Pennsylvania's privileges under it on the influence of British politicians whom he had met and cultivated during his first mission to England. Although Franklin had made little impression on the leading figures of the Pitt-Newcastle ministry, he had better luck with the men who succeeded them in the fall of 1761, and through-

---

[23] Wrote the anti-royal pamphleteer, the "Plain Dealer," in the spring of 1764: "It is very probable that we shall soon have stamp-offices, customs, excises, and duties enough to pay, we don't want to pay tythes into the bargain." *Paxton Papers*, 350.

out the period he enjoyed the friendship of numerous sub-ministers. Certain of these men had assured him of their assistance in establishing an acceptable royal government, and he expected—naively, as it turned out—that, if applied to, they would keep their word. Like most political influence, theirs would be exerted privately, and Franklin perceived that the surest way to forfeit it would be to announce to the Pennsylvania public who they were and what he expected them to do for the province. These sensitive politicians would resent such public predictions of their behavior[24] and would doubtless repudiate their previous promises. Therefore, Franklin would not publicly divulge his reasons for believing that Pennsylvania would be safe under a royal government. But in the privacy of the Assembly chambers, where he could speak freely of his connections and conversations in England, as he did during the 10-24 March fortnight, when the campaign for royal government was being planned, he dispelled virtually every doubt about its desirability.

Because Franklin's communications about his dealings with British politicians were confidential, it is impossible to discover precisely what he said. There are clues in his papers, in the comments of his friends, and in the accusations of his enemies, who seem to have obtained their information from John Dickinson or one of the other two or three anti-royal government Assemblymen. According to one foe, Franklin told the Assemblymen that "persons of weight at home" had "encouraged" him to try to change

[24] See, e.g., Richard Jackson's letter to Franklin of 11 Aug. 1764, in Labaree, ed., *Papers of BF*, XI, 314.

the government.[25] Another enemy claimed that he had specifically identified his supporters as the whole Grenville ministry, but a third declared that he had said he was "not at Liberty to mention" the "great Men" who had counselled him. On one point all accounts agreed, however: Franklin said that his talks in England made him "sure" that Pennsylvania could obtain royal government, that the province need only ask and it would be given.[26] So positive was he about this, so convincingly did he communicate his certitude, that a sober Quaker confidant bet a friend £100 that the King would be governing the province in a short time.[27]

Franklin professed to be equally "sure" that royal government would cost Pennsylvania nothing—neither money nor modification of its singular rights and privileges. In promising something for nothing, pleasure without pain, the Doctor resembled a quack peddling nostrums, but his colleagues in the Assembly were receptive to his pitch. His claim that Pennsylvania could obtain royal government free of charge was based on the 1712 contract between William Penn and the government of Queen Anne in which Penn agreed to sell the proprietorship to the crown for £12,000. Franklin, we will recall, had discovered the exist-

[25] William Allen to Thomas Penn, 11 March 1765, Penn Papers, Hist. Soc. Pa. The two following quotations are from the broadside *To the Freeholders and Electors of the Province of Pennsylvania* [28 Sept. 1765], APS, and *Pa. Journal*, supplement, 27 Sept. 1764.

[26] On Franklin's confidence, see William Allen to Thomas Penn, 13 Dec. 1764 and 11 March 1765, Penn Papers, Hist. Soc. Pa. John Dickinson, *Reply to Galloway's Speech*, in Paul L. Ford, ed., *The Writings of John Dickinson*, II (Phila., 1895), 89.

[27] See the broadside cited in note 25.

ence of this contract at the beginning of his mission to England and made it an important element in his intrigue with Springett Penn. Just as he had assumed that the contract was binding upon Springett, so he averred that it was binding upon Thomas and Richard Penn. "The Crown will be under no Difficulty in compleating the old Contract made with their Father," he assured the province in his pamphlet *Cool Thoughts*.[28] Franklin conceded that the Penns might equitably demand more for the province in 1764 (a proprietary pamphleteer asserted that it was worth at least £40,000)[29] than its market price in 1712. But he was prepared for this contingency, too. The crown, he declared, was entitled to one-half of the quit rents in the three lower counties on the Delaware, which the Penns were obliged to collect and pay. But they had never done so, he charged, and as early as 1722 owed the crown £18,000 on this account.[30] Therefore, whatever the fair purchase price of the province was in 1764, Franklin affirmed that the crown could afford it simply by cancelling the debts the Penns owed it. Specious though his arguments were, the Assembly accepted them at full value, for in its resolves of 24 March it spoke of petitioning the King to assume the government of Pennsylvania "by compleating the Agreement heretofore made with the first Proprietor for the Sale of the Government to the Crown."[31]

[28] Labaree, ed., *Papers of BF*, XI, 172; Franklin, *Preface* to Galloway's *Speech*, *ibid.*, 293-94.

[29] [Hugh Williamson], "Plain Dealer," No. III, *Paxton Papers*, 381.

[30] *Cool Thoughts*, in Labaree, ed., *Papers of BF*, XI, 172; Franklin to Jackson, 29 March 1764, *ibid.*, 148.

[31] *Ibid.*, 132-33.

Franklin's confidence that Pennsylvania could retain its rights and privileges under a royal government rested on the legal opinion he received from Pennsylvania's agent, Richard Jackson, on 24 April 1758. We will recall that at Franklin's request Robert Charles drew up a case in which he enumerated the province's privileges, explained that they had been conferred by the royal charter of 1681 and William Penn's charter of 1701, and emphasized that for additional security the Pennsylvania Assembly in 1705 had embodied them in laws which had received the royal confirmation. What, he asked Jackson, would their fate be under a royal government? The lawyer's answer was very comforting: "the Crown cannot introduce or establish any other Mode of Government within the Province than that now in Use there . . . except by an Act of the Legislature of Great Britain."[32] In other words, he appeared to be saying that in a change of government Pennsylvania had nothing to fear from the malevolence or machinations of ministers, for their instruments of governance—circular letters, instructions, and orders-in-council—were constitutionally inferior to colonial statutes confirmed by the crown; only Parliament, by its sovereign act, could deprive the province of its rights. And who, his implied question seemed to ask, could believe that that palladium of British freedom would oppress its fellow subjects?

In 1764 Franklin used Jackson's opinion as a talisman to ward off the Assembly's apprehensions about a change of government. "We confide in the Opinion you once gave on the Case stated," he wrote Jackson on 31 March 1764,

[32] For Franklin's case and Jackson's opinion, see *ibid.*, VIII, 6-27.

"that our Priveleges could not, on such a Change, be taken from us, but by Act of Parliament."[33] The agent's opinion inspired confidence because of his formidable reputation for learning—Samuel Johnson pronounced him "Omniscient," Franklin said that in England he was "esteem'd the best acquainted with our American Affairs, and Constitutions, as well as with Government Law in general"[34]— and, more importantly, because of his position in the government. When the Grenville ministry came to office in April 1763, Jackson was appointed the prime minister's secretary. Pennsylvanians assumed that this position gave him vast power and influence—local newspapers wrote as though he had as much power as Grenville himself—and, therefore, the Assemblymen concluded that, if so important a man said their privileges would be safe in a change of government, they would be.

Not everyone was so sanguine, however. It was recognized, for example, that there was a flaw in Jackson's opinion, caused by an error in Charles's statement of the case on which it was based. The agent had averred that the Pennsylvania statutes of 1705, which guaranteed the province's privileges, had received the royal confirmation. They had not. They had been considered by the Queen-in-Council, which declined to approve them and resorted to the device of letting them become law by lapse of time in ac-

[33] *Ibid.*, XI, 151. See also the Pennsylvania Assembly committee report, 21 Sept. 1764, in 8 *Pa. Arch.*, VII, 5640; James Pemberton to Samuel Fothergill, 13 June 1764, Pemberton Papers, Hist. Soc. Pa.; *The Speech of Joseph Galloway*, 23; Dickinson, *Reply to Galloway's Speech*, 138.

[34] See *Dictionary of National Biography* (DNB), *s.v.* Jackson; Labaree, ed., *Papers of BF*, VIII, 88.

cordance with the proprietary charter. Could laws so sanctioned safeguard the province's liberties? Some doubted that they could. And then there was the problem of Parliament's response to a change of government. There was no ironclad guarantee in Jackson's opinion that Parliament would refrain from intruding if a change were being contrived. Moreover, the acts and regulations it was supposed to be preparing for the colonies undermined belief in its benevolence and shook the customary assumption that it was solicitous of colonial liberties. Quakers, in fact, were reported to be "exceedingly afraid" that it would intervene to strip them of their singular privileges.[35] Franklin tried to quiet these fears by discounting the possibility of parliamentary intervention. But an opponent charged that he was "willing to say any thing, that may be like to persuade us that we may get a change of Government without coming through the hands of Parliament, tho' he knows very well that the thing is impracticable, for he has made enquiry and found it so, but he dishonestly conceals that story."[36] (Pennsylvanians would have been considerably more skeptical about Parliament's attitude had they seen a confidential opinion Jackson had given Franklin on 24 April 1758 which blasted the notion that the British legislature was a bastion of popular liberties; "we may rest satisfy'd," he advised, "that an Administration will probably for the future always be able to support and carry in Parliament

[35] George Bryan to ———, 13 April 1764, in Konkle, *George Bryan*, 47; on 14 Oct. 1765 William Young wrote Thomas Penn that "the quaker friends wish indeed that Franklin may succeed, but they are still in fear that if he brings a change about by the parliament they might lose many things." Penn Papers, Hist. Soc. Pa.

[36] *Paxton Papers*, 381.

whatever they wish to do so; [and] that they will almost always wish to extend the Power of the Crown and themselves both mediately and immediately."[37] Ominous words these, and ones which Franklin wisely kept to himself.)

What, then, was Jackson's opinion really worth? The agent himself answered this question in the summer of 1764. In a letter of 1 June Franklin asked him for specific advice on the feasibility of a change of government. In his reply Jackson warned against attempting it. He feared that an application for a change would "meet with some mortifying circumstances of Reception," that Pennsylvania might lose some of its privileges, and that consequently it would be better to remain under a proprietary government.[38] By his own admission, then, his opinion was worth very little.

What, therefore, were Franklin's motives in parading it before the Pennsylvania Assembly as a surety for the province's privileges? Was he, as his opponents charged, using it to dupe his colleagues, to make them the unwitting servants of his and his supporters' unholy ambition to overthrow proprietary government and monopolize public office under a new royal government (Franklin was accused of coveting the governor's chair, Galloway the chief justice's seat, other cronies other offices)?[39] Some men did, to be sure, climb aboard the royal government bandwagon wholly to gain power and preference under the new

[37] Labaree, ed., *Papers of BF*, VIII, 26.

[38] *Ibid.*, 313, 464.

[39] *Pa. Journal*, supplement, 27 Sept. 1764; William Goddard, *The Partnership: or the History of the Rise and Progress of the Pennsylvania Chronicle* (Phila., 1770), 62-63; George Bryan to ————, 26 April 1764, in Konkle, *George Bryan*, 50.

dispensation.[40] How much personal ambition motivated Franklin and Galloway is not clear, although one would assume that they were not blind to the possibility of serving themselves while serving what they took to be the public's interest in a change of government. Surely, they must have talked about the disposition of offices under a new regime, for their design of delivering the province from Thomas Penn's "tyranny" would have been defeated by the appointment of despotic royal officials. But this does not mean that the royal government movement was solely an office-seeking scheme and that Franklin was disingenuously using Jackson's opinion to promote it.

Nor was he artfully using it to avenge himself upon Thomas Penn for his insulting actions during his first mission. Although time had not assuaged his anger at Penn—in December 1763 he confessed to "cordially dislike and despise" him[41]—he did not, after his return to Pennsylvania in 1762, play the fanatic and preach a constant crusade against him, nor did he pluck at every pretext to plague him. When John Penn arrived as the province's chief executive in December 1763, Franklin "consider'd Government as Government, paid him all Respect, [and] gave him on all Occasions my best Advice." But when the young man's policies proved to be intolerable, Franklin joined the effort to replace the proprietorship with a little extra zest, for he perceived in it the opportunity to repay Thomas Penn for his earlier affronts. Nevertheless, in leading the movement for royal government Franklin was

[40] Nicholas Waln and Isaac Hunt, for example. See Labaree, ed., *Papers of BF*, XII, 311, and XIII, 281.

[41] *Ibid.*, X, 401; the quotation in the following sentence is from *ibid.*, XI, 103.

motivated as much by a concern for the public's interest, by a desire to relieve it of what he regarded as tyrannical government, as by a desire to gratify his personal resentments. In producing Richard Jackson's opinion in March 1764, therefore, he was acting with honorable intentions; months passed before Jackson's letters, virtually repudiating it, arrived. There were, to be sure, loose ends and loopholes in the opinion and in Franklin's reasoning about the cost of royal government, but these did not bother him because he assumed that the difficulties they presented would be resolved in Pennsylvania's favor by his principal British patron, the Earl of Bute.

The precise nature of Franklin's relationship with Bute is one of the major mysteries of his career. Before leaving for England in 1757 his opponents warned Thomas Penn that he would be a "Dangerous Enemy" because of "His reputation gained by his Electrical Discoveries which will introduce him into all sorts of Company."[42] Although Penn scoffed at the idea, science almost certainly brought Franklin and Bute together. The Earl was a "great Philosopher," as a Philadelphia newspaper put it.[43] He was an accomplished botanist, a patron of all branches of natural philosophy, and the owner of one of eighteenth-century Europe's largest and best collections of scientific instruments.[44] His collection of "electrical machines" was especially fine, and it can hardly be doubted that Franklin, who after the Privy Council hearings in 1760 spent much of his time

[42] *Ibid.*, VII, 110-11.

[43] *Pa. Journal*, supplement, 18 Sept. 1766.

[44] G. L'E. Turner, "The Auction Sale of the Earl of Bute's Instruments," *Annals of Science*, XXIII (Sept. 1967), 213-42.

conducting electrical experiments to gratify the curiosity of the British upper classes, favored Bute with visits and performances. Dr. John Pringle, the Earl's physician and Franklin's friend, probably made the initial introductions.[45] These experimental sessions evidently blossomed into personal friendship. Franklin, at any rate, thought that they had, for in 1764, when an opponent charged that he had no influence at the British court, he "forgot his usual reserve, and swore by his Maker, that it was false, that he had an interest with Lord Bute." Another, later account had Franklin claiming that he was "intimate" with his Lordship.[46]

When he returned to Pennsylvania, he advertised his relationship with Bute. No sooner had he debarked at Chester on 1 November 1762 than it was reported that he "speaks much of Lord Bute."[47] To make his point, he also hung the Earl's picture in the parlor of his new house. To the Assemblymen, wrestling with the proposal to seek royal government, he represented his connection with Bute, the King's favorite and the most powerful politician in the realm, as a gilt-edged guarantee that all would be well in a change. How did they know that he was telling the truth? His son William was the proof. In September 1762, to the "universal astonishment" of the citizens of Pennsylvania and New Jersey, young Franklin was com-

---

[45] For Pringle's role as intermediary between Franklin and Bute, see Labaree, ed., *Papers of BF*, x, 147n; *Pa. Journal*, supplement, 18 Sept. 1766.

[46] *Ibid.*; John Adams, "Autobiography," entry for 9 July 1778, in Lyman H. Butterfield, ed., *Diary and Autobiography of John Adams* (Cambridge, 1961), IV, 150.

[47] Richard Peters, "Diary," entry for 1 Nov. 1762, Hist. Soc. Pa.

missioned governor of the latter colony. "Every body here concludes that this must have been brought about by some strong Interest his Father must have obtained in England," Pennsylvania Governor James Hamilton wrote Thomas Penn on 21 November 1762. Lord Bute had arranged the appointment, Penn answered on 11 March 1763.[48] Franklin was not backward about broadcasting this fact, and the Assemblymen consequently were persuaded that, if his influence with Bute was strong enough to transform his son, the illegitimate offspring of a Philadelphia floozy, into a colonial governor, it was strong enough to procure a change of government and protect the province's privileges in the process.

That Bute had resigned as first lord of the Treasury on 8 April 1763 and held no public office thereafter did not upset these calculations, because most residents of the British Empire believed that he continued to run the government through his protégé, George Grenville, whom he had installed as his successor at the Treasury Board. Indeed, for several years after 1763 people on both sides of the Atlantic believed that public affairs in Britain were controlled by a "conspiratorial cabal"[49] headed by Bute. In 1767 the Marquis of Rockingham was convinced that Bute's "secret influence" had destroyed his administration during the preceding year, and three years later William Pitt railed against the Earl's "pernicious counsels" to which he attributed "all the present unhappiness and disturbances

[48] Hamilton to Penn, 21 Nov. 1762; Penn to Hamilton, 11 March 1763; both in the Penn Papers, Hist. Soc. Pa.

[49] This and the following quotations are from Bernard Bailyn, *The Ideological Origins of the American Revolution* (Cambridge, 1967), 144-48.

in the nation." Pennsylvanians readily adopted the notion of Bute as a "well nigh indestructible machinator," as Britain's political "Primum Mobile," to use James Logan, Jr.'s expression.[50] Their belief in his paramount, though private, influence was a principal prop of the royal government movement, for as long as they imagined that he could change their government by a wave of his wand, so long would the movement retain its vitality. And their faith in the Earl and in Franklin's power over him did not fade easily.

The persuasiveness of Franklin's account of his influence with Bute, Jackson, and other British politicians was demonstrated by an Assembly vote of 23 May on whether to send its own petition to the King requesting royal government: 27 out of 30, or ninety percent of the members present, voted affirmatively.[51] But if this figure is contrasted with the 3,500, or somewhat less than five percent of the adult males, who signed the royal government petitions, Franklin's misunderstanding of the popular temper becomes apparent. He evidently believed that among the people there was a vast reservoir of goodwill for royal government which could be tapped merely by denouncing Penn and suggesting that the province put itself under the King. He seems to have supposed that the citizenry did not need to be convinced of the advantages of royal government and that it was unnecessary (had it even been possible) to give them the careful, chapter-and-verse explanation of its acceptability which he gave his fellow Assemblymen.

---

[50] James Logan, Jr., to John Smith, 19 Feb. 1765, Smith MSS, Hist. Soc. Pa.

[51] Labaree, ed., *Papers of BF*, XI, 193.

But this was precisely what the people wanted and precisely what would have been necessary to enlist their support. The truth, which Franklin did not discern, was that they feared royal government and needed to have their apprehensions of losing their civil and religious privileges under it thoroughly allayed before they would support it.

The Proprietary Party read the popular pulse much better than Franklin and his colleagues. Its members sensed the people's fears and played upon them. Until June 1764, however, they did very little, principally because they were accustomed to doing very little. So rarely, in fact, did the Proprietary Party engage in concerted political activity that it hardly deserves to be called a political party. One of its problems was a lack of goals. Unlike its Quaker counterpart, it was not the guarantor of a religious denomination. Thomas Penn wore his religion lightly—he drifted from a nominal Quakerism to the Church of England out of political expediency—and did not, therefore, transmit to his followers in Pennsylvania any measure of sectarian fervor. Consequently, no sense of stewardship impelled them to intervene in public affairs to protect their religious persuasion, as it did their Quaker adversaries.

The Proprietary Party lacked political goals, too. As we have seen, Thomas Penn was guided by a clear design, the creation of "balanced government" in the province by means of the establishment of proprietary control over the Assembly's expenditure of the public monies. As we have also seen, Penn's partisans in the province refused to a man to support this scheme. Neither did they support his subsequent political initiatives, especially his various attempts to exempt his estate from taxes. And they failed to develop a program of their own, the closest approximation being occasional suggestions that the council be raised to the status of a legislative upper house, a proposal which they never pushed in a public forum.[52]

The absence of a religious cause or a political blueprint or vision which could generate enthusiasm and command broad assent caused the Proprietary Party to be crippled by apathy and a lack of cohesion. The council, the seat of the Penns' most important and, presumably, most loyal supporters, illustrates how triumphant indifference was in the proprietary ranks. As a general rule, no more than four councillors attended meetings, and for considerable stretches during various administrations fewer members appeared. Dissension among proprietary leaders was constant at the highest and lowest levels, the most spectacular squabble occurring in 1768, when Richard Penn, with the support of several councillors, broke with his brother John and sailed to England to try to supplant him, a move which resulted in the brothers refusing to speak to each other in the 1770s.[53]

Without cause or cohesion the Proprietary Party could muster little popular support. Its membership consisted principally of proprietary officeholders, who were recruited from the friends and relatives of the Penns, from county magnates like Colonel John Armstrong who could return, pocket borough style, a few well-disposed men to the Assembly, and from the parishioners of William Smith and

---

[52] *Ibid.*, XI, 301.

[53] Thomas Wharton to Benjamin Franklin, 29 March 1768, Franklin Papers, Yale University Library. Thomas Balch, *Letters and Papers Relating Chiefly to the Provincial History of Pennsylvania* (Phila., 1855), 232.

his allies in the Anglican priesthood. That this group was hardly an indomitable host is attested by William Allen's inability to garner more than three votes in one Assembly election.[54]

Acute though its organizational problems were, they are not the reason one hesitates to call the Proprietary Party a political party or even a political faction, as that term is generally understood. The *raison d'être* of a party or a faction is to gain power through the electoral process and to perpetuate its control by continual victories at the polls. The Proprietary Party was not committed, however, to winning elections; indeed, it was not even committed to contesting them. In September 1753 a committee of the Pennsylvania Assembly observed that "there has not been for some Years, nor was there expected to be, nor has there since been, any Contest at Elections between the Proprietary and popular Interests."[55] In fact, the Proprietary Party did not seriously challenge the Quaker Party for an interval of twelve years, from 1742 to 1754.[56] Nothing reveals its true nature better than the reasons which prompted it to enter the political arena in those two years. In 1742 Philadelphia's merchant commerce, a substantial portion of which was owned by proprietary supporters, was threatened by French and Spanish privateers hovering in the mouth of the Delaware River; in 1754 the French and Indians had invaded western Pennsylvania and were

---

[54] Norman S. Cohen, "The Philadelphia Election Riot of 1742," *Pa. Mag. Hist. and Biog.*, XCII (July, 1968), 318.

[55] Pennsylvania Assembly committee report, 11 Sept. 1753, in Labaree, ed., *Papers of BF*, V, 47; Cohen, "Election Riot of 1742," 318.

[56] For this election, see Isaac Norris to Robert Charles, 7 Oct. 1754, Norris Letters, 1719-56, Hist. Soc. Pa.

threatening to carry the war deep into the settled areas of the province, perhaps even to Philadelphia itself. Constrained by the imperatives of pacifism, the Quaker Party was unable to provide what the proprietary people regarded as sufficient protection for their persons and property. Therefore, they opposed it at the polls in an effort to elect Assemblymen who favored military preparedness. Their failure—so little support did they obtain that in 1742 William Allen was obliged to recruit sailors from the vessels in the port of Philadelphia to assist him,[57] while in 1754 their candidates were trounced and in 1756 (another war year) Allen was obliged to enter the Assembly through the back door of Cumberland County on Colonel Armstrong's interest[58]—demonstrated the ineffectuality of a group whose occasional political outings were manifestly motivated by a desire to protect their material interests. When these were not threatened, as they were not between 1742 and 1754, the Proprietary Party acted as a centerfold advertisement for consensus historians, acquiescing with great good humor in the Quaker Party's control of the political process. Describing the party's characteristic posture, William Allen wrote Thomas Penn on 8 October 1767: "our elections are now over, and have been carried without any heats. Our friends having determined to sit still to convince the better sort of Quakers we are not grasping at power, but were willing to let them order matters to their liking."[59]

[57] Cohen, "Election Riot of 1742."

[58] Richard Peters to Thomas Penn, 2 Oct. 1756, Peters Papers, Hist. Soc. Pa.

[59] Penn Papers, Hist. Soc. Pa.

The adoption by the House on 24 March 1764 of the resolves launching the royal government campaign guaranteed that 1764 would be one of those infrequent years in which the Proprietary Party roused itself from what a caustic young critic called its "old passive humor of submitting the conduct of public affairs" to its Quaker "State Pilots,"[60] for the effort to overturn the proprietary government was a portentous challenge to the self-interest of the party's members, threatening, as it did, to deprive them of their government positions and perquisites. Never, however, had the Proprietary Party been more ill-prepared for a political campaign. In the first place, none of the stalwarts who had guided its affairs during the past decades were available for action. Richard Peters, for years the provincial secretary, had withdrawn from public life and was on the verge of sailing for England to be treated for a debilitating case of kidney stones. James Hamilton had retired to his country estate, also in ill health. William Smith was in England raising money for the College of Philadelphia. And William Allen was also in the mother country, vacationing. The absence of these men, coupled with the usual apathy of the proprietary supporters, virtually deprived the party of activists. Meetings of the council reflected this. Besides John Penn, the only men who attended were his brother Richard, his uncle Lynford Lardner, and his "Prime Minister," Benjamin Chew. Twice during the spring of 1764 no one at all showed up for meetings.[61] The governor's indolence made the situa-

[60] Samuel Purviance, Jr., to James Burd, 20 Sept. 1765, in Balch, *Provincial History of Pennsylvania*, 208.

[61] John Penn to Thomas Penn, 16 June and 22 Nov. 1764, Penn Papers, Hist. Soc. Pa. For the persistence of this problem, see also

tion worse. And even had he been a political dynamo, he would have been handicapped by his inexperience, by his unfamiliarity with Pennsylvania's political terrain, by his ignorance of what levers to pull, whom to see, and what to say. Perplexing matters more was Richard Penn's distrust of Benjamin Chew.[62] The result of this host of shortcomings was that from March through May, while the royal government campaign rolled along in high gear, the corporal's guard which was the Proprietary Party took no action to oppose it, even though it promised to deprive the Penns of their patrimony and to put their appointees out of business. Like sheep in an abattoir, the proprietary partisans patiently awaited the executioner's knife.

The first group to oppose royal government was the province's Presbyterians, who took a stand against it within a week of the adoption of the resolves of 24 March. On 30 March the Presbyterian leaders in Philadelphia, the Reverends Gilbert Tennent, Francis Alison, and John Ewing, wrote a joint letter to their fellow ministers—a hostile Quaker writer described it as a "circular Apostolical Letter wrote by the Presbyterian Pope in Philadelphia, and his two Cardinals, to all the inferior Brethren and their Flocks throughout the Province"[63]—suggesting that they oppose the royal government movement and use their influence to prevent the signing of petitions supporting it. The Presbyterians were not enamored of proprietary government. On the contrary, they were prejudiced against it

---

Joseph Shippen, Jr., to Thomas Penn, 25 Sept. 1765, and John Penn to Thomas Penn, 21 March 1766, Penn Papers, Hist. Soc. Pa.

[62] Richard Penn to Thomas Penn, 15 June 1764, Penn Papers, Hist. Soc. Pa.

[63] *Paxton Papers*, 311-12.

by the large numbers of frontiersmen in their denomination, who resented what they considered the Penns' exorbitant quit rents and land prices (especially compared to those in the colonies immediately to the south) and who were furious about the chicanery and extortion in the proprietary Land Office, where ordinary people could not "get anything done in the Common Way without Extraordinary Fees . . . under the specious false name of *Dispatch Money*."[64]

If the Presbyterians disliked proprietary government, why did they oppose royal government? Was it simply because the Quakers supported it? Yes, but there was more to their opposition than that. The Presbyterians believed that the royal government movement had been conceived by Franklin and his Quaker Party colleagues, not to deliver the province from the oppressions of proprietary government, as they piously proclaimed, but to perpetuate oppressions of their own. What did they mean? In the wake of the march of the Paxton Boys the citizens of western Pennsylvania, substantially Presbyterian, began deluging the Assembly with petitions—some of them fifteen yards long[65]—praying for the redress of the chief grievance enunciated by the Paxtoneers, the underrepresentation of the west in the House. How did the Assembly respond to their requests? Instead of redressing them, it launched the movement for royal government. Was not its motive "to divide and divert the Attention of the injur'd Frontier

[64] Labaree, ed., *Papers of BF*, XI, 140; "S. B." to "T. P.," 7 Jan. 1765, Penn Papers (1730-66 and undated file), Hist. Soc. Pa.

[65] William Logan to John Smith, 25 March 1764, Smith MSS, Hist. Soc. Pa.; see also George Bryan to ———, 13 April 1764, in Konkle, *George Bryan*, 46-47.

Inhabitants from prosecuting their Petitions," as the writers of the 30 March circular letter charged? Did it not intend to "set the province in a ferment about another affair, lest the groans of the injur'd should be heard," to "lead us another dance" now that "the voice of misery and distress is no longer to be stifled," as the indignant "Plain Dealer" put it?[66] The Presbyterians believed, in short, that the royal government campaign was a diversionary tactic hit upon by the Quakers to continue the political domination of their denomination. There is evidence to suggest that they were not entirely wrong, either. James Pemberton, for example, wrote an English Friend on 11 April 1764 that royal government was an ideal way of "curbing the Insolence of Presbyterian Cabals," and two months later he wrote another English Friend that one of the reasons Pennsylvania Quakers were supporting royal government was their "fearfull apprehensions of their [the Presbyterians] getting the Legislative . . . part of Government into their hands."[67]

The notion that they were the intended victims of a Quaker plot supplied a vindictive vigor to the Presbyterian opposition to royal government. Laymen were as active as clerics: a Philadelphia merchant, Samuel Purviance, Jr., displayed a "peculiar Zeal" in the cause, visiting congregations throughout the province, weaving them into a network of committees of correspondence, and communicating with them by express, when the occasion demanded.[68] By

[66] *Paxton Papers*, 344-45, 350.

[67] James Pemberton to John Hunt, 11 April 1764, and to Samuel Fothergill, 13 June 1764, Pemberton Papers, Hist. Soc. Pa.

[68] William Allen to Thomas Penn, 8 March 1767, Penn Papers, Hist. Soc. Pa.

the end of May labors like his had united the denomination in its opposition to royal government.

Because of a split in the Quaker Party, other men had also gone into opposition by the end of May. Typical was John Dickinson, who was disgusted by the arbitrary actions of proprietary government but believed that royal government posed a far greater threat to the province's liberties. Therefore, in the midst of an Assembly debate on 24 May 1764 on the adoption of a petition for royal government, he parted ways with his colleagues by delivering a powerful speech against it. His example may have encouraged Speaker of the House Isaac Norris to declare his own opposition to a change of government. For some years Norris's resentment of Joseph Galloway, William Franklin, and their younger Quaker Party associates had been building, evidently because he feared that this "Set of Hottspurs"[69] was planning to stage a generational coup to curtail his and his elder colleagues' influence in the party.[70] "Isaac's rage is predominant against his new enemy," Galloway, wrote William Allen to Thomas Penn on 25 March 1761, "and I suppose will continue, for his hatred and ill will are known not to be fleeting."[71] And, indeed, they

[69] See Norris's memo of 30 Aug. 1760, Norris Letterbook, 1756-66, Hist. Soc. Pa.

[70] For evidence that what we would call a generation gap had developed in the Quaker Party leadership by 1764, with the younger men supporting royal government and the older opposing it, see William Allen to David Barclay, 25 Sept. 1764, in Lewis B. Walker, ed., *The Burd Papers, Extracts from Chief Justice William Allen's Letter Book* ([Pottsville, Pa.], 1897), 56-57; [William Smith], "Answer to the Remarks," in Labaree, ed., *Papers of BF*, XI, 515; William Allen to Thomas Penn, 12 Nov. 1766, Penn Papers, Hist. Soc. Pa.

[71] Allen to Thomas Penn, 25 March 1761, Penn Papers, Hist. Soc. Pa.

were not, although Norris's opposition to royal government stemmed at least as much from genuine reservations about the wisdom of the policy as from animosity toward Galloway and its other supporters. On 25 May 1764 he asked for and received permission to speak against a change of government on the floor of the House and dramatized his opposition the following day by resigning his speakership.

Of the two defections, Dickinson's was the more important. Norris was better known and he hurt the pro-royal government Quaker Party candidates in the fall elections by turning a number of voters against them, but both his political influence and his health were slipping away, and he died in 1766. The future belonged to the young, vigorous Dickinson, who over the next decade exercised profound influence on Pennsylvania's political life. Not a little of it stemmed from his speech of 24 May which, when printed and circulated throughout the province, became the bible of the anti-royal government cause. It was "a sensible, manly impartial performance," Thomas Penn wrote his nephew, and it was to Dickinson "we are chiefly obliged for the change in sentiments in a great number of People."[72] Another result of the speech was that, in graphically showing how royal government could endanger Pennsylvania's privileges, it converted a number of the province's younger and more aggressive politicians to Dickinson's side and induced them to desert the Quaker Party. Of particular importance were George Bryan and Charles Thomson, who

[72] Thomas Penn to Richard Penn, 7 Dec. 1764, Penn Papers, Hist. Soc. Pa.

as Presbyterians were already disenchanted with the Quakers and were happy to have a respectable reason to part company with them. Finally, Dickinson's speech made an enemy of Joseph Galloway with whom he had been linked, as late as 5 May, as a "Tribune of the People."[73] It was not Galloway's spirited rebuttal to the speech on 24 May which drove a wedge between the two men; they disagreed respectfully and over a matter of principle, whether royal government would be more or less repressive than proprietary government. Rather, it was versions of the speeches published later in the summer, dishonorably revised (it was alleged) and with vitriolic partisan prefaces, which poisoned their relations. Savage exchanges in the press followed, so enraging the men that a challenge to a duel was issued (apparently by Dickinson).[74] As if this were not unbecoming enough for two Quaker-bred gentlemen, they engaged in a fistfight as they were leaving an Assembly session in the fall.[75] These conflicts produced a mortal enmity between the two men which decisively influenced Pennsylvania politics up through 1775. It also guaranteed that Dickinson would never again be affiliated with a Galloway-led Quaker Party.

What existed, then, at the end of May 1764 were the components of a formidable countermovement to the royal government campaign. Numbers were present in the province's Presbyterians, talent in the persons of Dickinson,

[73] William Peters to Thomas Penn, 5 May 1764, Penn Papers, Hist. Soc. Pa.

[74] Paul L. Ford, ed., *The Writings of John Dickinson*, II (Phila., 1895), 71.

[75] David Hall to William Strahan, 12 June 1767, Hall Letterbooks, APS.

Thomson, Bryan, and Purviance. How incredible, therefore, that the Proprietary Party politicians sat on their hands and did nothing to marshal these forces against their Quaker Party adversaries! What was needed, clearly, was an artisan who could forge these elements into a political broadsword. Fortunately for the Penns, a smith arrived early in June, the Reverend William Smith, back from his fund-raising drive in England.

Smith was typical of the Proprietary Party supporters in that his political activities were motivated by a desire to protect his personal interests. Thomas Penn annually paid him a retainer of £50 for his services as provost of the College of Philadelphia,[76] and before sailing from England in April 1764 his "pension," as his enemies called it, was sweetened by Penn's giving him a share of the receipts of the Chester County prothonotary's office.[77] Obviously, then, self-interest obliged Smith to help preserve the proprietary government. He was also a characteristic proprietary politician in being continually at odds with his colleagues. Few people in the province liked him, principally because of his soaring ambition. This made him an object of suspicion and disgust and caused even close associates like James Hamilton and Benjamin Chew to entertain "unfavourable Impressions" of him.[78] His relations with William Allen were far from idyllic, too,[79] but their troubles were primarily a reflection of the tension between the prov-

[76] Labaree, ed., *Papers of BF*, VIII, 45-46.
[77] Thomas Penn to Smith, 17 May 1764, and 15 Aug. 1765, William Smith Papers, Hist. Soc. Pa. John Penn to Thomas Penn, 12 Sept. 1766, Penn Papers, Hist. Soc. Pa.
[78] Richard Peters to Smith, 28 May 1763, in *Pa. Mag. Hist. and Biog.*, X (1886), 351.
[79] *Ibid.*

ince's Anglicans and Presbyterians, of whom Allen was perhaps the most influential lay leader.

As a legacy of their common opposition to the Great Awakening, the Anglicans and the Old Side Presbyterians cooperated after a fashion through the 1750s. But behind a guise of goodwill each side measured the other apprehensively, for both recognized that they were the principal rivals for religious hegemony in the province. The Anglicans were reported in 1755 to "dread" the expanding Presbyterians of both the Old and New Side;[80] for their part, Presbyterians feared that through the countenance of the British government the Anglicans would be allowed to dominate them. Smith exacerbated the differences between the two denominations to the point of virtual open warfare by his actions during his English fund-raising drive. Preceding him to the mother country was the Reverend Charles Beatty, a minister dispatched in 1760 by Pennsylvania's Presbyterians to raise money for their Fund for the Aid of Ministers' Widows and Orphans. Since Beatty was a competitor for donations, Smith tried to undercut him by intimating that he was an emissary, not of an eleemosynary foundation, but of Presbyterian imperialism, which was seeking a bankroll to dominate the middle colonies. Smith's actions angered Allen and infuriated Francis Alison, who regarded the Ministers' Fund as his brainchild. His differences with the latter were aggravated by trouble in the College of Philadelphia, where both taught. By the early 1760s the College had become a cockpit of Anglican-

[80] Isaac Norris to Robert Charles, 29 Aug. 1755, Norris Letters, 1719-56, Hist. Soc. Pa.

Presbyterian infighting in which the Reverend John Ewing, Alison's ally, was also engaged.[81] Thus, when Smith arrived in the province in June 1764 and tried to coordinate the opposition to royal government, the Presbyterian leaders did not welcome him with open arms. Alison, in fact, was so wary of his embrace that he concluded that, instead of fighting each other, the Presbyterians and Quakers should compose their quarrel and "unite most heartily in defense of liberty" against the Church of England.[82] Being carried along, however, by the resentment of the masses of their denomination, the Presbyterian religious leaders were in no position to call off the contest with the Quakers, even though Alison feared "the mice and Frogs may fight, till the Kite devours both." But for the time being the kite had to be accommodated in uneasy cooperation.

Smith also encountered difficulties in securing Dickinson's cooperation with the Proprietary Party. With the lawyer personally he had little trouble. Dickinson welcomed his initiative in publishing and circulating his speech, and although he claimed not to have been consulted about the vitriolic preface which the parson wrote for it, he does not seem to have objected strenuously to its tone.[83] But

[81] For the Anglican-Presbyterian rivalry and the exacerbation caused by the Beatty mission and the controversies in the College of Philadelphia, see Leonard J. Trinterud, *The Forming of an American Tradition: A Re-examination of Colonial Presbyterianism* (Phila., 1949), 213-15.

[82] This and the following quotation are from Alison to Ezra Stiles, 15 April 1764, in Franklin B. Dexter, ed., *Extracts from the Itineraries . . . of Ezra Stiles* (New Haven, 1916), 425-26.

[83] Thomas Penn to Smith, 15 Feb. 1765, William Smith Papers, Hist.

obtaining Dickinson's active cooperation with the proprietary politicians was another matter altogether, for an "invincible hatred" existed between him and "Prime Minister" Benjamin Chew,[84] which foreclosed the possibility of common action. Unlike Dickinson's feud with Galloway, which was caused by a policy disagreement, his conflict with Chew turned on the distribution of power and place in Delaware, where each man had substantial interests. The result of both quarrels was the same, however: just as the one ensured that Dickinson would never rejoin the Quaker Party so long as Galloway shared in its leadership, so the other ensured that he would never participate in the Proprietary Party so long as Chew directed it. Nevertheless, during the time the province was threatened by the royal government movement, Dickinson worked to frustrate it, sharing at least a common goal with the Proprietary Party.

Smith encountered the least resistance in enlisting the aid of the province's German church groups, the Lutherans and the Reformed. By the end of the French and Indian War these denominations, which had formerly floundered in virtual anarchy, had become fairly well organized and were ready to flex their political muscles.[85] Between their leaders and the Proprietary Party there was, moreover, a tradition of cooperation, motivated principally by a mutual distaste for the German sectarians, who supported the Quaker Party. In 1754, for example, the Reverend

---

Soc. Pa.; Labaree, ed., *Papers of BF*, XI, 268n; Ford, ed., *Writings of Dickenson*, II, 118-19.

[84] John Penn to Thomas Penn, 22 Nov. 1764; Thomas Penn to John Penn, 11 Jan. 1765; John Penn to Thomas Penn, 12 Sept. 1766; all in the Penn Papers, Hist. Soc. Pa.

[85] Dietmar Rothermund, *The Layman's Progress* (Phila., 1961), 120.

Michael Schlatter, the Reformed leader, and to a lesser degree the Reverend Henry Muhlenberg, the Lutheran leader, assisted the proprietary leaders in establishing German charity schools, whose stated aim was to Anglicize the Germans and whose tacit one was to make them members of the Proprietary Party.[86] There was also a considerable amount of denominational cooperation between the Anglicans and the German church people; Dr. Carl Wrangel, the influential Lutheran minister, even favored a merger of the two groups, and certain Reformed leaders made similar suggestions.[87] Thus, the Germans seemed to offer considerable promise of support in the struggle against royal government.

Not only prior collaboration but also the nature of their membership made the German church groups potential allies. The bulk of the Lutherans and Reformed lived in the west, were subject to the horrors of Indian warfare (remember John Hambright and the irate German frontiersmen he led against the Assembly in 1755), and shared the attitude of their Presbyterian neighbors toward the royal government campaign, believing that it was a Quaker contrivance to cheat the west out of its proper share in the governance of the province. A German frontiersman, in fact, approached Muhlenberg on 29 March 1764 and denounced the royal government campaign in precisely these terms. Then he asked him to issue "a circular letter to our United Preachers," as the Presbyterian triumvirate was preparing to do the next day, attacking royal government

[86] *Ibid.*, 91-93; see also Whitfield J. Bell, Jr., "Benjamin Franklin and the German Charity Schools," *Studies on Benjamin Franklin*, 381-87, in *Proceedings of the American Philosophical Society* (1955).

[87] Rothermund, *The Layman's Progress*, 108, 126.

and urging the Germans to oppose it. Muhlenberg declined "to interfere in such critical, political affairs" and two days later pleaded with his parishioners to avoid them.[88] But Smith's arrival and his blandishments and cajolery converted Muhlenberg and Wrangel (who needed little cultivation) into active political partisans, who translated anti-royal government literature into German and harangued their congregations and those they visited around the province against a change of government.[89] Judging from petition signatures and voting patterns, their impact was considerable.

The arrival of William Smith in Pennsylvania in June saved the day for the proprietary cause, because he put together a confederation—the term "coalition" would be misleading, for it implies a degree of cooperation which the suspicious and antagonistic opponents of royal government could never achieve—which was more than a match for the Quaker Party. Another of Smith's contributions lay in conceiving the idea of circulating petitions opposing royal government throughout the province. On 12 July 1764 Franklin noted that these were being handed around and remarked that particular emphasis was being placed on procuring the signatures of the Presbyterians.[90] Observers charged that the Presbyterian clergy "turned their pulpits into Ecclesiastical drums for politics" and prostituted their altars by permitting petitions to be signed upon

[88] Theodore G. Tappert and John W. Doberstein, trs. and eds., *The Journals of Henry Melchior Muhlenberg* (Phila., 1945), II, 55, 56.

[89] *Ibid.*, 91, 99, 100, 101, 102, 107, 111.

[90] Franklin to Richard Jackson, 12 July 1764, in Labaree, ed., *Papers of BF*, XII, 256.

them.[91] Petitions were circulated and signed in the German churches as well, as Muhlenberg's diary attests.[92]

The petitioning process and the anti-royal government movement received a shot in the arm with the return of William Allen from England on 13 August 1764. While in London Allen had fraternized with Thomas Penn, hobnobbed with members of the ministry, and befriended Richard Jackson.[93] He created a sensation, therefore, by conveying to the Pennsylvania public what he said were these men's sentiments about royal government. Jackson, he asserted, had declared that the Assembly would be compelled to pay Penn £100,000 for his proprietorship, plus an additional £5,000 annually to the new royal governor.[94] Lord Halifax, he revealed, had fulminated against the royal government movement and had denounced it as tantamount to rebellion. Everything he had seen and heard convinced him of the correctness of the thesis of Dickinson's speech of 24 May: royal government would not relieve the province of the rigors of external control but would, on the contrary, be more repressive than any proprietary regime. "Put these refractory people into our Hands, and we'll soon make them feel the Difference be-

[91] Hugh Neill to Daniel Burton, 18 Oct. 1764, in William S. Perry, ed., *Papers relating to the History of the Church in Pennsylvania, A.D., 1680-1778* ([Hartford, Conn.], 1871), 364-65; *Observations on a late Epitaph*, Evans microcards, No. 9772.

[92] *Journals of Muhlenberg*, II, 106, 107.

[93] David A. Kimball and Miriam Quinn, "William Allen–Benjamin Chew Correspondence, 1763-1764," *Pa. Mag. Hist. and Biog.*, XC (1966), 202-26.

[94] For this and the following quotations, see Franklin to Jackson, 1 Sept. 1764, in Labaree, ed., *Papers of BF*, XI, 327-28.

tween a Proprietary and a Royal Government!" he quoted Lord Mansfield as saying. And in an epigram which epitomized the entire case against royal government, he warned the Assembly that "the King's little Finger we should find heavier than the Proprietor's whole Loins."[95]

In England Allen had also sought out leaders of the Society of Friends, men like Dr. John Fothergill and David Barclay, and had solicited their opinion about royal government. Finding that they opposed it, he wasted no time when he returned to Pennsylvania in conveying their sentiments to Quaker religious leaders, to Israel Pemberton in particular.[96] By 1764 Pemberton had been actively opposed to the Quaker Party political leadership for almost a decade. His disillusionment with it dated roughly from Franklin's ascendancy in its ranks. The Doctor, with his plans for militias and defense appropriations, represented, in Pemberton's view, a deadly threat to the soul of Quakerism—so much so that in 1756 Pemberton's camp regarded him as even more dangerous than the Presbyterians.[97] The royal government scheme appeared to be far more menacing than any of Franklin's previous measures, and Pemberton opposed it with a passion unbecoming his peaceable profession: "Israel Pemberton at present is violent against Franklin's Party," John Penn re-

[95] *Ibid.*, 432; John Hughes's "Letter," *Pa. Gazette*, 10 Jan. 1765; Hughes to the commissioners of the Stamp Office, 12 Oct. 1765, *Pa. Journal*, supplement, 4 Sept. 1766.

[96] James Pemberton to John Fothergill, 3 Sept. 1764, Pemberton Papers, Hist. Soc. Pa.; Allen to Thomas Penn, 21 Oct. 1764, Penn Papers, Hist. Soc. Pa.

[97] For an analysis of the origins of the Franklin-Pemberton antagonism, see my "Benjamin Franklin and Pennsylvania Politics, 1751-1755: A Reappraisal," *Pa. Mag. Hist. and Biog.*, XCIII (1969), 313-14.

ported, "he abuses them tooth and nail."⁹⁸ Although Allen
was an ancient enemy, Pemberton welcomed his information and cooperated with him in opposing royal government, trying, among other things, to persuade the Quakers not to vote in the October elections.⁹⁹ Despite his
diligent efforts, however, Pemberton did not accomplish
much, in Allen's judgment, for Franklin's hard core of
pro-royal government Quakers in Philadelphia "were so
much inflamed that they would listen to no terms of
accommodation."¹⁰⁰ Yet the cooperation of the two men
was significant, for it set a precedent for the increasing collaboration during the ensuing years of what might be
called the Quaker Establishment and the Proprietary
Establishment.

Allen's arrival and his dramatic and widely publicized
revelations—straight from the horse's mouth, as it were—
about the perils of royal government gave a powerful
thrust to the tide which, thanks to William Smith, was
already strongly running against a change of government.
Citizens searched for petitions to sign against it, and none
more eagerly than those German church people who, according to Allen, had been duped earlier into signing pro-

⁹⁸ John Penn to Thomas Penn, 12 Sept. 1766, Penn Papers, Hist. Soc.
Pa. The description was equally apt in 1764.

⁹⁹ William Logan to John Smith, [Oct. 2, 1764], Smith MSS, Hist.
Soc. Pa. Assisting the Allen-Pemberton cooperation was a visit to Pennsylvania of a respected London Quaker, John Hunt. This merchant-
preacher arrived at Philadelphia on 9 Sept. 1764, confirmed everything
that Allen had said, and urged opposition to royal government. Samuel
Purviance, Jr., to James Burd, 10 Sept. 1764, in Balch, *Provincial History of Pennsylvania*, 206; Israel Pemberton to David Barclay, 6 Nov.
1764, Pemberton Papers, Hist. Soc. Pa.; William Allen to same, 25
Sept. and 20 Nov. 1764; Walker, ed., *The Burd Papers*, 56-57, 63-64.

¹⁰⁰ Allen to Thomas Penn, 21 Oct. 1764, Penn Papers, Hist. Soc. Pa.

royal government petitions.[101] The result was that by September some 15,000 people had signed petitions against royal government.[102] The importance of this figure consists in its comparison with the total of 3,500 people who signed petitions for royal government, for this gives us a yardstick, perhaps unique in American colonial history, for measuring the popularity of George III and his government on the eve of the revolutionary agitation. The petition signatures may be considered a kind of public opinion poll, a referendum on the King's popularity at a propitious moment for him, at a time when his image had not been sullied by the Stamp Act or other hateful measures. It is of considerable significance, then, that five out of every six Pennsylvanians who signed petitions rejected his government, preferring to remain under the morally discredited government of an unpopular proprietor. What this means is that in 1764 over eighty percent of a significant sample of Pennsylvanians, by no means a "radical" people, were imbued with suspicions, fears, or hatreds of royal government active enough to impel them to register them publicly. Such a figure makes the Revolution easier to comprehend.

---

[101] Allen to Thomas Penn, 25 Sept. 1764, Penn Papers, Hist. Soc. Pa.

[102] *Pa. Journal*, 27 Sept. 1764; Remonstrance from Philadelphia Inhabitants, 26 Oct. 1764, in 8 *Pa. Arch.*, VII, 5688. This figure may be somewhat suspect, because both sources for it were documents composed by proprietary partisans. By 7 Dec. 1764 Thomas Penn had received anti-royal government petitions signed by 8,600 people; by 10 April 1765 he had received petitions "signed by between ten and eleven thousand People and Doct' Smith gives me reason to expect a great many more." Penn to William Smith and to Benjamin Chew, 7 Dec. 1764, and to Joseph Shippen, Jr., 10 April 1765, Penn Papers, Hist. Soc. Pa.

The summer surge of anti-royal government sentiment produced two major political changes. One was the alteration of the strategy, devised in England by Thomas Penn, to blunt the threat of Franklin and his confederates. We will recall that, when Penn received letters from his nephew, at the end of May, describing the dispute with the Assembly over the assessment of his located, uncultivated lands, he conferred with his lawyer, Henry Wilmot, who had represented him at the Privy Council hearings in 1760, and who advised him that the Assembly's interpretation of the Council's second amendment was justified. Penn immediately sent his nephew a copy of Wilmot's opinion, dated 30 May 1764, covered by his own letter of 1 June 1764,[103] ordering the young man to reverse himself and accept and be guided by the Assembly's interpretation of the amendment.

Penn's decision was dictated by the fear that his nephew had jeopardized his proprietorship. He overestimated the inflammatory impact of the assessment demand and assumed that its flagrant injustice had turned the entire province against him. He believed that he must either quench the flames or forfeit his position. Thus, he sent his nephew the order to reverse himself in the hope of convincing the populace of his fairness and dampening thereby the demand for royal government.

When Thomas Penn's letter reached Philadelphia in mid-August, John Penn and Benjamin Chew perceived that he had misjudged the temper of the province and that, because of the manifest unpopularity of royal govern-

[103] Both documents are in the Penn Papers, Hist. Soc. Pa.

ment, his interests would be best served by encouraging its partisans, not by pacifying them. Royal government had become a millstone around the necks of Franklin and his political supporters, and Penn and Chew saw that the Proprietary Party might defeat them in the forthcoming October Assembly elections by keeping it there. Consequently, they suppressed Thomas Penn's offer to appease them.[104]

The obvious liability of the royal government issue widened the split between the rural and urban wings of the Quaker Party. In the countryside, where royal government had never generated much enthusiasm and where it incurred more and more enmity as the summer advanced, Quaker Party politicians perceived that it was political poison, that to support it was to invite defeat. Therefore, they broke with their urban brethren, came out against it, and presented themselves to the electorate as patrons and protectors of proprietary government.[105] The October elections proved the wisdom of their policy. In their rural strongholds of Chester and Bucks counties they lost no seats to the Proprietary Party,[106] and they reelected their three representatives from Lancaster County, giving

[104] John Penn to Thomas Penn, 1 Sept. 1764, Penn Papers, Hist. Soc. Pa.

[105] William Allen described the tactics of the country Quakers to Thomas Penn in a letter of 21 Oct. 1764: "In the Country, all but Northampton, the Quakers had the address, or I might say, Craft, to delude the Dutch by false Storys, so that they . . . were induced to oppose our friends, and carried the elections against them. *They were made to believe that, if they changed the Assembly, the Government would be changed.*" Penn Papers, Hist. Soc. Pa.

[106] Peter Shepherd, a new member from Bucks County, might be counted a loss, but he voted on only three issues and then withdrew from the House, making it impossible to judge his true allegiance. See Labaree, ed., *Papers of BF*, xi, 393.

them a total of nineteen seats, a majority in the malapportioned Pennsylvania Assembly.

The Quaker Party was not so fortunate in the Philadelphia area. In that hotbed of royal government the faithful were not swayed by the surge of opposition to their cause and continued to support it and its leaders. Smelling blood, their adversaries worked unremittingly and refused to concede a single vote. In the city of Philadelphia they courted the Quakers' working-class supporters, trying with "unwearied Endeavours . . . to prejudice the minds of the lower class of people" against Franklin and his coadjutors,[107] an effort they continued the following year by cozying up to "Presbyterian and Dutch Tinkers, Cobblers &c."[108] They had some success, because Franklin and his running mate, Samuel Rhoads, were defeated in the city by approximately 700 to 600 votes[109] and "the wiser and better sort," as the proprietary partisans called themselves,[110] did not amount to anything like the former number. Furthermore, the opponents of royal government carried the province's Presbyterians "to a man," as William Allen informed Thomas Penn on 21 October 1764,[111] and some Philadelphia workingmen were obviously Pres-

[107] James Pemberton to Dr. John Fothergill, 11 Oct. 1764, Pemberton Papers, Hist. Soc. Pa.

[108] Samuel Wharton to William Franklin, 29 Sept. 1765, Franklin Papers, APS.

[109] For these figures, see Labaree, ed., *Papers of BF*, XI, 391-92. One craves more information on the election of 1764 in the city of Philadelphia, especially a breakdown of the vote by district, which might make it possible to see precisely how the working-class areas voted.

[110] For the use of this term, see Franklin, *Preface* to Galloway's *Speech*, in Labaree, ed., *Papers of BF*, XI, 292, 297, 300; Thomas Wharton to Franklin, 2 March 1766, *ibid.*, XIII, 191.

[111] Penn Papers, Hist. Soc. Pa.

byterians. But Franklin and Rhoads retained the support of the White Oaks and of many other mechanics.[112] This meant that in the October elections a substantial number of Philadelphia workingmen opposed the predominantly Presbyterian frontiersmen, just as they had in February when the capital's mechanics filled the ranks of the volunteer militia summoned to stop the Paxton Boys. Therefore, the thesis, first formulated by Charles H. Lincoln in 1901 and adopted by most historians since, that the march of the Paxton Boys and the turmoil of 1764 in general produced, or at least foreshadowed, the coalition between the "lower elements" of the east and the frontiersmen of the west which overthrew the old order in 1776 must be qualified.[113] Most mechanics of Philadelphia opposed the frontiersmen with bullets in February, and many opposed them with ballots in October. Instead of a "sympathetic link" between the two groups,[114] between important segments of each there was settled hostility. If 1764 produced any ties between east and west, it was through the looms of religion, through the province-wide network of commit-

[112] For the White Oaks' support of Franklin at the October 1764 election, see my "An Investigation of the Inarticulate: Philadelphia's White Oaks," 3 *WMQ*, xxviii (1971), 13-18.

[113] See Charles H. Lincoln, *The Revolutionary Movement in Pennsylvania, 1760-1776* (Phila., 1901), 109, 112-13. For more recent statements of this thesis, see Theodore Thayer, *Israel Pemberton* (Phila., 1943), 190, 201, 202; J. Paul Selsam, *The Pennsylvania Constitution of 1776* (Phila., 1936), 43; Brooke Hindle, "The March of the Paxton Boys," 3 *WMQ* (1946), 485-86; Leonard J. Trinterud, *The Forming of an American Tradition: A Re-examination of Colonial Presbyterianism* (Phila., 1949), 232-33; David L. Jacobson, *John Dickinson and the Revolution in Pennsylvania, 1764-1776* (Berkeley and Los Angeles, 1965), 26, 42.

[114] William S. Hanna, *Benjamin Franklin and Pennsylvania Politics* (Stanford, 1964), 153.

tees of correspondence spun by Purviance and his fellow Presbyterians, rather than through any putative community of grievances between the dispossessed of the two sections.

Too much attention must not be given to the Presbyterians, however, not in the county of Philadelphia, at least, for the Germans were the decisive factor in the October elections there (in which the Quaker Party lost four of its eight seats).[115] Franklin, who ran in both city and county, Galloway, and other defeated Quaker Party stalwarts acknowledged this with surprise and resentment. "They carried (would you think it!) above 1000 Dutch from me," Franklin wrote Jackson on 11 October—"low drunken Dutch," Samuel Wharton added with a sneer.[116] The success of the Proprietary Party with the German vote was, in one way, a testimony to William Smith's success with the German church people. Smith and other proprietary leaders had perceived the importance of involving the Germans in the political process, and in August 1764 the parson had joined with Muhlenberg and Wrangel in petitioning Governor Penn to appoint county justices of the peace from the Lutheran and Reformed congregations.[117] The logical conclusion of this policy was the placing of Germans on the Proprietary Party ticket for Philadelphia County in the October elections, and Henry Keppele and Frederick Antis were duly included. Both men were prominent Ger-

[115] Henry Pawling, who defeated a Quaker Party candidate, supported the party faithfully nevertheless. Thus, the Quaker Party only lost three votes. See Labaree, ed., *Papers of BF*, XI, 393.

[116] *Ibid.*, XI, 397; Samuel Wharton to William Franklin, 29 Oct. 1765, APS; Goddard, *The Partnership*, 11.

[117] *Journals of Muhlenberg*, II, 111.

man laymen, Keppele being an elder in Muhlenberg's church. To assist them, Smith, Allen, and "several English gentlemen" disbursed large amounts of money in the country (primarily through William Young) to pay the fees for naturalizing prospective German voters.[118] Their efforts would probably have been unavailing, however, had it not been for the assistance of Christopher Sauer, Jr., publisher of the influential *Pensylvanische Berichte*, who vigorously attacked royal government and its supporters in the pages of his newspaper and wrote pamphlets in German against it.[119] It seems highly unlikely that Smith or any of the German church leaders recruited Sauer, for he was a Quaker Party ally and an ardent sectarian, who passionately opposed the province's organized churches and their leaders, whether English or German. If anyone enlisted his assistance, it was probably Israel Pemberton, whose religious convictions were close to those of the German sectarians and who frequently served as their counselor. (Norris also had some influence with Sauer and his followers, but how or whether he exerted it is not clear; he and his old rival Pemberton, though both opposed to royal government, do not appear to have cooperated in working with the Germans.)[120] What seems most likely, however, is that Sauer's opposition to royal government stemmed from his own convictions about the danger it

[118] William Young to Thomas Penn, 14 Oct. 1765, Penn Papers, Hist. Soc. Pa.

[119] See, e.g., his *Anmerkungen uber ein noch nie erhort und gesehen Wunder Thier in Pennsylvanien* . . . , Evans microcards, No. 9578, and his *Eine zu dieser Zeit hochstnothege Warnung und Erinnerung* . . . , No. 9828.

[120] Norris did, however, encourage Dickinson's opposition to royal government. Labaree, ed., *Papers of BF*, XI, 527.

posed to the civil and religious rights of the German people. He and the rest of the Germans were intelligent men and their actions need not be attributed to the manipulation of Englishmen or, as Franklin and his followers assumed, to the power of the Proprietary Party's scurrilous election propaganda.[121] The Germans voted, it seems clear, according to their own perception of their best interests.

In the final analysis it was not even the tide of German votes which defeated Franklin and the royal government supporters in the city and county of Philadelphia; it was their own mismanagement and complacency. "Upwards of 3900" citizens voted in the Philadelphia County elections; Franklin was defeated by a mere eighteen votes, Galloway by a scant seven.[122] Twice during election day the royal government supporters committed blunders which cost them victory. At three o'clock on the morning of 2 October the Proprietary Party moved to close the polls, but the Quaker Party strategists, having "a reserve of the aged and lame," insisted on keeping them open. They prevailed, and forthwith roughly two hundred supporters limped or were led to the polls. The proprietary partisans reacted by dispatching horsemen and footmen to Germantown, and soon the Dutch began "to pour in, so that after the move for a close, 7 or 800 votes were procured; about 500 or near it of which were for the new ticket [Proprietary Party], and they did not close till 3 in the afternoon. . . ."[123]

[121] For the unprecedented abusiveness of the 1764 election, see J. Philip Gleason, "A Scurrilous Colonial Election and Franklin's Reputation," 3 *WMQ*, XVIII (1961), 68-84.

[122] For a careful analysis of the election returns, see Labaree, ed., *Papers of BF*, XI, 390-94.

[123] *Ibid.*, 391.

Having kept the polls open too long earlier, the Quaker Party now closed them too soon, for thirty royal government supporters "came to the Doors after they were shut, but could not get admittance."[124] So, for want of another hour, the election was lost.

The Quaker Party could have survived even the miscalculations of its managers had it not been overconfident. In an election post mortem Franklin explained that the Proprietary Party had prevailed "by great Industry against great Security."[125] What he meant by "great Security" was complacency, although the receipt of nearly half of 3,900 ballots, a record turnout, showed that the Friends had not exactly been twiddling their thumbs throughout the campaign. Nevertheless, the long years of easy, often uncontested victories had conditioned them to believe they could not really be defeated, no matter how ominous the threat, and they did not, therefore, put forth a maximum effort. Chastened by defeat, they pulled out all stops in 1765, beat every bush and shook every tree for voters, with the result that at least 4,332 people went to the polls, more than 400 higher than in any previous year, almost all of whom evidently voted for the Quaker Party candidates, for its lowest vote getter, Galloway, defeated his nearest rival, Dickinson, by 420 votes.[126] Had the party

[124] William Logan to John Smith, 4 Oct. 1764, Smith MSS, Hist. Soc. Pa.

[125] Franklin to Jackson, 11 Oct. 1764, in Labaree, ed., *Papers of BF*, XI, 397.

[126] See "Election Returns, 1765," Franklin Papers, APS. A good treatment of the election is Benjamin H. Newcomb, "Effects of the Stamp Act on Colonial Pennsylvania Politics," 3 *WMQ*, XXIII (1966), 257-72.

displayed such energy in 1764, the result would not have been in doubt.

The defeat of Franklin and Galloway, the leaders of the royal government campaign, and three of their coadjutors stunned the Quaker Party. By riding the crest of the anti-royal government wave, the Proprietary Party, which in the past had often been happy to receive two dozen votes, obtained two thousand and emerged a winner. But just as Franklin and Galloway were far from finished by the election defeat, so the Proprietary Party had not suddenly become invincible by virtue of its victory. Its crucial test would come when the issue of royal government, on which Franklin and his followers had so egregiously misjudged the popular temper, receded from the stage.

CHAPTER IV

The Mirage of Royal Government

BECAUSE THE people of Pennsylvania, by petition and by ballot, had rejected royal government, many politicians expected the Assembly to repudiate it officially, when it convened on 15 October. The issue was raised on 20 October, when a member asked what the House proposed to do with the royal government petitions it had sent to agent Richard Jackson in June. After "considerable Debate" a motion to recall them was made and rejected. Then a motion, sponsored by Speaker Isaac Norris (who had been re-elected in October), that the House put "an entire Prohibition on the Agent's presenting the said Petitions, without further and express orders from the House," was also defeated. Finally, the House passed a motion which repeated almost verbatim the orders it had given Jackson on 28 May, when the royal government campaign was at its apogee: he was to proceed in presenting "the Application for a Change of Government," taking care, however, to use "the utmost Caution" to protect the province's civil and religious liberties.[1]

The House's action in persisting in a policy which the electorate had just rejected was severely censured. Norris once again resigned in disgust (on 24 October), while William Smith upbraided the Assemblymen, the Bucks County delegation in particular, for duplicity; they promised "at

[1] 8 *Pa. Arch.*, VII, 5682-83.

last election to use all their endeavours to recall the petition for a change of government, and yet voted for continuing it," he indignantly charged.[2] John Penn and Benjamin Chew blamed the House's action on Franklin and Galloway, whom they likened to sorcerers manipulating the members at secret conventicles. Although they had not been elected, they had, according to Chew, "the entire direction of Matters within doors, the measure and plan of each days proceedings being settled by them every evening at private meetings and cabals with their Friends in the House."[3]

Chew's allegation did great injustice to the Assembly, for the election to fill the speakership on 24 October showed that it was anything but a rubber stamp in the hands of Franklin and Galloway. Their candidate, nominated by their spokesman in the House, John Hughes, was George Ashbridge. He was defeated by the veteran Assemblyman Joseph Fox. Fox's election was a setback for Franklin, because the new Speaker was "one of the warmest friends of the [proprietary] Government."[4] His victory proved that the rural Quakers, who were a numerical majority in the House and who favored and had campaigned for the retention of Penn's government, were in

---

[2] [William Smith], *To the Freeholders and Electors of the Province of Pennsylvania*, [28 Sept. 1765], APS. For the authorship and dating of this broadside, see Samuel Wharton to William Franklin, 29 Sept. 1765, APS.

[3] Chew to Thomas Penn, 5 Nov. 1764; John Penn to Thomas Penn, 19 Oct. 1764; both in the Penn Papers, Hist. Soc. Pa.

[4] For Fox's election, see John Dickinson to Isaac Norris, 24 Oct. 1764, Norris Letterbook, Hist. Soc. Pa. For his pro-proprietary attitude, see William Allen to Thomas Penn, 27 Feb. 1768, Penn Papers, Hist. Soc. Pa.

command. Although people like William Smith did not perceive it, the vote of 20 October keeping the royal government petition alive was part of this group's plan to retain proprietary government. And so was the appointment of Franklin as agent on 26 October to return to England to assist Jackson. Sending the Doctor to England and keeping the royal government petition cocked and ready were intended as bluffs. The Assembly hoped that Penn would interpret them as evidence that it meant to make a maximum effort to obtain royal government and that he would be frightened into offering it extensive reforms to divert it from its objective. "They never intended the petition should be presented," William Allen wrote Penn on 11 March 1765, "but only kept as a rod to hang over you to bring you to agree to their measures."[5]

The members assumed that Penn would accommodate them, because his instructions to his nephew to accept their position on the assessment of his vacant lands seemed to show a conciliatory disposition. Although John Penn had tried to keep these orders secret, his uncle had advertised

[5] Allen to Penn, 11 March 1765, Penn Papers, Hist. Soc. Pa. James Hamilton, who arrived in London in January 1765 to seek medical treatment, confirmed Allen's statement. "He tells me he was told the Petition was not to be presented," Thomas Penn wrote Richard Hockley on 12 Jan. 1765, Penn Papers, Hist. Soc. Pa. John Dickinson and the nine other assemblymen who signed the "Protest" against Franklin's appointment as agent, 26 Oct. 1764, affirmed that the petition was sent to England, not to procure royal government, but "to obtain a Compliance with some equitable Demands." Labaree, ed., *Papers of BF*, XI, 409. The Assembly itself clearly stated its intentions in instructions to Richard Jackson of 1 Nov. 1764; "The present Assembly, hoping an Accommodation with our Proprietors may take Place, and that he will in due time make such Concessions as will fully satisfy the Assembly and Freemen of this Province have determined not to withdraw those Petitions to his Majesty. . . ." *Ibid.*, 423-24.

them in England and letters reaching Pennsylvania had adverted to them, so that the province buzzed with rumors about his "healing Instructions." On 26 October William Allen officially announced their contents to the House.[6] He disclosed them for the same reason they had previously been concealed: to damage Franklin. By announcing them just a few hours before the members voted on sending the Doctor to England, Allen hoped to defeat his adversary's appointment by proving it to be superfluous. If the members knew that Penn had conceded the point of previous spring's controversy, would they send an agent to England to negotiate with him about it? But Allen and the Proprietary Party did not grasp the real nature of the Assembly's grievances. Although the members were incensed by Penn's tax dodging, they were far more distressed by his ability to force them to sanction it by means of inflexible instructions. His exercise of external control was what bothered them, and this concern could not be appeased by concessions on the assessment of his property. Therefore, Allen's announcement did not dissuade them from appointing an agent who they hoped would go to England and win significant concessions on the governance of the province.

But Franklin could not accomplish their intentions, proprietary partisans protested; his "rooted Enmity" to Penn and Penn's to him precluded all possibility of an accommodation.[7] The members evidently agreed, for it appears that they did not expect Franklin to negotiate with

[6] *Ibid.*, 409-10, 435-36; Israel Pemberton to David Barclay, 6 Nov. 1764, Pemberton Papers, Hist. Soc. Pa.

[7] See, e.g., the Philadelphia Remonstrance, 26 Oct. 1764, in 8 *Pa. Arch.*, VII, 5689, and the "Protest" against Franklin's appointment as agent, 26 Oct. 1764, in Labaree, ed., *Papers of BF*, XI, 409.

Penn. His function in England they conceived rather as that of an intimidator. They hoped that, when Penn learned of his arrival, he would assume that Franklin's hatred for him virtually guaranteed the presentation and prosecution of the royal government petition and that the only way to prevent this was to negotiate sweeping concessions with the Assembly.

But with whom would he negotiate? The Assembly apparently expected him to deal with English Quakers who had remained friendly with both him and the people of the province, men like his physician, Dr. John Fothergill, and merchants like Henton Brown and David Barclay. Although no documents commissioning Quakers to negotiate with the proprietor have survived,[8] they were evidently written, because in 1765 London Friends acted as the Assembly's plenipotentiaries in important, and heretofore unknown, negotiations with Thomas Penn. Franklin, on the other hand, may have communicated oral instructions to the Quakers when he arrived in England on 9 December 1764 after a short, thirty-day voyage from Pennsylvania. Whatever the case, the Friends swung into action in early

---

[8] A letter from Israel Pemberton to David Barclay, 6 Nov. 1764, though not an official commission, spells out the role the Pennsylvania Quakers wanted their London counterparts to play: "the aversion the Proprietaries and Franklin have to each other I am sensible will render the measures necessary for an amiable accommodation difficult, yet I hope, not impracticable, by the united assistance of such friends who may have some interest with them, if such who can influence the agent could prevail with him in a proper manner to make such proposals as they think reasonable, and those, with such other friends as have weight with the Proprietaries, would engage them favorably to receive and calmly to consider what they may offer, and seriously to reflect on the importance of this crisis, by which the connection between them and the people seems likely to be determined." Pemberton Papers, Hist. Soc. Pa.

February,[9] just as Franklin was being caught up in the politics of the Stamp Act.

Most historians have supposed that Franklin's immersion in the Stamp Act controversy signaled the end of the campaign for royal government, which they have treated as a political aberration he was happy to have an excuse to forget. But this is a mistaken assumption. If his letters during the final half of 1765 say nothing about royal government, thereby giving the impression that he had washed his hands of the affair, it was because the Quakers and Thomas Penn were negotiating secretly about provincial grievances (against the tacit threat of an appeal for royal government in the event of failure)[10] and he considered it imprudent to comment on their progress.

Quaker overtures were apparently made to Thomas Penn about the first of February, and a few days later a meeting was held between Penn, his brother Richard, and their attorney, Henry Wilmot, on one side and Dr. Fothergill and Richard Jackson (who was not a Quaker) on the other.[11] At this meeting Fothergill handed the Penns a

[9] Curiously enough, in a letter to John Ross of 14 Feb. 1765, Franklin represented the Quakers as acting on their own initiative. However, William Allen, who as a member of the Assembly received accurate information about the Doctor's actions, stated that the Friends had intervened at his solicitation. "I hear," wrote Allen to Thomas Penn on 19 May 1765, "that he [Franklin] had ingratiated himself with Dr. Fothergill, and friends with you, and induced them so far as to interest themselves in his affairs as to propose terms of accommodation." Labaree, ed., *Papers of BF*, XII, 67; Penn Papers, Hist. Soc. Pa.

[10] The Penns immediately recognized this. On 11 Feb. 1765, just after negotiations with the Quakers had begun, Richard Penn wrote his brother Thomas that he believed "they keep it [the petition] back only till they can find what is likely to be done with Us in regard to their several articles of Complaint." Penn Papers, Hist. Soc. Pa.

[11] *Ibid.*

paper containing the Assembly's "Articles of Complaint," a list of grievances which the House wanted redressed. For reasons that are obscure, the Penns did not prepare an answer to the articles until 9 May, on which date a response, drawn by Wilmot, was sent to Fothergill. A copy of the articles and the response follow:[12]

Articles of Complaint

1st. That Publick Houses and Dram Shops have much encreased of late to the great Injury of the Moralls of the People, and the Proposals made for reducing the Numbers of them have been rejected.

2d. That the Power of appointing Judges *during Pleasure* is dangerous and oppressive; and that it ought for the mutual Good of the Proprietarys and the People to be at least *during good Behaviour* if not *for Life*.

3d. That there ought to be only one Mode of Taxation for the Proprietarys and the People.

4th. That the Deputy Governor ought not to be restrained by private Instructions under a Penal Bond from Cooperating with the People for their mutual benefit as Exigencies may require.

5th. That a proper inquiry has not been made after the Authors of the Massacre of the Indians, and

---

[12] The articles and a heavily corrected draft of the response, both on the same sheet, dated 6 May 1765, were also found. See, at the appropriate dates, Pennsylvania Miscellaneous Papers, Penn and Baltimore, 1756-68, and Penn Manuscripts, Assembly and Provincial Council of Pennsylvania.

Riotts, and just Punishment inflicted on the Delinquents and their Abettors.

Proprietary Response

1st. The Proprietaries will direct their Governor to assent to a law in which it shall be provided that no Licenses for Publick Houses shall be granted but such as shall be recommended by the Grand Jurys to the Justices in open Court, and by them to the Governor.

2d. The Judges of all the Colonies and of Ireland are appointed during Pleasure and the Proprietarys have received so many Cautions from the Kings Ministers to be watchfull that the Prerogatives of the Crown be not given up that they do not think themselves to be at liberty to consent to an Alteration. But if the Province of Pennsilvania can convince the Kings Ministers of the Utility of such an Alteration, and they will from the King recommend it to the Proprietarys to grant Commissions to Judges during good Behaviour, the Proprietaries will grant Commissions accordingly.

3d. The Proprietors apprehend this Matter was settled by the Orders they gave that their located uncultivated lands should be taxed according to their Situation and Quality agreeable to the Forms prescribed by the Act. Vide the N. B. below.[13]

[13] The following footnote occurred at the bottom of the manuscript: "upon this Occasion the Proprietarys cannot help observing that there

4th. The Proprietarys have been so well advised of the Legality and fitness of Instructions and Bonds to enforce such Instructions that they cannot think of sending over a Governor without. But (the 3d Article and the making Paper Money a Tender being at an End) they think there are no Instructions They shall give which can be the Cause of any Difference between the Governor and Assembly.

5th. The Proprietarys are as desirous as the People that all Means may be used to bring the Authors of the Massacres of the Indians and of Riotts to Punishment and they do not know that any thing hath been omitted by the Governor for that Purpose.

Fothergill took his time in replying to the Penns' response. On 8 June he told the proprietor that he would

---

are severall Objections to the last Tax Act, which they apprehend ought to be altered. The Governor informed the House how impracticable it was to present an exact List of the Proprietary Quit Rents agreeable to the Forms of that Act. The Land Office hath been for sometime shutt and the Receiver of the Proprietarys closely confined in order to comply with the Act, but it is impossible. The Names of Places and Bounds of Townships have undergone such a Variety of Changes that the Receiver knows them not by their present Names. Many, perhaps one third of the Settlers are under Warrants only, many, under no Survey at all. The Proprietors can demand no Rent from either of these, and from the latter the Rent is not known. This Inconvenience might be effectually remedied by laying the Tax for the future on the Occupiers, as if the Lands were not lyable either to any money remaining due for the Land or to any Quit Rents, and enabling the Occupyers to deduct the Tax when they pay the Interest or the Quit Rent to the Receiver. There are some other parts of the Act which they apprehend ought to be altered, not necessary here to be taken notice of."

answer "soon" and a meeting was duly scheduled; it had to be postponed, however, because an illness befell Mrs. Richard Penn which required her husband's constant attendance. A conference with Fothergill and the Quaker merchant Henton Brown was finally held on 12 July, but no agreement was reached. Differences on fundamental points were so great, in fact, that Fothergill and Brown concluded that further meetings would be fruitless, and none were held.[14]

In the conference on 12 July both sides adhered to the positions contained in the document just printed. By analyzing it, we can form a clear idea of the course of the negotiations. Fothergill's "Articles of Complaint" expounded grievances which had been troubling the Assembly for years[15] and which, with the exception of article five, were included in the House's comprehensive bill of particulars against the proprietors, its twenty-six resolves of 24 March 1764. The Penns' response was not uncompromising. They agreed, for example, to redress the complaint about the proliferation of public houses. In Pennsylvania justices of the peace recommended public house licensees to the governor, who granted them licenses for a fee. The

[14] Thomas Penn to John Penn, 8 June and 6 July 1765; to Benjamin Chew and William Allen, 13 July 1765; all in the Penn Papers, Hist. Soc. Pa.

[15] Complaints against the excessive number of public houses had been heard for decades; see, e.g., the Remonstrance of the Philadelphia Grand Jury, 3 Jan. 1744, *Pa. Mag. Hist. and Biog.*, XXII (1878), 497-99. The Assembly protested against Penn's commissioning judges during pleasure on 22 Feb. 1757. Labaree, ed., *Papers of BF*, VII, 140. It attacked proprietary instructions enforced by penal bonds as early as Sept. 1753. Hutson, "Benjamin Franklin and Pennsylvania Politics, 1751-1755: A Reappraisal," *Pa. Mag. Hist. and Biog.*, XCIII (1969), 342-43.

Assembly contended that this system prompted the justices to recommend an inordinate number of licensees as a pay-off for continued appointment to office by the governors. The reform which the Penns offered was designed to limit the number of licensees, the effect of which would, of course, be to reduce their governors' income. Early in the negotiations Fothergill suggested that the Assembly would be willing to compensate them for this concession, but whether a precise sum was agreed upon is not clear.[16] The Penns' position on judicial reform was also reasonable. Recent British ministries had taken a hard line against the appointment of colonial judges during good behavior. The Privy Council had repealed several colonial statutes, including one passed in Pennsylvania in 1759, which granted this tenure, and in 1762 the governor of New Jersey was removed from office for passing an act which conferred it. Thomas Penn rightly feared that by approving such a measure he would put his proprietorship in peril. His willingness to grant this tenure if the Assembly received prior royal approval seems to have been sincere, even if he suspected that none would be given. The Penns believed that the third article was unnecessary, for they had already granted its complaint in their letter to John Penn of 1 June 1764, whose contents William Allen had announced to the Assembly on 26 October 1764. They tried to be accommodating on the fifth article, too, indicating that they were "desirous" of seeing the Paxton Boys brought to justice and stating during the negotiations that they would be

[16] The agreement on public house licenses never went in effect; when Penn and the House failed to resolve other grievances, he cancelled all concessions. See his letter to John Penn, 30 Nov. 1765, Penn Papers, Hist. Soc. Pa.

happy to see the governor and the Assembly make "such Provisions as they shall think necessary for this purpose."[17]

Only on the fourth article did the Penns show no disposition to compromise. Their intransigence may have been encouraged by Fothergill's negotiating tactics. Not appreciating Pennsylvania's antipathy toward proprietary instructions, he minimized their importance early in the negotiations, concentrating instead on the public house and judicial tenure issues. Proprietary instructions the Doctor professed to regard as "a mere Moon Shine which was to be given up upon a Compromise of the other two."[18] When he learned of the line Fothergill had taken, Franklin evidently set him straight by stressing that an understanding on proprietary instructions was the *vital* issue for Pennsylvanians. Accordingly, Fothergill put more emphasis on them later in the negotiations, demanding their abolition[19] and convincing Thomas Penn that ending them was "the only point they want."[20] But Penn would not budge on this issue. In requesting that he refrain from giving his deputies instructions enforced by penal bonds, the Assembly was

[17] Thomas Penn to William Allen, 13 July 1765, Penn Papers, Hist. Soc. Pa.

[18] Richard Penn to Thomas Penn, 11 Feb. 1765, Penn Papers, Hist. Soc. Pa.

[19] Thomas Penn to John Penn, 6 July 1765, Penn Papers, Hist. Soc. Pa.

[20] Penn wrote William Allen, 13 July 1765, that "the only point they want is . . . the disposal of the Publick Money." His meaning was that the Assembly wanted him to rescind his instruction through which since 1751 he had ordered his governors to demand a voice in the expenditure of the Assembly's surplus from the provincial excise and of the interest it received from the emission of paper money on loan. For an explanation of these matters, see Hutson, "Benjamin Franklin and Pennsylvania Politics," 322-23.

asking him to surrender control over the province. He refused to do so, and since the Assembly was adamant on the issue, negotiations collapsed at the end of July.

Franklin, who had anticipated failure,[21] did not attempt to exploit the situation by immediately applying for royal government. One assumes, although no documents survive to prove it, that his caution was induced by instructions to consult the Assembly in the event that negotiations miscarried. The fall of the Grenville ministry on 10 July 1765 must also have given him pause. Swept from office were Jackson and the two Treasury secretaries, Charles Jenkinson and Thomas Whately—friends who had given him influence with the ministry by seeing that he was consulted on American patronage and that his nominees were appointed to office: John Hughes to the Pennsylvania Stamp Distributorship, William Coxe to the New Jersey Stamp Distributorship, Zachariah Hood to the Maryland Stamp Distributorship, and James Parker to a landwaitership in the New York Customs.[22] Now Franklin was confronted with Lord Rockingham and a retinue of strange peers and placemen, whose attitude toward his plans was unknown.

---

[21] Labaree, ed., *Papers of BF*, XII, 67.

[22] Thomas Penn wrote William Allen, 13 July 1765, that Franklin "valued himself" much on his friendship with Jenkinson and Whately. Penn Papers, Hist. Soc. Pa. For his procuring the appointment of Hughes, see Labaree, ed., *Papers of BF*, XII, 234-35n; Thomas Penn to John Penn, 13 April 1765, and to William Smith, 28 Sept. 1765, Penn Papers, Hist. Soc. Pa. For his appointment of Coxe, see [Charles Lloyd], *The Conduct of the Late Administration Examined* (London, 1767), 28; for Hood, see [Smith], *To the Freeholders and Electors*, APS; for Parker, see Labaree, ed., *Papers of BF*, XII, 227-28n.

He wasted no time, however, in sounding out the new ministers. On 9 August he wrote Hughes that he had arranged an audience the next Wednesday with the Secretary of State for the Southern Department, Henry Seymour Conway. We know nothing about the results of this meeting (if, indeed, it was ever held), but in his letter to Hughes Franklin expressed his characteristic optimism about an application for royal government: "I have very little doubt of a favourable Progress and advantageous issue," he wrote.[23] Nothing decisive happened over the next few weeks, as Franklin apparently awaited instructions from Pennsylvania. These evidently arrived at the beginning of November in a letter from Galloway, describing the Assembly election of 1 October.[24]

The future of royal government was again contested in that canvass. The coalition opposing it wanted to trounce the Quaker Party so thoroughly that it could dominate the Assembly and end the movement for royal government once and for all: "to recal our dangerous enemy, Franklin, with his petitions . . . is the great object we have now in view," wrote Purviance on 20 September 1765.[25] The issue

[23] Labaree, ed., *Papers of BF*, XII, 235-36.

[24] Galloway's letter has not been found. He mentions having written it in a letter to Franklin of 8-14 Oct. 1765 (*ibid.*, 305), which means that it was written before that date and probably a day or so after the 1 Oct. election, on 2 or 3 Oct. presumably. The letter, he wrote, went by Bristol. *Pa. Gazette*, 3 Oct. 1765, mentions the brig *Newport Packet*, Capt. J. Corser, as being outward bound for Bristol, so this must have been the ship which carried the letter. If the vessel sailed on 3 Oct. or a day or so later, it could have reached Bristol by 1 Nov. (a fast passage, but not an impossible one) and Galloway's letter could have reached Franklin by 3 Nov.

[25] To James Burd, in Balch, *Provincial History of Pennsylvania*, 208.

which it hoped to use to defeat the Quaker Party was the Stamp Act. Representing that tyrannical stature as typical of royal government, the coalition dared its advocates to deny that its advent in the province would be fatal to Pennsylvania's liberties. Since Franklin and his Quaker Party supporters favored royal government and since royal government had passed the Stamp Act, could they not be considered friends of that hideous statute? The anti-royal government coalition strove mightily to stamp this syllogism on the electorate's consciousness. This is not to say that its opposition to the Stamp Act was solely a campaign gambit. Both the Presbyterians and German church people opposed the statute on principle, with the latter bearing it a special grudge because it imposed double taxes on documents written in their language. But even though partisan advantage may not have been the anti-royal government forces' sole motive in attacking the Stamp Act, the prospect of gaining it added to the gusto with which they assailed it.

The Stamp Act played havoc with a policy devised by the Quaker Party leadership to assist Franklin's quest for royal government in England. This policy presupposed a symbiotic relationship between events in Pennsylvania and the Doctor's mission to the mother country; for him to succeed in his negotiations in London, his supporters (and he himself) believed that they had to shape Pennsylvania politics to please the British ministry. Encouraged by Franklin's assurances, they concluded that it would be easy enough for him to persuade the ministers to remove Thomas Penn, but they feared that it might be difficult for him to convince them that they would be suitable replacements. The ministers might assume, as detractors of America alleged, that Pennsylvanians, like the other colonists, were ungovernable anarchists who would roil a royal government as readily as they had a proprietary one. To counter such an impression, the Quaker Party leaders believed they had to demonstrate that they would be reliable recipients of royal government. And what better way to prove this than to obey in the fullest measure possible the policies of the ministers in whatever form they appeared—acts of Parliament, orders-in-council, royal proclamations, and so on? The Quaker politicians hoped that their obedience not only would prove them to be worthy custodians of royal government but would encourage its bestowal. They hoped, as Franklin put it, that "it might by Government be thought as good Policy to show Favour where there has been Obedience as Resentment where there has been the Reverse."[26] Individuals also expected to profit from their obedience, their thinking being that, when royal government was granted, those who had been conspicuously loyal would be appointed to public office. Galloway, who was constantly being accused of seeking the chief justiceship under a royal government, exemplified this mentality when he argued that those Pennsylvanians who, because of their opposition to the Stamp Act, had "already forfeited all favor that might be expected from a New Government" were trying to implicate Quaker Party members in their guilt that "they may equally Share in their Disgrace, and be entitled to no more favor."[27] Obedience to the policies

---

[26] Franklin to Galloway, 13 June 1767, in Labaree, ed., *Papers of BF*, XIV, 182.
[27] *Ibid.*, XIII, 373.

of the British government was thus expected to pay multiple dividends: it would help Franklin; it would, in consequence, help the province; and it would help deserving individuals in it. Therefore, as long as the Quaker Party leaders believed that Franklin could procure royal government, they made it their business to conduct public affairs so as to please the British ministry. The result was that from 1765 to 1768 they practiced—and gave Pennsylvania—what we may call a politics of ingratiation.

The Stamp Act put these politics to a severe test. Most Quaker Party leaders regarded it as unjust and tyrannical, yet they realized that by resisting it they could not hope to please the British politicians who supported it. A handful of men, like John Hughes and his followers in the Assembly, escaped this dilemma by denying that the act was illegitimate, proposing to obey it, and trying to obstruct efforts to negate it, opposing, as Hughes did, the sending of Pennsylvania delegates to the Stamp Act Congress and coming within one vote of preventing their dispatch.[28] Joseph Galloway took a different tack, writing a long letter in the *Pennsylvania Journal*, 29 August 1765, over the signature "Americanus" in which he apologized for the Stamp Act and found extenuating circumstances for it.[29] But Galloway prudently kept his authorship anonymous, for he perceived that few Pennsylvanians approved of his paper. His public conduct—disapproval of the Stamp Act coupled with efforts to please the British by confining opposition to it to conspicuously legal methods and by trying to prevent its nullification by force, as had happened in other

[28] *Ibid.*, XII, 265n.   [29] *Ibid.*, XII, 219n, 269-70.

colonies—more nearly suited the taste of the supporters of royal government.

Pennsylvania was first threatened with mob violence on the night of 16 September when bells rang, bonfires blazed, and "every Demonstration of Joy"[30] was made at the news received the preceding day of the Grenville ministry's resignation. A crowd collected at the nerve center of the opposition to the Stamp Act, the London Coffee House, owned by the Presbyterian printer and "Son of Liberty" William Bradford, where threats were made that the houses of Franklin (who was accused of helping plan the Stamp Act), Hughes, and others "should be leveled with the Street." Galloway and the Quaker Party leaders quickly mobilized a counterforce of about 800 White Oaks, mechanics, and tradesmen.[31] These men, stationed in various parts of the town, completely overawed the anti-Franklin mob, and it meekly melted away. Hughes, whom the mob hoped to frighten into resigning his Stamp Distributorship, scorned its intimidation and defiantly remained in office.

Trouble threatened again on 5 October when a ship arrived from London carrying Hughes's commission and the province's allotment of stamped paper. A large crowd, estimated by some to be in the thousands, assembled at the State House, where Hughes heard that "it was publickly declared . . . that if I did not immediately resign my office, my house should be pulled down and my substance

---

[30] For this and the following quotation, see *ibid.*, 315.

[31] The White Oaks and their role during the Stamp Act crisis are discussed in my "An Investigation of the Inarticulate: Philadelphia's White Oaks," 3 *WMQ*, XXVIII (1971), 3-25.

destroyed."[32] Franklin's wife, Deborah, reported that James Allen, son of Proprietary Party leader William Allen, was "Sperriting up the mobe,"[33] and Hughes weighed in with a denunciation of those "Presbyterians and proprietary emissaries" who were "animating and encouraging the lower class."[34] Quaker Party supporters sought in vain to have Proprietary Party officials control the crowd, but John Penn and Benjamin Chew had vanished into the countryside and no other magistrate could be found "to discourage the mob, or to give the least aid or protection." The same "700 or 800" men who had turned out on the night of 16 September again came to Hughes's rescue, forming themselves around his house and taking positions at strategic locations in town.[35] Apparently these men and Galloway and the Quaker Party politicians who led them struck a bargain with Hughes. If he would agree not to enforce the Stamp Act "until his Majesty's further pleasure was known, or until the act should be put into execution in the neighbouring provinces," they would prevent the mob from forcing him to resign and would defend his person and property against its aggressions. This Hughes agreed to do, and when a seven-man delegation from the mob visited him, including Bradford, Thomson, and the Secretary of the Proprietary Land Office, James Tilghman,

[32] Hughes to Stamp Office Commissioners, 12 Oct. 1765, in *Pa. Journal*, supplement, 4 Sept. 1766.

[33] To Benjamin Franklin, 8-13 Oct. 1765, in Labaree, ed., *Papers of BF*, XII, 301.

[34] 12 Oct. 1765, *ibid*. The following quotation is from the same letter.

[35] Hughes to Stamp Office Commissioners, 12 Oct. and 2 Nov. 1765, *Pa. Journal*, supplement, 4 Sept. 1766. Labaree, ed., *Papers of BF*, XIII, 294.

he informed them of his intentions. Evidently intimidated by his supporters from attempting to force him to do anything more, they accepted his offer, returned to the State House, and urged the crowd to retire in peace, which it did.[36]

One more attempt was made to force Hughes's resignation. During the second week of November Thomson, with Bradford one of what passed for the "Sons of Liberty" in Philadelphia, called a mass meeting at the State House. To the 200 people who attended, he proposed that Hughes be compelled to "totally and fully resign his Office."[37] No action was taken, however, for everything Thomson suggested "was hissed or opposed by Some of the W Oaks . . ." and the meeting "broke up without effecting anything." Hughes, nevertheless, was alarmed by the attention of Thomson and his friends and feared that his house would at last be destroyed. Galloway was not about to let this

[36] The royal government campaign also helped persuade the leaders of the State House mob to restrain it. They knew that in England Franklin was arguing for royal government on the grounds that proprietary government was too weak to preserve the public peace (the march of the Paxton Boys, which was repelled only by organizing volunteers, was the principal evidence he was citing of its debility). If Philadelphia were wracked by violence over the Stamp Act, Franklin's charge would be confirmed and royal government might be hastened. Therefore, the leaders of the State House mob, supporters of proprietary government all, were almost as anxious to prevent violence as Hughes was. "The present precarious state of our charter at home by no means admitting of our exerting ourselves in this seditious way, or else we have spirit and resentment enough among us to sacrifice the villain [Hughes] to his injured country," wrote Benjamin Rush on 18 Nov. 1765. Lyman Butterfield, ed., *Letters of Benjamin Rush* (Phila., 1951), I, 20.

[37] This and the remaining quotations in this paragraph are from Labaree, ed., *Papers of BF*, XII, 372-74.

happen, however. He went to a tavern to speak to his "friends—and there proposed an Union for the preservation of the Peace of the City, Several of the White Oaks and Hearts of Oak [another ship carpenters' organization] were there—they all Declared they would be ready—Since which J[ohn] H[ughes] has had a Meeting with them and they are determined to defend him to the Utmost." Galloway reported that this pact had frightened Hughes's enemies and predicted that it would keep Philadelphia calm, "for you may be assured," he wrote William Franklin, "we can Muster ten to their one." He was correct, for in the months remaining before the repeal of the Stamp Act neither Hughes nor the city was disturbed.

The frustration of Thomson's plans by the White Oaks, the Hearts of Oaks, and the other laboring men who composed Galloway's ten-to-one majority makes it clear why the Sons of Liberty never caught on in Pennsylvania, why they had less impact there than in any other colony.[38] The Pennsylvania Sons of Liberty had the chiefs, but not the Indians; the mechanics who swelled their ranks in the other colonies were mostly on the other side in the Quaker Commonwealth. Thomson's failure shows something else, too: despite assiduous cultivation of the mechanics and artisans of Philadelphia—of the "presbyterian and Dutch

[38] Edmund S. and Helen M. Morgan note that "although there were local Sons of Liberty in Pennsylvania the intercolonial organization seems to have made little headway there." *The Stamp Act Crisis* (Chapel Hill, 1953), 202, n. 72. William Bradford in a letter to the New York Sons of Liberty, 15 Feb. 1766, admitted that the Pennsylvania organization was "not declared numerous." Quoted in Frances Von A. Cabeen, "The Society of the Sons of Saint Tammany of Philadelphia," *Pa. Mag. Hist. and Biog.*, xxv (1901), 439.

Tinkers and Cobblers," as a Quaker Party grandee contemptuously called them—the opponents of royal government had not succeeded in rallying the mass of them to their standard by the fall of 1765 and were no closer than they had been in the preceding year to forging a formidable coalition between the farmers of the frontier and the workingmen of the city.

When measured against events in the other colonies, the achievement of Galloway and his Quaker Party colleagues during the Stamp Act crisis was impressive. They had prevented violence against persons and property (they had even prevented the hanging of effigies),[39] and they had made Pennsylvania the only colony on the continent whose Stamp Distributor had not been forced to resign. Their actions had the intended result—they pleased the British ministry—but they did not pay the expected dividend. Ironically, the principal beneficiary of the goodwill they created was Governor John Penn, whom the Quaker Party suspected of condoning the opposition to the Stamp Act by absenting himself from Philadelphia on 5 October 1765. Yet in letters to Secretary of State Conway on 10 and 19 February 1766 young Penn took credit for the colony's good behavior, and on 31 March he received the minister's congratulations: "assure [your Assembly] of his Majesty's Approbation of the wise and prudent, as well as dutiful Behaviour, which the Province of Pennsylvania has held amidst the too prevailing Distraction, which has so generally agitated the other Colonies. *This Behaviour of your Province reflects on your Administration*; and I have the

[39] Labaree, ed., *Papers of BF*, XII, 270, and XIII, 294.

Satisfaction to inform you, that your own Conduct meets with his Majesty's Approbation."[40] Conway's response was characteristic of the politics of ingratiation; although the Quaker Party generated abundant goodwill in Britain, it never profited from it. But it kept trying to please the British ministry in the hope that it would.

A greater irony still was the reversal of the roles of the province's parties in the wake of the Stamp Act. Prior to 1764 the Quaker Party regarded itself, in the idiom of the time, as the "patriot" party or, alternatively, as the "country" party. According to contemporary terminology, such parties were supposed to oppose the pretensions of the executive on behalf of the legislature, to be anti-prerogative, pro-popular rights. This description fit the Quaker Party in its struggle with the proprietor, just as it fit the parties in the other American colonies which opposed the royal governors and their cliques. The beginnings in earnest of the controversy with the mother country in 1764 did not interrupt the political rhythm in most American colonies. Royal governors and their partisans supported the imperial policies as best they could, and the popular, "country" parties opposed them in the name of popular rights. Only in Pennsylvania was there a rupture. Here the political world was turned upside down, for the Quaker Party leadership, to obtain the salvation from proprietary tyranny it promised itself in royal government, adopted a policy of ingratiating itself with the British ministry, which in 1765 meant becoming the apologists for and, as far as possible, the defenders of the royal prerogative as it ravaged colonial rights in the Stamp Act. Thus, the royal government cam-

[40] 8 *Pa. Arch.*, VII, 5878-79. The italics are my own.

paign forced it to forfeit its role as a "country" party and perform the functions of a "court" party.

The goad of the royal government campaign also forced the Proprietary Party to change its role, if only temporarily and imperfectly. As an organization—the term "party," we should keep in mind, has been applied to it throughout this book more for convenience than for descriptive correctness—whose leader was the chief executive in the province and whose continuation as an entity depended on the sufferance of the King whose power constituted the proprietor his deputy, the Proprietary Party would have been (as in England it was) expected to support the royal prerogative as it was embodied in the Stamp Act. But because the Stamp Act was the vehicle it could use to defeat the Quaker Party's threat to its existence, it opposed it, in varying degrees. The diversity of its opposition was not a matter of policy. Rather, it reflected the lack of discipline and coherence which characterized the Proprietary Party under John Penn. While some proprietary partisans like James Allen and James Tilghman contended against the Stamp Act openly and conspicuously, other and more important of their compatriots would not venture beyond the covert opposition of Penn, Chew, and William Allen, who made themselves inaccessible to those wanting to suppress the demonstrative opponents of the Stamp Act, whom they were accused of secretly encouraging. "Nothing was left unessayed by them," wrote Joseph Galloway, "to incite the People to Acts of Violence, which coud be done, without publickly joining the Mobs and exposing themselves."[41]

[41] To Franklin, 7 June 1766, in Labaree, ed., *Papers of BF*, XIII, 294.

Public exposure was the line which most of the proprietary partisans would not cross in protesting the policies of the British government, because to oppose them openly was to invite the dissolution of the proprietorship for insubordination. Thus, there were insurmountable restraints on the Proprietary Party's capacity to change its role, as the Quaker Party had done, and become the province's "country" party, its adversary of ministerial politics. In fact, not a few proprietary stalwarts like Penn, Chew, and William Allen were uncomfortable even in their tacit opposition to the home government and were relieved when the repeal of the Stamp Act and the diminution of the threat of royal government permitted them to assume a posture more personally congenial and more attuned to the self-interest of the Proprietary Party, one of supporting where possible, or at least acquiescing in, the policies of the British ministry.

The movement for royal government created a remarkable political landscape in Pennsylvania. It transformed what was formerly the popular, anti-prerogative party into a suitor of the British ministry's goodwill, while demonstrating that many members of the venerable court party were inhibited from openly opposing the home government and, in fact, coveted its goodwill as avidly as its political adversaries. By the conclusion of the Stamp Act crisis both of Pennsylvania's established political parties wanted to be friends of the British ministry. As we will shortly see, to oppose ministerial policies Pennsylvanians were forced to form a new political party in the midst of the imperial controversy, an event which occurred in no other American colony.

The excitement of John Hughes's confrontation with the anti-Stamp Act mob and the tumultuous events attending it have frequently diverted historians' attention from the significance of the Assembly elections of 1 October 1765. Hughes's intrepid advocacy of the Stamp Act and his resolute attempt to prevent the House from sending delegates to the Stamp Act Congress paved the way for a Quaker Party victory in the election, although it ruined his own political career. However much his actions might have been privately approved by some Quaker politicos as a means of pleasing the British ministry, they offended the citizenry at large and led to the perception that by disavowing them the Quaker Party could establish an image as an advocate of moderate, constitutional opposition to the Stamp Act. Hence, Hughes was purged from the party ticket in the October elections. This step refurbished the Quaker Party's reputation and, coupled with its unprecedented efforts to get out the vote, enabled it to win the election and recapture almost all of the seats lost in the preceding year's debacle. Frosting was added to the cake by Galloway's victory over Dickinson in Philadelphia County.[42]

Galloway reported the election returns by letter to Franklin.[43] The news, which reached the Doctor at the begining of November, was music to his ears, for he had been sitting in London, awaiting word as to how to proceed, since the failure of negotiations with Thomas Penn in mid-

[42] An excellent account of the 1765 election may be found in Benjamin H. Newcomb, "Effects of the Stamp Act on Colonial Pennsylvania Politics," 3 *WMQ*, XXIII (1966), 257-72.

[43] See note 24, above.

summer. Information that his coadjutor in the royal government campaign had been victorious evidently convinced him that the electorate had thereby signified its approval of the campaign and would now support a determined effort to change the government. Therefore, on 4 November he presented the petition for royal government to the Privy Council, assuring the Assembly once again that he had "no reason to doubt of its success."[44]

Eighteen days later the Council dismissed the petition. There are different accounts of the manner in which it did so. According to Thomas Penn, it acted ruthlessly. The petition was "resolved not proper for further consideration," he wrote his nephew on 30 November, "but by his Majesty's order postponed, sine die, that is (to use my Lord President's own expression) for ever and ever." Later Penn qualified himself by confiding to William Allen that the President's statement was not the official language of the Council, but merely a private communication. Still later he confessed that the Council had acted "in a less harsh way" than he wished by not rejecting the petition outright. To his friends Franklin represented the petition as having been only temporarily laid aside, remaining "ready to be proceeded on, as soon as . . . other Affairs are out of hand." The official *Acts of the Privy Council* simply state that consideration of the petition had been "postponed for the present."[45]

[44] Labaree, ed., *Papers of BF*, XI, 145-47, 193-200, XII, 420, and XIII, 35. Thomas Penn to Richard Peters, 15 Nov. 1765, Penn Papers, Hist. Soc. Pa.

[45] Thomas Penn to John Penn, 30 Nov. 1765; to William Allen, 15 Dec. 1765; to William Smith, 1 April 1766; all in the Penn Papers, Hist. Soc. Pa. Labaree, ed., *Papers of BF*, XIII, 240; *Acts Privy Coun., Col.*, IV (1745-66), 741.

Disagreement over the precise status of the petition could not disguise the fact that the Privy Council's decision constituted a staggering setback for Franklin, for which his poor political judgment was alone to blame. While in England he heard officials of all ranks damn proprietary regimes and express desires for their demise. These sentiments were open and widespread, as Thomas Penn could attest.[46] But Franklin mistook a general bureaucratic pique with proprietary governments for a high-level resolve to rid the empire of them—hence his confidence, with which he consistently misled his supporters in Pennsylvania, that royal government was theirs for the asking. Richard Jackson, who as Grenville's secretary knew the ministerial mind, warned him that he had misread it, that an application for royal government was likely to "meet with some mortifying circumstances of Reception"; Thomas Penn, who also knew the ministerial mind, confirmed Jackson's reading of it, telling Benjamin Chew on 20 July 1765 that he had received the "strongest assurances" that Franklin would not be encouraged.[47] Nevertheless, the Doctor would not heed Jackson's warning and steered straight ahead. Perhaps he had made a secret bargain with Lord Bute, in which his Lordship had promised to use his influence to procure royal government for Pennsylvania. But if he were close enough to Bute to make such an arrangement, he should have known that, despite the public's notions about the Earl's private power in govern-

[46] See Penn to Richard Peters, 13 May 1767, Penn Papers, Hist. Soc. Pa.

[47] Labaree, ed., *Papers of BF*, XI, 313; in addition to Penn's letter to Chew, see his letter to John Penn, 11 Jan. 1765, Penn Papers, Hist. Soc. Pa.

ment, Grenville refused to tolerate his interference and that after May 1765 Bute ceased to try to exert any influence over the King and his servants. Since the Earl's "abdication" and the fall of the Grenville ministry did not dampen Franklin's invincible optimism about the prospects for royal government, one assumes it was formed principally by his personal appraisal of what was in Britain's best political interest. Although Jackson continued to express reservations about the reception of the royal government petition up to the moment it was presented, he did not deter Franklin.[48] The man who had disarmed lightning evidently refused to believe that his judgment about a political petition could be wrong. But science and politics were governed by very different laws, as the Privy Council showed him on 22 November.

The Privy Council's decision represented, not the first, but the last in a series of major political miscalculations made by Franklin in 1764 and 1765. He had badly misjudged the mentality of the people of Pennsylvania when in 1764 he expected them to support the royal government campaign without extensive explanation. He compounded this mistake in 1765 by procuring his friend, John Hughes, the Stamp Distributorship on the assumption that Pennsylvania (and, indeed, all the colonies) would docilely submit to the Stamp Act. And his stubborn, arrogant decision to present the royal government petition showed that he had misjudged the British political temper as profoundly as he had that of his own countrymen. Rare is the politician

[48] Labaree, ed., *Papers of BF*, XIII, 35. On 9 Nov. 1765, after the petition was presented but before the Privy Council acted on it, Jackson suggested that the Assembly withdraw it; see Assembly committee of correspondence report, 21 Jan. 1766, in 8 *Pa. Arch.*, VII, 5837.

who can make, much less survive, so many major mistakes in so short a time. But Franklin was barely bruised by these blunders.

The Privy Council decision did not extinguish the movement for royal government in Pennsylvania.[49] Galloway and his Quaker Party colleagues, who had staked their reputations on its speedy, painless acquisition, swallowed hard and accepted Franklin's hopeful account of the decision, rather than Thomas Penn's apocalyptic one, and continued to persuade themselves that royal government could be obtained and that it was worth working for. Proprietary partisans naturally credited Thomas Penn's version of the decision. His letter to his nephew, announcing the postponement of the Assembly petition "for ever and ever," they printed in the *Pennsylvania Journal* on 27 February 1766 and saw that copies of it were "industriously sent all over the Province,"[50] as if to show the citizenry that the threat to their positions and perquisites was over. The news aroused some apprehension, however, for it was feared that the diminution of the royal government thrust would cause the confederation which had mobilized against it to disintegrate. Foreseeing this possibility, the proprietary leaders had, throughout 1765, courted the Presbyterians and German church people and tried to cement them to their cause with patronage and palatable public policies. "Since the Pextang riot" they "have remarkably caressed these people," wrote James Pemberton on 12 December 1765.[51] And so, indeed, they had. After the October 1764 elections

[49] For a contrary opinion, see William S. Hanna, *Benjamin Franklin and Pennsylvania Politics* (Stanford, 1964), 169.

[50] Labaree, ed., *Papers of BF*, XIII, 179-82.

[51] To John Fothergill, Pemberton Papers, Hist. Soc. Pa.

John Penn began appointing large numbers of Presbyterian justices of the peace,[52] and to gratify the Germans, Allen, Chew, and Smith persuaded him to violate his instructions and issue charters of incorporation to their churches.[53] To please both groups, the majority of whose members were frontiersmen and farmers, the following steps were taken: the practices of the Provincial Land Office were reformed in July 1765 with an eye to remedying abuses and simplifying purchasing procedures; a new Land Office secretary, James Tilghman, was appointed with a higher salary, intended to discourage the corruption which had disgraced the tenure of his predecessor, William Peters; and proprietary land prices were reduced by two-thirds.[54] These measures failed to hold their beneficiaries in the proprietary orbit, however. With the abatement in the winter of 1766 of the threat of royal government, the fear of which alone united them, previous rivalries reasserted themselves, the confederation collapsed, and some of its members were soon at sword's point.

The principal friction developed, predictably, between those self-conscious religious rivals, the Presbyterians and the Anglicans, with the activities of the Reverend William Smith provoking the difficulties. As early as 1756 Smith had been accused of wanting to become "Bishop of America" in case the Anglican church was established in the

---

[52] See Hutson, "Franklin and Pennsylvania Politics," 307n.

[53] John Penn to Thomas Penn, 14 Oct. 1765, Penn Papers, Hist. Soc. Pa.

[54] Shepherd, *Proprietary Government in Pennsylvania*, 34, 72ff; Thomas Wharton to Franklin, 2 March 1766, in Labaree, ed., *Papers of BF*, XIII, 92.

colonies.[55] As the fear of such a development became acute
at the end of the French and Indian War, his opponents
eyed him with increasing apprehension. The Presbyterians
bore with him while the threat of royal government lasted,
but as soon as it abated, they challenged him. "Doctor
Smith has said something in religious Polliticks that has
greatly Iretated the Prisbetearen Clerge," John Reed informed Franklin on 17 June 1766. "The Sinod at New
York have nominated some wits of the laiety to handle
him it relats to the haveing of an American Bishop of
which Smith has great Hopes of the apointment."[56] According to Samuel Purviance, Smith had stabbed the Presbyterians in the back. Like Francis Alison, Purviance believed that the Anglicans "rejoyce at the Quarrel between
us and the Quakers and no doubt expect that in the midst
of our Contests theyle one day or other get the upper hand
of us both." Smith, he charged, had "betray'd our Cause"
during the summer of 1766 by secretly making "Overtures
to Governor [William] Franklin, that on Condition the
Quakers could be engaged not to oppose their Views of a
Bishop, the Churchmen should not longer oppose his
Father in the Scheme of changing the Government."[57] As
a result of these suspicions and Smith's manifest mitre
fever, the Presbyterians split with him and the Proprietary
Party in the summer of 1766. (Men like the Allens, Armstrong, and Purviance, who were both Presbyterians and

[55] See "Humphrey Scourge" in *Pa. Journal*, 25 March 1756.
[56] Labaree, ed., *Papers of BF*, XIII, 320.
[57] Purviance to Ezra Stiles, 1 Nov. 1766, in Franklin B. Dexter, ed.,
Extracts from the Itineraries . . . of Ezra Stiles (New Haven, 1916),
555.

proprietary officeholders and clients, tried to keep their feet in both camps, however, to the dismay of those historians who want their factional lines clean and sharp. They were appropriately called the "Half and Halfs,"[58] and their ambiguous position enormously complicates the comprehension of Pennsylvania politics down to the Declaration of Independence.)

Religion was not the only seam along which the abatement of the royal government threat caused Pennsylvania politics to rend. Ministerial policies were another. The Quaker Party leadership, which refused to concede that royal government was dead, continued to pursue the politics of ingratiating itself with the British ministry. The Proprietary Party leadership (with some exceptions) was freed by what it took to be the receding of the royal government threat from the dangerous necessity of attacking a policy of the home government (the Stamp Act) to help defeat the domestic royal government movement. With relief it assumed a posture more consistent with its self-interest, one of trying to cultivate the ministry's goodwill. With both of the province's established parties now anxious to please the British government, those who opposed its arbitrary policies and pretensions, as most recently manifested in the Declaratory Act, had no instrumentality through which they could channel their opposition. Hence, they were obliged to form a new party.

It was no coincidence that many who split from the two old parties in protest against their approach to British im-

[58] The first usage I have found of this term is in a letter from Sally to William Franklin, 3 Oct. 1766, Mason-Franklin Collection, Yale University Library.

perial policies were the same men who split from the Proprietary Party in the spring and summer of 1766 because of the fear of an American bishop. Politics and religion were often intertwined in eighteenth-century America, and in this instance they certainly were. If Americans conceded to the British government the power to bind them in all cases whatsoever, as the Declaratory Act put it, then they would jeopardize more than their civil liberties. A government with such unlimited power could imperil their religious liberties as well by riveting an Anglican establishment upon them. These considerations motivated the formation of the new party in mid-1766 and gave it both a political and religious dimension. Appropriately, it was called the "Presbyterian Party" after the denomination whose apprehensions about its Anglican rival prompted it to furnish most of the members and most of the leaders: Thomson, Bradford, Bryan and later Reed, Cannon, Rittenhouse, Rush, and Wilson.

"Presbyterian Party" was a pejorative term used by the organization's opponents consistently from 1766 to 1776; its partisans preferred the term "Whig Party," which gained currency after 1774.[59] Like the Quaker Party, the

[59] For the existence of a separate Presbyterian Party in 1766, Sally Franklin's letter (cited immediately above) is again as good evidence as any. "How strong is the Cause of Truth," she wrote her brother. "We [the Quaker Party] beat three party's, the Proprietary, the Presbeterean's, and the Half and Halfs." Galloway affirmed the existence of a separate Presbyterian Party in 1770, when he wrote of a group deserting from the Quaker Party who, he feared, "will go over to the Presbyterians, and yet I believe the Proprietary Party will not stir." To Benjamin Franklin, 27 Sept. 1770, APS. Joseph Reed wrote of the province's three parties in 1774, using the term "Whig" for Presbyterian. In June 1774, he wrote, there was "a full meeting comprised of all ranks and interests. These were the proprietary interest, the sons of

Presbyterian Party contained important members who were not communicants in the denomination. John Dickinson, for example, who until the early seventies was generally acknowledged to be the leader of the party (although at times he was closer to being a figurehead), was not a Presbyterian. Neither was he a religious fanatic, oppressed by nightmares about an Anglican establishment. He affiliated with the party for political and personal reasons: he deplored British imperial policy and detested both Proprietary Party "Prime Minister" Chew and Quaker Party leader Galloway so much that he could cooperate with neither. The Presbyterians sealed the marriage with Dickin-

---

the principal officers of Government, the Quakers, the Whigs. . . ." "Joseph Reed's Narrative," New-York Historical Society *Collections* (1878), 271. Charles Thomson described the existence of the same alignment in the winter of 1774-75. "A great majority of the Assembly," he wrote William Henry Drayton, "was composed of men in the Proprietary and Quaker interest, who heretofore opposed to each other, were now uniting . . . had the Whigs in Assembly been left to pursue their own measures. . . ." *Ibid.*, 280-81. Older and more recent historians have treated the province's political alignments, especially from 1774 to 1776, in two ways. Having perceived three groups, they have called them Conservative, Moderate, and Radical (or have used other terms which convey the same meaning). Or, recognizing that the Proprietary and Quaker parties were working closely together by 1774, they have reduced the political chaos to two groups, Moderates and Independents (or some variation on these terms). The first approach is used by, among others, William B. Reed in his *Life and Correspondence of Joseph Reed* (Phila., 1847), I, 151-52, and Kenneth R. Rossman, *Thomas Mifflin and the Politics of the American Revolution* (Chapel Hill, 1952), 16; the second approach is represented in its best form in David Hawke's excellent *In the Midst of a Revolution* (Phila., 1961). My thesis is that there were three distinct parties in existence until Independence (the term "party" is, admittedly, loose) and that, from 1774 on, one need not devise new labels to describe them, for they were the parties which had existed in the province for a decade to more than three quarters of a century.

son in the October 1766 Assembly elections by letting him run in place of their "Hero," George Bryan, for a Philadelphia city seat, for which Purviance received a letter "from Mr. Dick[inson] expressing the greatest Gratitude and inviolable Attachment to the Presbyterians for their generous Behaviour to him."[60]

Where did the Germans fit into the new political dispensation? The receding of the royal government threat detached them, as it had the Presbyterians, from the confederation with the Proprietary Party, but they settled into a far less active posture than the members of the Kirk. The Dutch "are now generally come over to the Assembly Party, and have lost their former Prejudices," wrote Galloway on 7 June 1766.[61] What he meant was that the German sectaries, who, like Sauer, had disagreed with the Quakers over the desirability of royal government, had drifted back into their traditional alliance. The church Germans, on the other hand, moved toward the Presbyterian orbit, although over the next several years they played a retiring and somewhat enigmatic role in provincial politics.[62]

The abatement of the royal government threat left Pennsylvania with a vastly different political landscape than it possessed before the royal government movement began. Some things were the same: the Proprietary Party,

---

[60] Purviance to Ezra Stiles, 1 Nov. 1766, in Dexter, ed., *Itineraries . . . of Ezra Stiles,* 557.

[61] Labaree, ed., *Papers of BF,* XIII, 296.

[62] Their historian, Arthur D. Graeff, claims that they were politically inert between 1766 and 1774. See his *The Relations Between the Pennsylvania Germans and the British Authorities (1750-1776)* (Norristown, Pa., 1939), 232-33, 235, 236n, 246-47.

unable to capitalize on the opportunity to acquire a meaningful constituency, had relapsed by the summer of 1766 into the decrepitude from which the miscalculations of the royal government supporters had temporarily raised it; once again it became an undisciplined collection of friends and relatives of the Penns, proprietary officeholders, and parishioners of William Smith and his allies in the Anglican priesthood. Other things had changed somewhat: the Quaker Party had lost a number of vigorous young leaders—Dickinson, Thomson, Bryan—in the disagreement over royal government and had also lost those Presbyterians and church Germans who had formerly followed it for want of a better alternative; but it retained much of its strength—the agricultural and milling magnates in the rural crescent formed by Chester, Philadelphia, and Bucks counties, the merchants and shopkeepers of Philadelphia, and a powerful body of the capital's mechanics, led by the White Oaks. Still other things were completely different: the Presbyterian Party had made its political debut, prompted by the dissipation of the royal government threat. Running under the party's colors in the October 1766 Assembly elections, Dickinson suffered a crushing defeat which exposed the weakness of the fledgling organization.[63] It was clear, though, how it would acquire political strength. Since the province's rural and urban elite had been preempted by the established parties, it must sink its roots among the ordinary farmers of the west and the tradesmen, artificers, and workingmen of Philadelphia. With the former group, among whom church Germans

[63] The Philadelphia city and county election results are in the Franklin Papers, APS.

and Presbyterians predominated, there was good reason for optimism. It was the latter group which posed the critical challenge, for the anti-royal government coalition had not been able to detach decisive numbers of "mechanics" from the Quaker Party, and unless the Presbyterian Party could, it would not be a major factor in provincial politics. It remains, then, to sketch the way in which the Presbyterian Party drew these men to its banners and how, as a result, the Quaker and Proprietary parties converged, until by the eve of the Revolution they were often functionally indistinguishable.

The repeal of the Stamp Act invigorated the Quaker Party's politics of ingratiation, because that statute could no longer be used as a brush to tar its every effort to please the British ministry. News of the repeal arrived in May 1766. Franklin had advised the Assembly's committee of correspondence that the Rockingham ministry would be incensed if the colonies treated the repeal as a triumph over the mother country and exulted over it in noisy celebrations. Consequently, the Quaker Party leaders tried to prevent the citizenry from conspicuously commemorating it. Although they failed to keep those whom they accused of being proprietary partisans from illuminating Philadelphia, they discouraged any public demonstrations by having their "Friends . . . constantly Patroling in the Streets"; they also tried to please the ministry by adopting, at Franklin's suggestion, an obsequious address to the King, thanking him for repealing the Stamp Act.[64] This memorial was presented to His Majesty in August by Lord Shelburne and was said to have made a good impression upon him.

[64] Labaree, ed., *Papers of BF*, XIII, 285, 384-85.

In September the Quaker Party leaders made another attempt to please the ministry by passing an act putting Pennsylvania in compliance with the Quartering Act of 1765. They knew that their action would be compared to that of New York, which was contesting the act and Parliament's right to pass it, and they emphatically wanted the comparison made, so that Pennsylvania would appear as a paragon of obedience to Great Britain. Their ploy accomplished its purpose, for it was favorably noticed by British politicians. Lord North, for example, declared from the floor of the House of Commons that he had a high "regard for Pensilvania, which had behaved so well in all the late Disturbances in America, and had shown such a dutiful Obedience to Parliament in the Billeting Affair."[65] But, typically, his goodwill did not help the province, because at the end of his speech he advised rejecting a petition from the Assembly without a hearing.

The politics of ingratiation would not have been viable had not the hope persisted that the British would grant royal government. What point would there have been, after all, in trying to please a ministry from which nothing could be gained? Hope was sustained principally by Franklin's optimistic reports from England. Proprietary politicians, who correctly saw that the Privy Council's action of 22 November 1765 had ended all chance for royal government, assumed that Franklin was deluding his supporters about its outlook, playing the pollyanna so that he could continue living off the fat of the land in London at the public's expense. He was "continually feeding the party

[65] Franklin to Galloway, 9 Jan. 1769, William L. Clements Library, University of Michigan.

with hopes of success in the old affair and amusing them with idle tales, in order to be kept in England," wrote John Penn in 1768.[66] If Franklin was, in fact, deceiving his supporters, it was only after he had deceived himself first, for he was too emotionally committed to royal government to make a sober appraisal of its possibilities. His conviction that it was Pennsylvania's panacea and his concern for his political reputation, which rested on his predictions about the ease with which it could be obtained, produced in him, as the months passed, a desperate optimism about its prospects. He succumbed, in fact, to the seduction of wishful thinking and began perceiving in the faintest signs reasons to hope that a change of government was still possible.

On 10 June 1766, for example, after complaining to the Assembly committee of correspondence that the past year's fluctuations in the personnel of the British ministry had played havoc with his negotiations—" 'tis a kind of Labour in vain to attempt making Impressions on such moveable Materials; 'tis like writing on the Sands in a windy Day"— he welcomed the latest ministerial change: "if the present Ministry should be confirmed, as I sincerely pray they may, I hope another Winter will bring our Affairs all to a happy Conclusion."[67] But the reshuffled Rockingham

[66] John to Thomas Penn, 8 Feb. 1768, Penn Papers, Hist. Soc. Pa.

[67] This quotation and those that follow in this paragraph are from the following sources: Franklin to the Pennsylvania Assembly committee of correspondence, 10 June 1766, in Labaree, ed., *Papers of BF*, XIII, 299; Franklin to Galloway, 11 Oct. 1766, *ibid.*, 448; same to same, 13 Dec. 1766, *ibid.*, 522; Franklin to John Ross, 11 April 1767, Hist. Soc. Pa.; Franklin to Galloway, 8 Aug. 1767, William L. Clements Library, University of Michigan; Franklin to Thomas Livezey, 20 Feb. 1768, in Smyth, ed., *The Writings of Franklin*, V, 184.

ministry expired on 30 July and the Pitt-Grafton ministry replaced it. The new Secretary of State for the Southern Department, Lord Shelburne, was married to the niece of Thomas Penn's wife. Proprietary politicians gloated over this connection, declaring that it guaranteed that Shelburne would champion proprietary government, but Franklin nevertheless professed to be encouraged by the appointment. Shelburne was "of Opinion," he wrote Galloway on 11 October 1766, that "Mr. Penn ought to part with the government voluntarily, and said he had often told him so." "Nothing in my Power shall be wanting," he continued, "to push the Matter vigorously to a Conclusion if possible this Winter." By December Franklin's determination had not abated, for on the 13th he wrote Galloway that he and Richard Jackson were "making all the Impressions possible wherever we can be heard, preparatory to reviving the Petition." Came the spring of 1767 and the Doctor was once again lamenting the difficulties imposed upon him by the instability of the ministry, but he comforted himself and his friends in Pennsylvania with the information that "there is scarce a Man of Weight in or out of the Ministry that has not now a favorable Opinion of the Proposed Change of Government." By August the persistent disequilibrium in the ministry had made him despondent, and he broadly hinted to Galloway that royal government was unobtainable and that he might as well be recalled. But another change in the ministry in December 1767 and the appointment of Lord Hillsborough to be the Secretary of State for America revived his spirits, so that by 20 February 1768 he was telling a correspondent in Pennsylvania that Thomas Penn was terrified by the possibility of losing his government.

The Quaker Party leaders had committed themselves to royal government as wholeheartedly as Franklin had and wished for its attainment as ardently as he did. Therefore, they read his reports in the same spirit of wishful thinking as he wrote them and blotted out of their consciousness his occasional pessimistic passages. The result was that they permitted the reports to sustain their optimism about the prospects for royal government. Franklin, wrote William Allen to Thomas Penn in 1767, "keeps feeding his associates in mischief with hopes of wresting the power of government out of your hands . . . and they either really believe him, or pretend to do it."[68] A year later John Penn informed his uncle that the Quaker Party had "not yet lost sight of" its objective of a change of government. And Galloway, speaking at the same time, confirmed his assessment. The Quaker Party "had great expectations from the favour of the ministry," he declared in the midst of a diatribe against Dickinson's *Letters from a Pennsylvania Farmer*. "Such performances would injure the province at the British court, and show that they were as refractory as the other colonies, and they might thereby destroy their best hopes centered in their agent."[69]

By showing how the expectation of British favor created a fear of forfeiting it—and support for actions designed to

[68] 8 March 1767, Penn Papers, Hist. Soc. Pa.; the quotation immediately following is from John to Thomas Penn, 8 Feb. 1768, Penn Papers, Hist. Soc. Pa.
[69] [William Goddard], *The Partnership: or the History of the Rise and Progress of the Pennsylvania Chronicle* (Phila., 1770), 16.

obtain it—this last statement graphically reveals the rationale behind the politics of ingratiation. And it is appropriate that it does, for Galloway was the province's principal practitioner of these politics and in 1768 he used his power and prestige as Speaker (he had defeated Joseph Fox for the office in October 1766) to commit the Quaker Party to yet another trial of them, this time in response to the Townshend Acts.[70] Galloway's attitude toward Charles Townshend's legislation was unconventional (to put it mildly), for he professed to believe that it would not harm Pennsylvania. "I don't well see how the Publick Weal of the Province can be affected by it," he wrote Franklin on 9 October 1767.[71] He assumed, in fact, that the province might profit from the acts. The revenue they generated was to be used to pay colonial governors and judges. Would the crown use this money to pay proprietary officials, "Men Who are Named by its Subjects"? Galloway thought that it would not, that if the King paid American officials, he would appoint them, the governor of Pennsylvania no less than the governors of New York and Massachusetts. He believed, in other words, that the Townshend Acts presupposed royal government in Pennsylvania. In his view this provided an extra incentive for obeying them. Not only would obedience please the British government, which he hoped would reward the Quaker Party with royal government, but it would enable the party

[70] To my knowledge, the only previous writer who has perceived that the response of Galloway and his colleagues to the Townshend Acts was dictated by their desire to procure royal government is David L. Jacobson; see his *John Dickinson and the Revolution in Pennsylvania, 1764-1776* (Berkeley, 1965), 59, 60.

[71] APS.

to capitalize on the logic of the acts, which also seemed to dictate royal government.

Galloway realized that few people shared his view that the Townshend Acts contained a silver lining for Pennsylvania and that to appease those citizens who did not relish being taxed without representation a gesture of protest, preferably as innocuous as possible, was needed. One was made on 20 February 1768 when the Assembly's committee of correspondence, headed by Galloway and his friends, drafted instructions to Franklin and Jackson, enjoining them to "co-operate with the Agents of the other Colonies, in any decent and respectful Application to Parliament" protesting the Townshend Acts, but only if the other agents first took the initiative.[72] Then the Quaker Party leaders got down to the business of promoting obedience to the acts in Pennsylvania. This they did, not in the positive sense of preaching their virtues to the public, but in the negative one of discouraging overt acts of disobedience. Their principal effort along these lines lay in preventing the province's merchants from being pressured into adopting a nonimportation agreement, as they had done at the time of the Stamp Act.

Proprietary Party politicians behaved far differently than they had during the Stamp Act crisis. Instead of overtly and covertly inspiriting opposition to the Townshend Acts, they followed William Allen's lead in trying to blend in with the most cautious of their countrymen and in doing nothing until the petitioning process, as well as every other constitutional remedy, was exhausted.[73] Leading the opposition to the Townshend Acts was the Presbyterian Party,

[72] 8 *Pa. Arch.*, VII, 6168.

spearheaded by John Dickinson. In his famous *Farmers'*
Letters Dickinson urged nonimportation to nullify the acts.
His proposal initially had greater impact in other colonies than in his own, however. The merchants of Boston
adopted a nonimportation agreement in March 1768, those
of New York in April. The Philadelphia merchants met
in both months and listened to harangues from Dickinson
and Charles Thomson on the necessity of commercial coer-
cion, but they ignored their exhortations, just as they
ignored their "unrelenting" newspaper crusade for nonimportation.[74] Many traders agreed with Thomas Wharton that the Townshend Acts were less harmful than the
Stamp Act and did not demand the same measure of
resistance.[75] Many were persuaded by Galloway's newspaper articles that nonimportation was a New England
trick, designed to destroy Philadelphia's competitive commercial advantage.[76] But, most importantly, the merchants

[73] In the fall of 1768 Allen commented on a studiously deferential
petition from the Pennsylvania Assembly to the British government,
praying for relief from the Townshend Acts: "If it should be unfavor-
able to us, then, and not till then, shall we begin our Constitutional
war with our mother country—we will set up M[anu] F[act]ers and
provide for ourselves." At approximately the same time Allen drew
himself up in the best Whiggish fashion and refused, in his capacity as
Chief Justice of the provincial Supreme Court, to issue writs of assistance
to the Philadelphia customs collector. The apparent inconsistency in his
conduct is illustrative of his ambiguous position as a "Half-and-Half"
in Pennsylvania politics, a Presbyterian who was also a high proprietary official. For the Allen quotation, see Theodore Thayer, *Pennsyl-*
vania Politics and the Growth of Democracy 1740-1776 (Harrisburg,
1953), 144.

[74] See Arthur L. Jensen, *The Maritime Commerce of Colonial Phila-*
delphia (Madison, Wis., 1963), 174.

[75] Wharton to Franklin, 29 March 1768, Hist. Soc. Pa.

[76] See, e.g., his articles signed "A Chester County Farmer," *Pa.*
Gazette, 24 June 1768, and "A.B.," *Pa. Chronicle*, 25 July 1768.

were not as intimidated by pressure from supporters of nonimportation as their counterparts in other provinces were. Although Presbyterian Party "radicals" thundered away at them in the newspapers, their rhetoric was not supported by the force of public opinion or by the menaces of a mob. The mechanics and the tradesmen, who had been mobilized behind nonimportation in the other seaboard cities, in Philadelphia still took their lead from Galloway and his Quaker Party colleagues and acted as they had done during the Stamp Act crisis, as bulwarks of law and order, refusing to support nonimportation or to countenance any forcible attempts to nullify the Townshend Acts. "Great Pains have been taken in this City by some hot headed Men, to raise a Spirit of Violence against the late Act of Parliament," Galloway wrote Franklin on 17 October 1768, "but the Design was crushed in its Beginnings by our Friends, so effectively, that, I think, we shall not soon have it renewed."[77] In predicting that no violence would attend Pennsylvania's response to the Townshend Acts, Galloway was right. But in presuming that he and his colleagues could control the course of provincial politics over the whole period the acts were being challenged, he was as wrong about the popular temper as Franklin had recently been.

Galloway and his friends doubtless flattered themselves that by preventing nonimportation during the first half of 1768 they had piled up points with the British ministry, for they had not only promoted acquiescence to the Townshend Acts in Pennsylvania but had also sabotaged intercolonial efforts to subvert them. The operation of the New

[77] APS.

York nonimportation agreement was contingent on the adoption by Philadelphia of a similar one by 14 June, so when Philadelphia refused to cooperate, the New York agreement collapsed. Pennsylvania thwarted another attempt at concerted intercolonial opposition, too. The famous Massachusetts circular letter of 11 February 1768 proposing such a step reached Galloway (copies were sent to all House Speakers on the continent) during the Pennsylvania Assembly's spring recess. When the House reconvened in May, the letter was given one perfunctory reading, tabled, and ignored. This action made the Pennsylvania Assembly "a byword among the patriots throughout the colonies; it was responsible, they declared, for 'all the Bloodshed and Calamities' that might follow the refusal to preserve colonial unity against the British government."[78] Scorn for the politics of ingratiation found its voice in Philadelphia in the writings of "Pacificus." "How beautiful does this prudent, peaceable, dutiful and submissive behaviour of this province appear," wrote this sarcastic opponent of the Quaker Party on 16 July 1768. "What applause do we not deserve, and shall we not receive— From his Majesty's ministers? And what rewards will those worthy men be entitled to, whose loyalty to their sovereign, and duty to Great-Britain, have lulled and composed us into so deep a love of public tranquility?"[79]

Galloway and his fellow worthies were paid for their loyalty in far different coin than they expected—Lord Hillsborough's "circular letter" of 21 April 1768. This

[78] John C. Miller, *Origins of the American Revolution* (Boston, 1943), 261.

[79] David L. Jacobson, "The Puzzle of 'Pacificus,'" *Pennsylvania History*, XXXI (1964), 414.

ministerial mandate was addressed to each of the colonial governors and ordered them to make their assemblies "take no Notice" of the Massachusetts circular letter; if they showed "a Disposition to receive or give any Countenance to this seditious Paper," they were to be prorogued or dissolved immediately. Hillsborough's ukase aroused a storm in all segments of Pennsylvania society. The Presbyterian Party organized a massive public protest meeting on 30 July, and Galloway and the Quaker Party leaders, though less demonstrative, were no less agitated; "those persons who were the most moderate are now set in a flame and have joined the General Cry of Liberty," John Penn wrote his uncle.[80] The reasons for the ferment were familiar to the Penns, for they were the very ones which had inspired the royal government campaign. Hillsborough's order to the governors to dissolve uncooperative assemblies threatened to deprive Pennsylvania of one of its most precious rights, the right of its Assembly to sit upon its own adjournment, while his Lordship's order to the Assembly to disregard a communication from a sister colony seemed to be an exertion of naked dictatorial power in no way different from Thomas Penn's demand for an exemption of his estate from taxation. Given the province's animosity to the exercise of external control, Hillsborough's letter was bound to inflame it.

The letter was a disaster for Galloway and his Quaker Party colleagues, because it punctured the assumptions on which their policies were based. They had promised the public that royal government would be freer than proprietary government—that royal liberty would supplant pro-

---

[80] Miller, *Origins of the American Revolution*, 263.

prietary slavery, as their 1764 campaign slogan put it. But Hillsborough showed (if any more proof were needed) that a king's government could be as arbitrary as a proprietor's. His Lordship's letter also showed that the assumption informing the politics of ingratiation, that there would be reciprocity between Pennsylvania and the British ministry, was wrong; instead of returning favor for obedience, Hillsborough returned fire and brimstone. Galloway was naturally disheartened by Hillsborough's actions, and on 17 October 1768 he wrote Franklin lamenting how "truly discouraging" his Lordship's conduct was to "a People who wish well to the Mother Country, and by their Dutiful Behaviour during these Times of American Confusion have recommended themselves to the Crown."[81] This turned out to be an epitaph for the politics of ingratiation, although Galloway did not know it at the time.

When the Assembly convened in September, it felt compelled to respond to Hillsborough's letter. The Philadelphia public meeting of 30 July had suggested that it counter the minister's mandate by petitioning the King, Lords, and Commons against the Townshend Acts and by collaborating with the other colonies in opposing them. To assert its corporate integrity, the House reconsidered the Massachusetts circular letter, which it had earlier ignored, but it refused to comply with the Bay Colony's recommendation for intercolonial cooperation; still trying to please the British ministers, Galloway and his colleagues evidently reckoned that thwarting colonial unity would satisfy them, if anything could. Nevertheless, they recognized that some remonstrance would have to be made and saw to it that on

[81] APS.

22 September 1768 the Assembly adopted respectful petitions to the King, Lords, and Commons. These petitions
were praised on the floor of the House of Commons—one
member commended Pennsylvania for being the "only
Colony that has paid them the Respect of Petitioning on
this Occasion"[82]—but, like earlier expressions of British
goodwill, these compliments produced no compensations.

What did produce results was Franklin's letter to Galloway of 20 August 1768 describing a "long Audience" he
had just had with Hillsborough about the prospects for
royal government. The Secretary told him that there were
none, and Franklin took him at his word and abruptly
dropped the long quest for a change of government. "I
shall therefore move the Matter no farther during the Administration of a Minister that appears to have a stronger
Partiality for Mr. Penn than any of his Predecessors," he
wrote in disgust.[83] When this letter arrived in Philadelphia
at the end of October, it dumbfounded Galloway and his
friends, for in a stroke it annihilated their long-nurtured
hopes for royal government, hopes which had been buoyed
a fortnight earlier by the reception of a hint from Franklin that Hillsborough was "now disposed to favour the
Petition." These men were also excruciatingly embarrassed
by this communiqué, because it destroyed their credibility
as politicians. For four years they had been telling the people of Pennsylvania that royal government was a sure
thing. What would they tell them now? Furthermore, it
was evident that the policies they had pursued since 1764
had been grossly misconceived, for it now appeared that,

[82] Franklin to Galloway, 9 Jan. 1769, William L. Clements Library,
University of Michigan.
[83] *Ibid.*

no matter what the province had done to please the British ministry, it would not have been rewarded with royal government.

Galloway and his colleagues were dazed, disappointed, and demoralized by the letter of 20 August 1768 and were incensed with Franklin, whom they blamed for deceiving them about the prospect of royal government and for causing them to make political fools of themselves. The deeper their commitment had been to royal government, the deeper their anger with the Doctor; no man, therefore, was more provoked with him than Galloway. The correspondence between the two men proves it. Until the end of October 1768 Galloway wrote Franklin a long, chatty letter almost every week. After receiving Franklin's letter of 20 August, he virtually stopped writing. From 6 November 1768 until 12 August 1769 he wrote nothing. Three months passed before he wrote again (8 November 1769), and after that he did not write until 16 May 1770.[84] Down to the Revolution letters followed at long intervals. All were short, stiff, and impersonal. What happened is clear: Franklin's letter of 20 August 1768 affronted Galloway and caused a split between the two men which was never repaired. What is more, the corrosive effect of nursing his indignation against Franklin and brooding over the wreck of his political program seems to have contributed to a rather serious illness which befell Galloway in the spring of 1769 and prompted him to retire from the Speaker's

---

[84] The correspondence between Franklin and Galloway can be followed in the card catalogue of the editorial offices of the Papers of Benjamin Franklin, Yale University Library.

chair for a season—so deep was the wound inflicted by the 20 August letter.[85]

Another of its casualties was the political motivation of the Quaker Party leaders. The expectation of royal government had, since 1765, provided them with the incentive to promote obedience to the policies of the British ministry. With the expectation destroyed by Franklin's letter, the incentive vanished. One immediate result was that in the fall of 1768 the Townshend Acts were suddenly without supporters in Pennsylvania. Most Quaker Party leaders had never liked them anyway, and they were now so angry with the British ministry for letting their past loyalty go unrequited and loosing Hillsborough upon them that they were not about to do anything to promote the acts. But neither would they nullify them by supporting nonimportation. This was the program of Dickinson and his devotees and was, on that account, taboo. Thus, in the fall of 1768 the Quaker Party leaders had no position on the major political issue of the day. They were adrift on a sea of indecision and ineffectuality—men who had lost their political goals, credibility, and confidence. Though continuing to hold seats in the Assembly, they became passive spectators in the struggle over the Townshend Acts. Galloway, for example, after recovering from his illness, went into a kind of self-imposed exile, spending the spring of 1770, when the fate of the nonimportation agreement was being

---

[85] Galloway's illness first began to interfere with his duties on 15 May 1769, and a week later he relinquished the Speaker's chair; his problems were compounded by what was diagnosed as a sunstroke, which he suffered about this time. 8 *Pa. Arch.*, VII, 6378, 6386; Cadwalader Evans to Franklin, 11 June 1769, APS.

contested in Philadelphia, on his father-in-law's farm in Bucks County.

The demoralization of the Quaker Party leaders had a profound effect on political alignments in Pennsylvania, especially in Philadelphia. Until the fall of 1768 they had succeeded in keeping both wings of the party in the metropolis, the merchants and the mechanics, working in harness to present a reasonably solid front of opposition against nonimportation. But with the collapse of their hopes for royal government they lost the incentive to impose party discipline on their supporters and left them to their own devices. Concurrently, Presbyterian Party leaders, having failed the preceding spring to cajole the merchants into voluntarily adopting nonimportation, tried to mobilize the city's populace to put pressure on them to act. The freshly foot-loose mechanics became the focus of their recruiting efforts.

It is difficult to define the term "mechanic" exactly, because eighteenth-century Philadelphians used it so carelessly. "Artificers, manufacturers, tradesmen, mechanics"— this whole mouthful of terms had roughly the same meaning to the editor of the *Pennsylvania Journal* on 24 May 1770, and his fellow citizens would have used them interchangeably as well. Philadelphians were quite clear, however, about what this order of men did and what rung of the social ladder it occupied. Mechanics worked with their hands, but many of them were also businessmen. With the possible exception of the shipyards, there were no equivalents in eighteenth-century Philadelphia of our modern factories with armies of industrial laborers. Indeed, even

certain groups of shipyard workers—ship carpenters, for
example—were specifically called tradesmen.[86] But the
more typical tradesman-mechanic was the craftsman who,
usually in conjunction with a journeyman or a partner, produced and sold his own goods. Thus, he was frequently
an incipient entrepreneur, a small businessman, a man on
the make. His fellow citizens ranked him among "the mid-
dling sort of people,"[87] although the term "lower middle
class" might have been more appropriate for many mechanics, who nevertheless were as ambitious and as determined
to rise in the world as any of their more established
colleagues.

Presbyterian Party leaders tried to enlist the mechanics'
support for nonimportation by appealing to their vanity
and to their enlightened self-interest. They flattered their
egos by addressing them as "the useful and necessary Inhabitants of this Province"[88] and as the repositories and
guardians of its freedoms. The repetition of these encomi-
ums, coupled with the compliment of being continually and
specifically appealed to in the public prints as potential
saviors of the province's liberties, helped win the mechanics over to nonimportation; it also instilled in them a group
consciousness and esprit de corps which made them a political force to be reckoned with in the future. The appeal to

[86] "A Pennsylvanian," writing in the *Pa. Gazette*, 23 Aug. 1770,
wrote of a certain proposal that it would "of Course considerably effect
the Ship-carpenters and all other Tradesmen employed in fitting out
Vessels to Sea."

[87] See, e.g., "Publius," writing in the *Pa. Chronicle*, 29 Aug. — 5
Sept. 1772.

[88] "A Brother Chip," *Pa. Gazette*, 27 Sept. 1770.

enlightened self-interest was a master stroke, for what mechanic could resist the opportunity, by supporting nonimportation, to thwart British tyranny while at the same time sealing the province off from every kind of competing manufactured product made in the mother country? The inspiration for selling nonimportation in this way to an audience of artificers probably came from the Presbyterian Party's master organizer, Charles Thomson; it was, in part, a projection of his own needs as a struggling iron manufacturer and distiller.[89]

The success of Thomson and his colleagues in drumming up public support for nonimportation and bringing it to bear on the merchants, together with the failure of the Pennsylvania Assembly's and the merchants' own petitions to obtain relief from the Townshend Acts, prompted the merchants to take the plunge into nonimportation in March 1769. A committee appointed to supervise the agreement soon fell under the control of Thomson, James Mease, and other Presbyterian Party members, and by the winter of 1769-70 so few substantial merchants remained on the committee that it "lost all pretense of speaking for those whose interests and views it was presumed to represent, especially the dry goods importers who were most deeply affected by the non-importation agreement."[90]

The committee's principal objective was to broaden support for nonimportation. If we can credit an opaque passage in a Thomson letter, written almost two decades after the event, it established enforcement subcommittees in the

---

[89] For Thomson's business interests, see Arthur M. Schlesinger, *The Colonial Merchants and the American Revolution* (New York, 1968), 118.

[90] Jensen, *Maritime Commerce*, 183.

rural and frontier counties.[91] Such an action would have been consonant with the Presbyterian Party's concern to retain and expand its following among the province's farmers. Beginning in the fall of 1768 it publicly courted and flattered them exactly as it did the mechanics[92] and constantly represented the two groups' interests and its expectations of them as identical. A good example of how the committee worked was its handling of the first apparent violation of the nonimportation agreement, a shipment of malt which arrived in Philadelphia in July 1769. Instead of adjudicating the matter itself, it called a mass meeting of the town's citizens and put the matter to their vote; the purpose was, of course, to promote massive participation in and identification with nonimportation.[93]

The first major crack in the intercolonial nonimportation agreement came in May 1770 when the Newport, Rhode Island, merchants unilaterally abrogated it. A mass meeting of Philadelphia mechanics on 23 May denounced the Rhode Islanders and vowed to "endeavour to render the non-importation, as it now stands, permanent."[94] What the mechanics proposed, in other words, was a perpetual protective tariff, so well had they come to like nonimportation. A meeting of the subscribers to the original nonimportation agreement was held on 5 June and agreed "almost unanimously" to persist in it, a result which one disaffected merchant ascribed to Thomson, who as "the

[91] To David Ramsay, 4 Nov. 1786, New-York Historical Society *Collections* (1878), 218-19.

[92] See, e.g., "A Tradesman," *Pa. Chronicle*, 10 Oct. 1768, "To the Farmers and Tradesmen of Pennsylvania."

[93] For an account of this meeting, see *Pa. Journal*, 20 July 1769.

[94] *Pa. Gazette*, 24 May 1770.

Leader, all along for the opposition . . . Introduc'd tis suposed the body of disaffected Mechanics, among the Subscribers, who were only appointed to meet & by this Artifice Carry'd his point."[95] Even New York's defection from the agreement did not immediately shake Philadephia. At a 14 July mass meeting of the citizens, joined by "a great number from the country,"[96] the resolution was taken to adhere to the nonimportation agreement come what may.

The ardent support of Philadelphia's mechanics for nonimportation was motivated, in the first place, by a recognition that the policy paid. "This Province has, during the Non-Importation, increased more in Wealth than it ever did, in any equal Space of Time, since its first Settlement," wrote a newspaper commentator on 23 August 1770.[97] Because of the prohibition of competing British goods, the mechanics shared fully in the boom. As a "Tradesman" wrote in a broadside on 24 September 1770: "The Tradesmen who have suffered by the Non-Importation Agreement are but few, when compared to the Number of those who have received great Benefit from it."[98] Benjamin Franklin also molded the mechanics' attitude. Hillsborough's rejection of Pennsylvania's request for royal government in the August 1768 interview had the effect of "radicalizing" the Doctor. With royal government declared to be unobtainable, Franklin's incentive to please the British ministry or to counsel his friends in Pennsylvania to please it drastically decreased (he was still somewhat restrained in his actions toward it by concern for the security

[95] Quoted in Jensen, *Maritime Commerce*, 189.
[96] *Pa. Journal*, 14 July 1770.
[97] "A Pennsylvanian," *Pa. Gazette*, 23 Aug. 1770.
[98] University of Pennsylvania Library.

of his postmastership). Unlike Galloway, Franklin bore no personal ill will toward Dickinson or Thomson, a Philadelphia neighbor with whom he corresponded regularly, and therefore was not emotionally inhibited from supporting their program of nonimportation. Beginning in January 1769 in letters to Galloway, Thomson, and other Pennsylvania correspondents, this is precisely what he did.[99] His letters were invaluable to Thomson, because of his popularity with Philadelphia's tradesmen and mechanics, who idolized him. Thomson publicized the letters among these men, and they helped bring them to his and Dickinson's side.[100] Because they did and because Franklin dared correspond with and support Thomson, the henchman of Galloway's arch enemy, Dickinson, his letters widened his split with his erstwhile ally.

Philadelphia's dry goods merchants refused to accept the results of the mass meeting of 14 July 1770 at which eternal fealty was sworn to nonimportation. By careful canvassing among themselves, they worked up strong sentiment for abandoning the agreement and managed to carry a vote to that effect at a public meeting of their brethren in September. Still somewhat shell-shocked by the collapse of the royal government campaign, Galloway and the Quaker Party leadership took no stand on this issue. They also saw a strategic reason for remaining noncommittal, hoping such

---

[99] See, e.g., Franklin to Galloway, 29 Jan. and 9 March 1769, William L. Clements Library, University of Michigan; Franklin to Thomson, 18 March 1770, in Smyth, ed., *Writings of Franklin*, v, 251-54; Franklin to Galloway, 21 March 1770, in Stan V. Henkels *Catalogue*, 13 Dec. 1921.

[100] See John J. Zimmerman, "Charles Thomson, 'The Sam Adams of Philadelphia,'" *Mississippi Valley Historical Review*, XLV (1958), 477.

a posture would enable them to muddle through without alienating either wing of their party in Philadelphia. But the tradesmen and mechanics resented their failure to endorse a continuation of nonimportation and allied themselves with the men who did—Thomson, Dickinson, and their party. "We are all in Confusion," wrote Galloway on 27 September 1770, on the eve of the Assembly elections. "The White Oaks and Mechanicks or many of them have left the old Ticket and 'tis feared will go over to the Presbyterians."[101] Go over they did and their votes elected Dickinson to one of the city's seats in the Assembly. Galloway's stock, on the other hand, fell so low that he was obliged to seek election from Bucks County.

The 1770 election signaled the disintegration of the Quaker Party, as the province had long known it. Although it maintained the support of some wealthy city merchants, it lost its urban working-class base and became a party whose power and orientation were primarily rural and whose purpose was primarily self-perpetuation. In this respect it resembled the Proprietary Party, whose members were principally concerned with preserving the government and their places under it. By 1770, in fact, a considerable community of interest had grown up between the two parties. The convergence began with the cooperation between Israel Pemberton and William Allen in opposing the royal government forces in the 1764 election. Thereafter the initiative came from the leaders of both parties, working within the framework of the accomplishments of the royal government campaign. Accomplishments of the royal government campaign? As acrimonious as it was,

[101] To Franklin, 27 Sept. 1770, APS.

it produced much that was positive and paved the way for the smoothest executive-legislative relations in America from 1770 to 1776. During the course of the campaign (including the preliminary skirmishing in the late 1750s) some of the most intractable and inflammatory issues between the two branches of government were resolved. The Assembly conceded to the executive the right to amend its supply bills and to have a voice in the expenditure of the monies it raised. It also exempted Penn's quit rents from payment in legal tender paper. For his part, Penn conceded to the Assembly the right to tax his estate in a manner it considered equitable. Problems which were not solved were carefully defined and put to negotiation in 1765. What the royal government campaign had given Pennsylvania was the resolution of some of its difficulties and an *éclaircissement* of the remainder, a situation which was conducive to political peace, if the province's principals were willing to improve it to that end.

Thomas Penn, for one, was more than willing. For him the royal government campaign had been a nightmare—threatening, expensive, exhaustive, and aggravating. At its conclusion he wanted nothing so much as to encourage the "possibility of burying the former Contests, and living in Peace" with his Quaker Party adversaries.[102] Therefore, he extended the hand of friendship to his opponents. To conciliate them, "to reconcile Partys,"[103] he took two steps: he tried to avoid rekindling unresolved conflicts with the Assembly, such as the one over the imposition of control through inflexible instructions; and he ordered his parti-

---

[102] To William Smith, 1 April 1766, Penn Papers, Hist. Soc. Pa.
[103] To John Penn, 14 Dec. 1765, Penn Papers, Hist. Soc. Pa.

sans to defer to the Quaker Party, to back away from con-
tending with it, to grant it, as far as they could, hegemony
in the province.[104] His advice conformed to the sentiments
of his supporters, who as early as 2 March 1766 were telling Quaker Party politicians that, "as the affairs of the
Petition are at an end, 'tis best for all Parties to be at
Peace,"[105] and who were willing, in order to promote that
end, "to set still" in the Assembly elections of 1 October
1767, "to convince the better sort of Quakers we . . . were
willing to let them order matters to their liking."[106] Although passivity was the characteristic Proprietary Party
posture, Thomas Penn's directives now elevated it to official policy. It was he, after all, who was now employing
the politics of ingratiation.

To make peace, no less than war, it takes two parties.
After the failure of the royal government campaign the
Quaker Party was ready to bury the hatchet and live in
peace with Penn and the Proprietary Party. Its main motive was fear of the Presbyterians. After the Presbyterians
had split with the Proprietary Party in 1766 because of
apprehensions about an American bishop, several of them
made overtures to the Quakers for a rapprochement.
Samuel Purviance, for example, was "so much more apprehensive of the Danger from the church, and displeas'd
with their double Conduct," that he was "fully determin'd
to meet the Q[uaker]s half Way, shake Hands and
be Friends . . . and endeavour to unite with them in

---

[104] To John Penn, 8 Nov. 1766, Penn Papers, Hist. Soc. Pa.

[105] Thomas Wharton to Benjamin Franklin, 2 March 1766, in Labaree, ed., *Papers of BF*, XIII, 191.

[106] William Allen to Thomas Penn, 8 Oct. 1767, Penn Papers, Hist.
Soc. Pa.

Opposition."[107] The Quakers, however, did not want the Presbyterians' company, for they regarded them as religious imperialists, intent on imposing their denomination on every man in the province.[108] Many Friends, indeed, had already begun flirting with measures which they had long opposed, as a means of counteracting the Presbyterians. Thomas Wharton, for example, a staunch supporter of Franklin and of royal government, tentatively endorsed the conversion of the governor's council into a legislative upper house, a pet project of the Proprietary Party, in order to arrest Presbyterian influence.[109] On the matter of an American bishop, Hugh Neil, an Anglican missionary, wrote a British superior on 16 November 1764 that "many of the principal Quakers wish for it in hopes it might be a check to the growth of Presbyterianism, which they dread," a statement which Wharton confirmed in a letter to Franklin of 26 April 1766.[110] The support by important Quaker Party politicians like Wharton of the religious and political objectives of the Proprietary Party, the resolution and clarification, midst the strife of the royal government campaign, of the political problems which had divided the two groups in the past, and the passivity which Thomas Penn imposed upon his governor and partisans led not only to a remarkable period of executive-legislative harmony from 1770 to 1776 but also to a kind of tacit alliance between the Quaker

[107] Purviance to Ezra Stiles, 1 Nov. 1766, in Dexter, ed., *Itineraries . . . of Ezra Stiles*, 556-57.

[108] See, e.g., Cadwalader Evans to William Franklin, 10 Feb. 1767, APS.

[109] Labaree, ed., *Papers of BF*, XI, 484-85.

[110] William S. Perry, ed., *Papers Relating to the History of the Church in Pennsylvania, A.D., 1680-1778* ([Hartford, Conn.], 1871), 368; Labaree, ed., *Papers of BF*, XIII, 251.

and Proprietary Parties, which lasted until Independence destroyed the political influence of both groups. Galloway acknowledged the collaboration on 12 October 1772. Commenting on the loss of some of the Quaker Party's traditional urban supporters, he wrote "that should it ever be my lot to stand in Need of Friendship, I should not know where to look for it among the latter, while I have a moral Assurance of meeting [with it] unasked among the former [the Proprietary Party]."[111] Thomson noted it in the winter of 1774-75. "A great majority of the Assembly was composed of men in the Proprietary and Quaker interest," he wrote, "who heretofore opposed to each other, were now uniting, the one from motives of policy, the other from principles of religion."[112] And Christopher Marshall and Thomas Paine remarked on it at the critical Assembly election of 1 May 1776. "Quakers, Papists, Church, Allen family, with all the Proprietary Party, were never seemingly so happily united as at this election," Marshall observed, while Paine as the "Forester" railed against the union of "testimonizing Quakers" and "proprietary dependents."[113]

If the election of October 1770 signaled the disintegration of the Quaker Party, it heralded the arrival of the Presbyterian Party. To its co-religionists on the farm and frontier it now added Philadelphia's workingmen (here, finally, was the coalition between the "ordinary" elements of the east and west, which historians have previously at-

[111] To Franklin, APS.

[112] To William Henry Drayton, n.d., New-York Historical Society *Collections* (1878), 280-81.

[113] William Duane, ed., *Extracts from the Diary of Christopher Marshall . . .* (Albany, 1877), 68; *Pa. Journal*, 8 May 1776.

tributed to the march of the Paxton Boys.) To Dickinson and Thomson it added Benjamin Franklin. With its stolid support among the German church groups, it promised to be the party of the future in the province and afforded the anti-establishment ambiance which attracted the aggressive men who spearheaded the Revolution in Pennsylvania— the peripatetic revolutionaries like Paine and Young, the patrician "radicals" like Reed and Mifflin, the intellectuals like Cannon and Rush, and the popular favorites like Matlack and Roberdeau. Thomson (for after 1770 it was he who took the helm of the Presbyterian Party) and his colleagues did not repeat the Proprietary Party's error during the royal government campaign of allowing a newly gained constituency to escape after the crisis which produced it had passed. From the collapse of the nonimportation agreement in September 1770 until armed resistance to Britain began, the Presbyterian Party assiduously cultivated Philadelphia's mechanics, using the same approach—appeals to their vanity and self-interest—with which it had won them over in the first place. Consider, for example, the party's efforts in 1772 to portray itself to the mechanics as a group devoted to the promotion of their welfare by making the government recognize and respond to their economic needs. The party's program as presented by its newspaper writers[114] was not doctrinaire; it opposed some kinds of government interference in the economy and supported others. It opposed a leather inspection act passed by the Quaker Party because it would burden the tanners and

[114] So far from being the quiet year it is generally thought to be, 1772 percolated with controversy, with which all three of the major newspapers, the *Gazette*, *Journal*, and *Chronicle*, teem. Curiously, the *Pennsylvania Packet* carried little, if any, political news.

because (with an eye to the lower-middle- and middle-class consumers) it would raise the price of shoes; it opposed an excise on spirituous liquors because it threatened the small retailer with inquisitorial regulations and because (with another glance to the mechanic-consumer) it would raise the price of liquor for the "men at the forges, the bricklayers, the carpenters, the ship carpenters, reapers &c";[115] and it opposed the operations of the British vice-admiralty court as intolerable intrusions in the workaday world of America. On the other hand, it favored government initiative in raising revenue by converting the excise to an import duty on spirits (thus assisting the local distiller), and it wanted the government to remedy the abuse of vendues, auctions at which cheap merchandise was sold, undercutting not only the established dry goods merchants but also the local artificers. Sponsoring these programs, encouraging Philadelphia's tradesmen to form political organizations, like the Patriotic Society, established in August 1772,[116] and assisting their efforts to make the Assembly more accountable by compelling it to publish weekly proceedings in the newspapers (as it began doing in January 1773) solidified the Presbyterian Party's hold on the mechanics. Philadelphia's monolithic opposition to the Tea Act (which, by conjuring up the possibility of British merchandising monopolies, threatened the interests of the mechanics as much as those of the merchants) testified to the success of the Presbyterian Party, which led and orchestrated it. The Stamp Act crisis, when a large body of me-

[115] "One of the Good People of Philadelphia," Pa. *Journal*, 13 Jan. 1773.

[116] For the "fundamental articles" of the Patriotic Society, see *Pa. Gazette*, 17 Aug. 1772.

chanics had defended the person of a proponent of the royal prerogative, was only a memory now.

Reflecting on the opposition to the Tea Act in Philadelphia, Joseph Reed wrote on 27 December 1773 that because of the "frequent appeals" to the citizenry it would be "more and more difficult to repress the rising spirit of the people."[117] Reed knew whereof he spoke, for by the spring of 1774 the rising spirit of numbers of ordinary Philadelphians was the motive force of the Presbyterian Party, now increasingly called the Whig Party. The mechanic, whose political consciousness had been aroused by the party and whose stake in the colony's economy had been catered to by it, was intensely jealous of his rights and was not prepared to let a government in London abridge them. Therefore, as the revolutionary agitation in Pennsylvania ran its complicated course through the complex interplay of three parties, he functioned as the point of the popular party's spear, and when the Presbyterian-Whig Party split in the spring of 1776 over the future of the charter form of government and over the pace of the repudiation of British authority, he swung Pennsylvania behind the movement for Independence and brought her into the new nation with a new constitution.

[117] To Lord Dartmouth, 27 Dec. 1773, in Reed, *Life and Correspondence of Joseph Reed*, I, 55.

CONCLUSION

The Implications of the Royal
Government Movement

WE HAVE demonstrated that the advocates of royal government were concentrated in Philadelphia and, almost
monolithically, in the Pennsylvania Assembly (27 of 30
members present voted to support it on 23 May 1764).
We have also demonstrated that, as in most human deci-
sions, there were plural, rather than singular, reasons for
the preference for royal government: many Philadelphians
believed that it would restore law and order to the province; some Assemblymen were beguiled by Franklin's
arguments on its behalf, while others saw it as a source of
office and personal profit. But we have insisted that one
principal factor prompted the Assemblymen to support
royal government: exasperation and outrage, which in 1764
could no longer be contained, over Thomas Penn's persistent efforts to impose policies on them from England without their consent, which violated what they considered to
be their rights and privileges. Beginning in the early 1750s,
Penn used inflexible instructions to his deputies to try to
control the revenue which the Assembly raised through
the provincial excise and through loans of paper money to
the inhabitants at interest. In 1755 and for a decade thereafter he tried, using the same instrumentalities, to force
the House to exempt his property from taxes. The Assembly responded to his actions by employing every conceiva-

ble channel of constitutional protest—petitions, agents, remonstrances, and so on. But these maneuvers failed and, with its patience and remedies exhausted, it tried in 1764 to overthrow his government. The Assemblymen and their supporters who countenanced this effort were not typical of colonists in other parts of America, for they were mostly Quakers who were by training and profession accommodating—"meek and long suffering," as they liked to style themselves (Thomas Penn and his followers would have insisted that they honored their precepts more in the breach than in the observance). How significant it was, then, that rather than accept the sustained, systematic violation of their rights by a ruler with whom they had no contact and over whom they had no control, they attempted to overturn his government. If Quakers displayed such a disposition in 1764, there can be no doubt about how citizens in other colonies, for whom conciliation was not a religious canon, would respond to similar provocations.

The majority of Pennsylvanians did not, as we have demonstrated, support the campaign against proprietary government, but it was not because they approved of, or were prepared to acquiesce in, autocratic external control. Far from it. When Penn's control of the expenditure of the excise was first suggested, Attorney General Tench Francis predicted that such a policy would precipitate "a downright Civil War in the Province, the people would hold out to the last as pro Aris & Focis," while Richard Hockley feared that the citizenry would cut the throat of any deputy who tried to control their excise money.[1] In

---

[1] Francis to Penn, 9 Feb. 1753; Hockley to Penn, 4 Aug. 1754; both in the Penn Papers, Hist. Soc. Pa.

1759 James Hamilton revealed the depth of popular opposition to external control by admitting that not a single person in the province favored Penn's attempt to force the Assembly to exempt his estate from taxes.[2] Penn himself provided the most decisive evidence of this attitude by confessing to the British ministry in 1756 that, even if his enemies, the Quakers, were purged from provincial government, he could not guarantee that those who replaced them would pass the laws he demanded.[3]

Why, then, did citizens who opposed external control oppose the effort to rid the province of a government which so imperiously exercised it? There were two reasons. In the first place, many of the people at large were not directly the victims of external control and were not, therefore, as consumed with indignation against it as some of the preceding quotations imply. The rights and privileges which Penn's instructions abridged were those which pertained particularly to the Assembly, were what might be called corporate rights—the right of the House (as it conceived it) to pass supply bills without amendment and to dispose of the people's money as it saw fit. Numbers of people in the province did not personally "feel" the violation of these "rights," and although they opposed external control, they did not share the resentment of their representatives upon whom Penn directly inflicted it. The second reason the people at large opposed royal government was the ineffectuality of its advocates, who operated under restraints which prevented them from making it appear to

[2] Hamilton, "Some Observations on Mr. Penn's Instructions," 18 June 1759, Penn Papers, Hist. Soc. Pa.
[3] Penn to Morris, 13 March 1756, Penn Papers, Hist. Soc. Pa.

be an acceptable alternative to the proprietary regime. Franklin, as we have seen, could not reveal to the public the assurances he privately gave the Assembly that the province's privileges would be safe under royal government, for fear that his patrons in England would repudiate the commitments he ascribed to them. He compounded this difficulty by grossly misjudging the popularity of royal government, assuming that the mere mention of direct government by the King would send people streaming to his standard and that, therefore, it was unnecessary to sell it to the public. What the prospect of royal government actually did was repel the people, overwhelming numbers of whom viewed it with trepidation; in fact, some 15,000 citizens signed petitions against it, whereas only 3,500 signed in support of it, a unique measure of the popularity of the British monarchy on the eve of the revolutionary agitation.

The royal government movement gives us this reading on the attitudes and mentality of Pennsylvanians in 1764: an overwhelming number of them feared the government of George III, while almost all of them opposed external control of provincial affairs. The resistance to external control varied in intensity with the extent of exposure to it. The Assembly, upon whom it was systematically inflicted over several years, was finally provoked into trying to overturn Penn's government. Had the citizenry at large been similarly victimized, it would doubtless have responded in the same way, probably with more alacrity, since it was not as inhibited by the accommodating imperatives of Quakerism as the Assemblymen were. Had the government of George III been the agent trying to impose direct external control, its unpopularity would surely have provoked a conflagration very quickly. That the flames were contained at the time of the Stamp Act is not really an anomaly, because the proponents of royal government kept order to promote the success of their campaign to relieve the province of the rigors of control exercised externally by the proprietors. They prevailed over fellow citizens who were opposed, in the broadest sense, to control exercised externally by the King. And they rapidly lost control of provincial politics to these people. Does this not suggest that by 1764 Pennsylvanians were temperamentally prepared for the Revolution which occurred twelve years later?

Did the forces which produced this frame of mind operate in the other colonies? Pennsylvania's animosity toward royal government seems to have been a product of Old World grudges against princes which the citizens carried across the sea and nurtured in the New World. Since most of the settlers of America had migrated from Europe because of dissatisfaction with conditions for which they could directly or indirectly blame crowned rulers, there was a tremendous reservoir of ill will toward royalty throughout America, although nowhere was it possible to measure it with the statistical precision afforded by the royal government campaign. Because Pennsylvania contained unusually large numbers of recently arrived Germans, who had been grievously oppressed by the potentates of their native land, it may have harbored more resentment toward royalty than its sister colonies, but of this we cannot be certain. Suffice it to say that ill will toward royalty was pervasive, though muted, throughout the continent.

Pennsylvanians opposed external control because by the middle of the eighteenth century they wanted to be the masters of their own destiny, wanted what the twentieth century calls "self-determination." Two factors produced this passion for autonomy: historical circumstance and environment. The Quaker settlers of the province wanted to govern themselves—they "despise all Dominion and dignity that is not in themselves," wrote Governor John Blackwell to William Penn on 13 January 1689[4]—and transmitted this temper to succeeding generations. But even had they not been determined to govern themselves according to their own lights, the early settlers of Pennsylvania would have been forced to use their own resources, ideas, and instincts to run the colony, because little or no direction emanated from England after the beginning of the eighteenth century. Soon after the century turned, William Penn became physically and mentally incapable of governing the province and, for years after his death, Pennsylvania drifted, while his heirs fought over his patrimony in the courts. Neglected by the proprietary family, the province was forced to govern itself, and by the time Thomas Penn took over in 1746 its people regarded de facto self-government almost as a prescriptive right.

The second force shaping Pennsylvania's mid-century mentality was the province's physical environment, or

---

[4] Lloyd MSS, Hist. Soc. Pa. Recently, Professor Gary Nash has found the desire for "local autonomy" strong and manifest among the populace in the province's first decade and sees it as one of the motivating forces in provincial politics from then onward. Nash, *Quakers and Politics: Pennsylvania, 1681-1726* (Princeton, 1968), 97, 126, 129, 201, 210, 231, 248.

rather the people's success in subduing it and fashioning from the wilderness a flourishing, expanding society. Pennsylvanians were intensely proud of this achievement and felt that it made them superior to the inhabitants of the Old World. Benjamin Franklin voiced this pride in 1754 by maintaining that, in comparison to their British cousins, Americans had the "most merit," because they had "most contributed to enlarge Britain's empire and commerce, encrease her strength, her wealth, and the number of her people, at the risque of their own lives and private fortunes in new and strange countries."[5] A corollary of this conclusion was that, having more merit than the British, the Americans deserved more political privileges. "There is a Power in the Crown," wrote Franklin on 18 December 1755, "for the farther Encouragement and Reward of such Merit, to grant additional Liberties and Priveleges, not used in England."[6] The bonuses he seems to have meant were those extraordinary privileges which the Pennsylvania Assembly had acquired during the long period of proprietary neglect, so that in his mind and in the minds of those whose thinking he reflected the American success in settling the wilderness entitled the colonists to the kind of functional self-government which Pennsylvania was exercising at Thomas Penn's accession in 1746.

It is clear that the forces just described operated over the same or longer periods of time in the other North Ameri-

---

[5] Labaree, ed., *Papers of BF*, V, 451; see also *ibid.*, 447, and VI, 229.

[6] *Ibid.*, VI, 299. See also Pennsylvania Assembly message, 25 Nov. 1755, *ibid.*, 264. For another statement of this point, see James Otis, *The Rights of the British Colonies Asserted and Proved* in Bernard Bailyn, ed., *Pamphlets of the American Revolution* (Cambridge, 1965), 436.

can colonies: almost all were settled by sectaries or by other peoples disaffected with their native societies who transmitted to their posterity the desire for free and unrestricted development which brought them to the New World; all forged strong and sophisticated political institutions with little help or direction from the mother country; and all were filled with pride—and pretensions— because they had subdued the wilderness and pushed the frontiers back with flourishing settlements. Did these forces produce in the other colonies the same self-governing temper as they did in Pennsylvania? That no colony except Pennsylvania tried during the 1750s and early 1760s to overthrow its existing government only proves that no colony except Pennsylvania experienced a determined attempt to impose political reforms from the outside during this period. When the French and Indian War was over, the other colonies caught up with Pennsylvania, in the sense that with the Sugar Act and the Stamp Act they were subjected to the same exertions of external control as Thomas Penn had applied before and during the war. The promptness and determination with which they opposed these acts showed that they were every bit as averse to external control as Pennsylvania had been, that the forces which had created in the Quaker Commonwealth a passion for autonomy and an abhorrence of outside interference produced the same mentality across the continent, and that only an absence of provocation prevented its earlier expression elsewhere.

As we have seen in the preceding pages, the people of Pennsylvania were impelled to try to overthrow Penn's government in 1764, not by indignation at a single instance of proprietary encroachment, but by exasperation at the efforts of a decade to impose the proprietary will upon them. The experience of the American colonies as a whole in the decade after 1764 was, of course, similar. They revolted against George III in 1776, not because of anger at a single act of his ministers, but because of accumulated outrage at a long series of attempts to force them to obey acts they opposed. In both cases it was the persistence of the exercise of external control which precipitated the attempted revolution in government. And this is precisely what we should expect, since men determined to govern themselves can excuse an isolated infringement of their power but cannot tolerate a settled, systematic effort against it. Therefore, it appears that in studying the period between 1764 and 1776 too much attention has been given to individual episodes like the Stamp Act and the Tea Act on the assumption that their singular odiousness or provocativeness was of transcendent importance in causing the Revolution. Rather, it appears that these acts were significant primarily because they were links in a chain of efforts to impose external control on people who were unwilling to accept it; another concatenation of entirely different kinds of acts of external control would, it appears, have produced the same results in America in 1776.

What is of importance, then, in the view of this writer, is not so much the character of the acts passed by the British after 1764 as the character of the people for whose governance they were intended. If, during the 1750s and early 1760s, their attitudes were similar to those of the people of Pennsylvania, as there is every reason to believe they were, then the crucial revolution "in the minds and hearts of the people," which John Adams believed "was effected before the war commenced,"[7] had, in fact, already taken place, and a revolution against Britain was insured as soon as she chose to try to establish her supremacy in the colonies. This, of course, is not a new idea, but by examining Pennsylvania during the years leading up to 1764 we have hopefully given it new force.

[7] To Hezekiah Niles, 13 Feb. 1818, in Charles Francis Adams, ed., *The Works of John Adams* (10 vols., Boston, 1850-56), X, 282-83.

Bibliographical Essay

THE STARTING place for any study of Pennsylvania colonial history is the Historical Society of Pennsylvania, one of the country's great research facilities. The collections I exploited most at the Historical Society were the Letterbooks and Official Correspondence of Thomas Penn, both of which are now available on microfilm. Other indispensable collections are the Pemberton Papers, the Etting Collection, which in part supplements the Pemberton Papers, the John Smith Manuscripts (formerly in the Library Company), the Shippen Papers, the Peters Papers, the Hamilton Papers, the Isaac Norris Letterbooks, the Gratz Collection, the Waln Collection, and the Thomas Wharton Letterbooks. This listing by no means exhausts the store of manuscripts at the Historical Society, examination of which is a prerequisite to understanding the period.

The American Philosophical Society holds the largest collection of Benjamin Franklin manuscripts in the country. It also has an important collection of Shippen Papers. Another important source for Franklin documents is the William L. Clements Library of the University of Michigan. Finally, the Mason-Franklin Collection in the Yale University Library is rich in Franklin documents for the pre-1776 period.

Unquestionably, the most important printed primary source for the study of Pennsylvania colonial history is the edition by Samuel Hazard and others of the *Pennsylvania Archives* (9 series, Phila. and Harrisburg, 1852-1935). The eighth series, which contains the proceedings of the Assembly, was exhaustively used in this study. The *Min-*

utes of the Provincial Council of Pennsylvania . . . (16 vols., Phila., 1838-53), referred to in this study as *Pa. Col. Recs.*, are only slightly less useful. *The Statutes at Large of Pennsylvania from 1682 to 1801* . . . (Vols. 2-16, [Harrisburg], 1896-1911) are also an indispensable source. The premier printed collection of personal papers is Leonard W. Labaree, ed., *The Papers of Benjamin Franklin* (14 vols. to date, New Haven, 1959-   ). This series should be supplemented by Albert H. Smyth, ed., *The Writings of Benjamin Franklin* . . . (10 vols., New York, 1905-7). *The Pennsylvania Magazine of History and Biography* prints many original documents along with its fine articles. John R. Dunbar's voluminous collection of documents, issuing from the march of the Paxton Boys, *The Paxton Papers* (The Hague, 1957), was invaluable.

In consulting the newspapers of the period one must not neglect the *Pennsylvania Chronicle*. It is livelier and contains more political "dirt" than either the *Pennsylvania Gazette* or the *Pennsylvania Journal*.

Several monographs cover Pennsylvania from 1746 to 1770. William R. Shepherd's *History of Proprietary Government in Pennsylvania* (New York, 1896) should not be underestimated. It is based on a careful and discriminating reading of the primary sources and still contains useful accounts of topics in Pennsylvania history which modern scholars often ignore. Charles L. Lincoln's *The Revolutionary Movement in Pennsylvania 1760-1776* (Phila., 1901) is a representative volume of Progressive era history with all the strengths and weaknesses of that genre. Theodore Thayer's *Pennsylvania Politics and the Growth of Democracy 1740-1776* (Harrisburg, 1953) is another volume which should not be underestimated. Although I disagree with Professor Thayer in places, I acknowledge the importance of his work, which was the first substantial monograph on pre-revolutionary Pennsylvania politics since Lincoln's book and which vastly broadened our knowledge of the subject. Dietmar Rothermund's *The Layman's Progress: Religious and Political Experience in Colonial Pennsylvania 1740-1770* (Phila., 1961) is an intelligent work which rightly stresses the importance of the interplay of religion and politics in colonial Pennsylvania. I profited from David L. Jacobson's penetrating *John Dickinson and the Revolution in Pennsylvania, 1764-1776* (Berkeley, 1965). By all odds, the most important recent monograph on pre-revolutionary Pennsylvania politics is William Hanna's *Benjamin Franklin and Pennsylvania Politics* (Stanford, 1964). Although I have disagreed with Professor Hanna about his interpretation of certain episodes, there can be no doubt that his reassessment of Thomas Penn's role in the shaping of provincial politics is a contribution which will change the direction of all future historical accounts of Pennsylvania. His observations on the course of Pennsylvania politics after 1764 are acute and anticipate, in some instances, my interpretation.

I owe a heavy debt to two rather more specialized studies. I used Arthur L. Jensen's *The Maritime Commerce of Colonial Philadephia* (Madison, Wis., 1963) with constant profit. David Hawke's superbly written *In the Midst of a Revolution* (Phila., 1961) enlightened me about the crucial political events in the spring of 1776.

Carl Van Doren's biography, *Benjamin Franklin* (New York, 1938), still holds its place as the best account of the

Doctor's life. Verner Crane's *Benjamin Franklin and a Rising People* (Boston, 1954) should be read by anyone interested in colonial America. A brief, but scintillating interpretation of Franklin, Ralph Ketcham's *Benjamin Franklin* (New York, 1965) is a welcome recent addition to the literature.

I profited greatly from the following articles: J. Philip Gleason's "A Scurrilous Colonial Election and Franklin's Reputation," 3 *WMQ*, xviii (1961), 68-84; Benjamin H. Newcomb's "Effects of the Stamp Act on Colonial Pennsylvania Politics," *ibid.*, xxiii (1966), 257-72; Glenn Weaver's "Benjamin Franklin and the Pennsylvania Germans," *ibid.*, xiv (1957), 536-59; John J. Zimmerman's "Benjamin Franklin and the Quaker Party, 1755-1756," *ibid.*, xvii (1960), 291-313; and the same author's "Charles Thomson, 'The Sam Adams of Philadelphia,'" *Mississippi Valley Historical Review*, xlv (Dec. 1958).

Index

Index

Fothergill, John, 166, 182, 183, 184-89
Foulke, Samuel, 91
Fox, Joseph, 87, 179, 220
Francis, Tench, 11, 12, 245
Franklin, Benjamin, accused of manipulating Assemblymen, 179; accuses John Penn of striking a bargain with the Paxton Boys, 112; anger at Thomas Penn persists, 143; animosity toward Thomas Penn, 42; antagonism of Israel Pemberton toward, 166-67; appointed commissioner to England, 33; architect of the royal government campaign, 135; arrives in England, 41; Assembly instructions to, 33-35; corrects misapprehension of Fothergill, 189; defeated in Oct. 1764 election, 171-77; despairs of obtaining royal government, 227; disillusionment with Parliament, 48-49; estrangement from Galloway, 228-29; favors dominion status for colonies, 40; favors royal government for Pa., 51-54; fears objectives of the Paxton Boys, 86; friendship with Bute, 144-47; immersion in Stamp Act crisis, 183; masterminds propaganda campaign for royal government, 125-27; on fear generated by the Paxton Boys, 108; opponents allege he favors Stamp Act, 192, 195; political miscalculations of, 205-7, 247; presents petition for royal government, 204; pride in American achievements, 250; proposes Pa. Assembly

emit non-legal tender paper money, 89-90; publishes *Cool Thought*, 126; rallies Philadelphians against Paxton Boys, 92-94; remains optimistic about royal government, 216ff; "rooted enmity" toward Thomas Penn, 181; rumored to be Pa. Assembly agent in England, 27; sent on second agency to England, 180-82; suggests address to George III, 215; supports non-importation, 234-35; threats against residence of, 195-96; writes "Explanatory Remarks," 125
Franklin, Deborah, 196
Franklin, Sarah, 210
Franklin, William, 34n, 145-46, 198, 209

Galloway, Joseph, accused of manipulating assemblymen, 179; accused of seeking Pa. chief justiceship, 193; accused of seeking personal profit in a change of Pa.'s government, 142-43; analyzes Pa. politics in 1770, 236; confers with Paxton Boys, 94; cooperates with Proprietary Party, 240; criticizes Thomas Penn, 47, 48; defeated in Oct. 1764 election, 175-77; describes Oct. 1765 election, 191; disillusioned with Hillsborough, 226; enmity toward Dickinson, 158; estrangement from Franklin, 228-29; fears objectives of Paxton Boys, 86; legal opinion of, 36; mobilizes White Oaks, 195; Norris's antipathy toward, 156; opinion on Thomas

260

Index

estate, 18-24; said to be afraid of losing his proprietorship, 219; seeks accommodation with Quaker Party, 237-38; seeks compensation for receiving depreciating currency, 63-66; strategy to thwart royal government campaign, 169-70; succeeds in exhausting Pa. Assembly's funds, 76-77; tries to repeal supply bill of 1759, 59

Penn, William, 56, 249

Peters, Richard, 62, 152

Peters, William, 208

Pitt, William, 71-72

Pitt-Grafton ministry, 218

Pitt-Newcastle ministry, 49

Pontiac, 73-75

Pratt, Charles, 42-45

Presbyterian Party, courts Pa.'s farmers, 233; formation of, 4, 211ff; opposes Hillsborough's circular letter, 225; party of the future in Pa., 240ff; recruits Phila. mechanics, 230ff; response to Townshend Acts, 221ff; seeks accommodation with Quaker Party, 238-39

Presbyterians, abuse Quakers, 100-102; courted by Proprietary Party, 207-8; difficulties with Anglicans, 208-10; oppose royal government campaign, 153-56; rivalry with Anglicans, 160

Presqu'Isle, Fort, 73

Pringle, John, 145

Proprietary Party, accused of bargaining with Paxton boys, 113; characteristics of, 148ff, 214; leads opposition to Pa. royal government campaign,

148ff; performance at Oct. 1764 elections, 170-77; policy toward Stamp Act, 201-2; response to Townshend Acts, 221ff; tries to maintain coalition supporting it, 207ff

Purviance, Samuel, 155, 173, 191, 209, 238

Quaker Party, as "country party," 200; attempts to overturn proprietary government, 3; composition of, 131ff; demoralization of, 228ff; eclipse of, 4; favors royal government for Pa., 51; leads campaign for royal government, 123ff; opposes Hillsborough's circular letter, 225; performance at Oct. 1764 elections, 170-77; persistence in support of royal government campaign, 207ff; politics of ingratiation of, 192-94, 215ff; prevents violence during Stamp Act, 199; suspects Proprietary Party bargains with Paxton boys, 113; tactics at Oct. 1764 elections, 175-76; uncontested by Proprietary Party, 150; urban-rural split in, 170-71; welcomes reconciliation with Thomas Penn, 238-40

Quakers, abuse Presbyterians, 96-99, 102; negotiations with Thomas Penn, 182-90; principal supporters of royal government, 127ff

Reed, John, 209

Reed, Joseph, 211, 241, 243

Rhoads, Samuel, 171-72

Rittenhouse, David, 211

Roberdeau, Daniel, 94, 130, 241